THE EVERYTHING COOKING FOR KIDS COOKBOOK

Dear Reader,

Our children mean everything to us. As we bring them into the world, we have plans to teach them and guide them until they are ready to soar as well-grounded, confident, bright, and self-sufficient young adults. As parents, we know this is no easy task; if only the children came with a manual!

The Everything® Cooking for Kids Cookbook is undoubtedly a component to your *nutrition* parenting manual! In the food cornucopia of life, it is our responsibility to assist our children in making good decisions and creating healthful eating habits that can last them a lifetime. Chapter 1 describes the concern we have today that our children are really not in good shape, and how we can (and should) educate them, from their first bite of solid food. Considering today's perilous statistics of diabetes, heart disease, cancer, and childhood obesity, eating healthfully is non-negotiable, serious matter—*much under our control.*

The remainder of *The Everything® Cooking for Kids Cookbook* will offer you a full array of fun, child-friendly, delicious, and practical recipes that I think you will appreciate for many child-rearing years to come. My best wishes in turning out healthful and happy children—just like mine!

P.S. There has been no rebellion yet!

Ronni Litz Julien

Welcome to the EVERYTHING® Series!

These handy, accessible books give you all you need to tackle a difficult project, gain a new hobby, comprehend a fascinating topic, prepare for an exam, or even brush up on something you learned back in school but have since forgotten.

You can choose to read an Everything® book from cover to cover or just pick out the information you want from our four useful boxes: e-questions, e-facts, e-alerts, and e-ssentials.

We give you everything you need to know on the subject, but throw in a lot of fun stuff along the way, too.

We now have more than 400 Everything® books in print, spanning such wide-ranging categories as weddings, pregnancy, cooking, music instruction, foreign language, crafts, pets, New Age, and so much more. When you're done reading them all, you can finally say you know Everything®!

QUESTION

Answers to common questions

FACT

Important snippets of information

ALERT

Urgent warnings

ESSENTIAL

Quick handy tips

PUBLISHER Karen Cooper

DIRECTOR OF ACQUISITIONS AND INNOVATION Paula Munier

MANAGING EDITOR, EVERYTHING® SERIES Lisa Laing

COPY CHIEF Casey Ebert

ACQUISITIONS EDITOR Katrina Schroeder

SENIOR DEVELOPMENT EDITOR Brett Palana-Shanahan

EDITORIAL ASSISTANT Hillary Thompson

EVERYTHING® SERIES COVER DESIGNER Erin Alexander

LAYOUT DESIGNERS Colleen Cunningham, Elisabeth Lariviere, Ashley Vierra, Denise Wallace

THE EVERYTHING®

COOKING FOR KIDS COOKBOOK

Ronni Litz Julien, MS, RD/LDN

Avon, Massachusetts

Without my dear magnificent children, Jamie and Jordan,
being a third-time author may never have come to fruition. I
dedicate The Everything® Cooking for Kids Cookbook *to them,*
with endless love. Their extraordinary patience and their
encouragement of my writing is a sensational blessing in my life.

An Everything® Series Book.
Everything® and everything.com® are registered trademarks of F+W Media, Inc.

Published by Adams Media, a division of F+W Media, Inc.
57 Littlefield Street, Avon, MA 02322 U.S.A.
www.adamsmedia.com

ISBN 10: 1-60550-665-6
ISBN 13: 978-1-60550-665-4

Printed in the United States of America.

10   9   8   7   6   5   4   3   2   1

Library of Congress Cataloging-in-Publication Data
is available from the publisher.

Contents

Acknowledgments

My writing has always been a group effort! I have an exceptional support team of family editors, researching friends, gourmet cooks, and an enormous cheerleading squad behind me, to whom I am eternally grateful. To each of you, I express my deepest gratitude for your unending patience and devotion, for without you, *The Everything® Cooking for Kids Cookbook* might still just be a floating concept in my mind.

Again, I must acknowledge my own precious children, Jamie and Jordan, ages seventeen and fourteen, not just for the time they allowed me to write, but for accepting the notion that we could all eat healthfully, make good choices, learn moderation, and not feel deprived of foods we love. You both have done a superb job, and I especially chuckle when Jamie is appalled at some of her friends' food choices, and when Jordan still asks in the grocery store "Mom, is this healthy?" Thank you for allowing me to give you healthy bodies.

To my parents, Sheila and Norman Litz—the co-presidents of my fan club. Words could not possibly express how lucky I feel that I was "given" to the two of you. With every one of my endeavors, whether it be my nutrition career, my teaching career, my writing, my community volunteer work, my child-rearing, you have been the backbone of my entire life—my forever soulmates.

To my brother and best friend, Steve, for trying to keep me sane, calm, and thinking clearly all of my life! It is not typical for siblings to have the kind of relationship we do and I don't take one minute of it for granted. You are a source of infinite pride to me and our friendship is priceless.

I would like to acknowledge and thank my dear friends, from the bottom of my heart: Donna Strans, Joni Meiselman, Belinda Tuckerman, Lisa Quintero, Alison Cohen, Cindi Schuetz and Sharon Smith; I am honored and privileged to have your everlasting support and belief in me, for so many years. Life wouldn't be the same without you. To my "gourmet" friends, Rebeca Lusky, Wendy Berman, Myra Sonshine, and Linda Martin Lazarus, who graciously bestowed upon me their family's favorite recipes. Forgive me, for I had to make a few "healthy" changes to your recipes, but they remain delicious! Dr. Margie Chiaralonzio, my friend, your creativity is invaluable and you were gracious to offer to be a part of this.

To Bob Diforio, my wonderful literary agent—keep those propositions coming. *You* have encouraged me to enter this world of authoring books and being a writer, and I am so appreciative of your confidence in me.

And, finally, to Adams Media and the *Everything*® series of books, I am honored to be part of this esteemed series.

Introduction

MY BROTHER AND I walked around as teenagers saying, "Mom, meat-loaf *again?*" It felt like every third day, we were having meatloaf for dinner. Today, having been a mom for seventeen years, I have *never* made that dish. Just can't bring myself to make it, or eat it. In fact, my Mom *did* make other things—but for some reason, those unpleasant meatloaf memories have stuck with me a very long time. I am sure we all have positive and negative meal remembrances while growing up. It's just part of growing up!

Every parent has their repertoire of foods that they make for their family—and use the same familiar recipes most of their children's growing-up years. But now with *The Everything® Cooking for Kids Cookbook*, there is a whole new non-meatloaf world out there. Everyday life is so different than in past generations—there is more running around, fewer family mealtimes together, more extracurricular early evening activities, more fast food, and less breakfast time. There doesn't seem to be a reason why it needs to be this way, or what the benefit is; however, that is today's world, and you have to make the best of it.

The Everything® Cooking for Kids Cookbook is a great handbook to help you teach your children healthful eating habits while running to the soccer game or making a birthday party. Additionally, this book offers an enormous collection of fantastic recipes and hints that will never bring on mediocre meatloaf memories! There will always be something fun and unique to choose from, for holidays, for birthdays, for desserts, for innovative vege-table ideas, for after-school snacks, and the list goes on and on. From the time you have picky toddler eaters, to the time where your teenager wants to make her own gourmet birthday cake, it can all be found within these pages.

Being a nutritionist and registered dietitian for the past twenty-three years, I would be remiss if I didn't remind you, as parents, that we are in the midst of the worst childhood obesity epidemic in history. Children have never been unhealthier than they are today, and they are not anticipated to have the same life expectancy that our present generation has—due to their poor eating habits, the abundant unhealthy choices available to them, and their preference for sitting at the computer, rather than playing baseball or tennis. Pediatricians have never diagnosed more childhood diabetes, high blood pressure, high cholesterol, and breathing issues from children being so overweight—not to mention the devastating feelings that weight issues create for children's self-esteem. There is a better way, and *The Everything®* *Cooking for Kids Cookbook* can certainly be the go-to guide when trying to feed your children, and their friends, in a healthier manner. There are fun and unhealthy recipes to be made, but the goal of the book is to become comfortable with preparing healthier foods, having that occasional "treat," and still enjoying them all immensely.

Finally, feel free to contact my own children and see how they have fared over the years, living with their mom, the nutritionist! They are none the worse for it—there are always food challenges, but we have created healthy children, who have learned the true meaning of moderation, self-control, and the proper place for food in our incredible world. Best of luck as you embark on your nutrition parenting journey!

CHAPTER 1

Creating That Healthy Family

Raising children today is quite different than raising children in past generations—the options available, the technology, the educational process, and so on. Everything is *so* different. Due to the accessibility of such abundance, many decisions made today by parents, caregivers, and children have created an epidemic of kids in poor health—the worst in history. As a parent you are in complete control of this situation when your children are small. You can train your children to make sound decisions, *and* love what they are eating, for a lifetime.

Molding Healthy Children Forever

When thinking of childhood illnesses, what generally comes to mind are colds, ear infections, and chicken pox, *not* high blood pressure, high cholesterol, diabetes, depression, and breathing issues. Yet these once "adult" diseases are becoming more prevalent in this generation of children. There are astonishing numbers of kids across the country who are dealing with adult medical issues, because they eat too much, have terrible eating habits, move too little, and are therefore too heavy. At the other end of the spectrum, there are children who are too thin, malnourished, or suffering from eating disorders (such as anorexia nervosa or bulimia). Today, the medical industry's concern focuses on these horrific eating habits and the lifelong repercussions that go along with them.

FACT

More than 30 percent of children in the United States are considered overweight. That number has increased over the past decade. This should really be an eye-opener for parents to pay attention to the choices they offer to children.

This book is an attempt to merge fun with food, combined with an insight into healthful food choices, creating great kids with impressive eating habits. This is not as difficult as it sounds, but it seems to be an integral part of raising well-rounded, healthy children. The best part is that it *can* be done. If children can be taught how to read and write, they can be educated on how to make better choices—all-around. There is one opportunity for you to do this while your children are young. *Your children need you*. They are under your complete guidance until they are preteens; you have their undivided attention in molding them and their eating behaviors. Teach them.

Help Is on the Way (Slowly)

Organizations and countless concerned individuals around the country have taken a front-and-center approach to the problem of unhealthy children—former President Bill Clinton's foundation, The American Heart

Association, The American Academy of Pediatrics, The Centers for Disease Control, The National Dairy Council, The American Diabetes Association, colleges and university programs around the country, and so many others—are creating programs to help parents, teachers, and caregivers get the message that kids can learn to make healthful choices without feeling dissatisfied or deprived. Unfortunately, kids have never been unhealthier than they are today, and sadly, the headway being made is just too slow. The statistics have not improved significantly over the past few years, since childhood obesity has entered the limelight. If you walk around a school cafeteria, you'll see that the students are still ordering pizza and French fries and a large chocolate chip cookie as their meal, rather than the healthier panini, tuna wrap, sushi, or salad. Recent medical studies have shown that due to the listless manner in which children are being guided, and their abysmal eating habits and food choices, this generation of children will live a shorter lifespan than their parents. Here are some sobering statistics:

QUESTION

Are there more children in the United States that are undernourished or overnourished?
There are certainly undernourished (or malnourished) children in this country; however, most children (and adults) are overnourished. Take protein for example—the protein need of a teenager is 0.8 grams per kilogram of body weight. For a teenage girl, 5'2" tall, weighing about 105 pounds, her protein needs for the day are 38–40 grams of protein for the day. This equates to a 6-ounce serving of fish, beef, or chicken (about the size of a normal adult hand). Most children and adults ingest far more than this amount of protein, along with most other nutrients.

- The rate of childhood obesity has increased by approximately 12 to 15 percent across most childhood age ranges. This refers just to the group of obese children (obesity classified as 20 to 30 percent above an ideal or healthy body weight). This is based on a NHANES—The National Health and Nutrition Education Survey—study from the years 1976–1980 and 2003–2006.

- Approximately 9 million children struggle with being overweight sometime during their childhood.
- Eighty percent of all children who are overweight between the ages of ten and fifteen become obese adults by the age of twenty-five.
- Children of obese parents have an 80 percent chance of becoming obese adults.

These are sobering statistics that demonstrate that we, as parents, are being neglectful, not only to the longevity of our children, but to the actual quality of their lives.

What Do They Really Need to Grow?

Believe it or not, at each stage of a child's growth and development, their caloric needs, among many other nutrients, are quite different. During the first four years of growth, substantial protein intake is critical for brain formation. During the pubescent period for girls, more iron is necessary (as they begin to menstruate). Until children's bones finish growing, calcium plays a crucial role in bone and teeth formation. So, at each stage of childhood, parents must be aware of the important nutrient groups necessary for their children's ultimate growth. A multivitamin is a great idea for every child—and adult, too. The caloric breakdown is as follows for each age group range:

Infants Through Age One

This group should have 14 to 40 ounces of breast milk or formula per day. Begin baby solid foods at about six months old (not necessary to begin before that). Start with about two to four tablespoons of iron-fortified cereals (preferably oatmeal and mixed grains, after they tolerate the rice cereal well). At about month seven, increase to two to four ounces of solid food daily, and advance them as you read their hunger cues. Please begin with green vegetables, advancing to the sweet ones (since they might not like the green ones after they've tasted the sweet ones), and then the protein foods (chicken, lamb, beef). By about month ten, introduce finger foods such as dry oat cereal (e.g., Cheerios), bits of crackers, scrambled egg, and bite-size pieces of turkey or chicken. At one year, begin introducing dairy products such as slices of cheese, and so on. Be very cautious about giving small children foods that are choking risks, for example, carrots, grapes, nuts, hot dogs, raisins—food items that are the shape of their small throat.

Toddlers

Generally, the rule of thumb for feeding toddlers is: one tablespoon of food per food group at each meal—for each year of age. Therefore, one tablespoon of protein (ground meat), one tablespoon of a vegetable (cooked carrots), one tablespoon of carbohydrate/starch (mashed potato), and one tablespoon of fruit (mashed banana)—for a one-year-old. For a two-year-old, two tablespoons from each food group at each meal, and so on. Snacks are required to increase calories, such as two to four ounces of low-fat yogurt, a slice of low-fat cheese, four to 6 ounces of low-fat milk with a few low-fat cookies, or ½ mashed plum or peach.

Never give a child under two years old any food that is "low-fat," "nonfat," "low sugar," or "sugar free." Do not limit their calories or fat intake until they are older than two years old. Then, offer low-fat milk and low-fat cheeses and other lower-fat foods.

School Age Through Teenage Years

This is the time of the growth spurt, hopefully. So, if you see your child eating as if he were a "bottomless pit," keep an eye on him; though, in most cases, it is a "growing" appetite for a growing body. The pubescent period (preteen) is the second greatest growth spurt in a child's life. Calorie intakes range in school-age children between 1,200 and 1,500 calories per day, whereas, as teenagers grow and develop (gender dependent), daily calorie intake should be somewhere between 1,500 and 3,000 calories per day. Obviously, the 3,000 calories per day may be for your male or female athlete. Here is a guideline of the "servings" per day needed at this age:

- **Dairy servings per day: 3 (or more)**—a serving specified as: 1 ounce (slice) of low-fat cheese, 8 ounces low-fat yogurt or low-fat milk, a 1 cup serving of broccoli or 4 ounces of salmon or sardines with bones. The calcium in vegetables and fish (above) are not as well absorbed as the dairy products. If you see your child is not getting in sufficient servings of calcium, discuss a calcium supplement with your dietitian or pediatrician. Bones only have one chance at getting strong, for as humans age, the density of bones tends to decrease.
- **Protein servings per day: 2–3**—a serving specified as: 1–2 eggs, 12–15 nuts, 3–6 ounces lean beef, poultry, fish, veal, pork, or tofu; ½ cup beans or legumes; 2 tablespoons of peanut or almond butter.
- **Fruit servings per day: 3**—a serving specified as: a medium piece of fresh fruit, e.g., an orange, pear, apple, peach, plum, or banana; or ½–1 cup berries or fresh fruit salad, ½ cup canned fruit (in light syrup or own juice), 15 grapes, 1 cup melon chunks.
- **Vegetable servings per day: 2–3**—a serving specified as: ½ cup any vegetable, fresh, frozen, or canned (starchy vegetables such as corn, peas, and potatoes are higher in calories than the traditional green beans, carrots, zucchini, squash, broccoli, and so on).
- **Bread and grain servings per day: 3–5**—a serving specified as: ½ cup brown rice or pasta, corn or peas; a small baked white or sweet potato; 1 slice whole grain bread, ½ whole wheat bagel, ½ cup quinoa, a whole grain English muffin, or ¾–1 cup whole grain cereal (check cereal box for further details and portion sizes).

Can They Eat Too Much or Too Little?

Children can *absolutely* eat too much or too little food. If children are not guided well, or they are guided inappropriately by parents who have their own food issues or are uneducated, this could make for serious problems. Of course, not teaching kids to recognize when they are full or satiated can certainly set them up for eating too much—increasing their risk for overweight and obesity. Parents need to learn what a child's portion size is—kids are not mini-adults, and should not be served that way. Overeating, or super-sizing in a fast food restaurant, for instance, is undeniably the fastest way to a weight problem. Limits must be set in terms of how much children eat, how much snacking they partake in, and what favorites might be brought into the house that might promote overeating.

Eating too little, at the other end of the spectrum, is a very serious issue, with potentially severe consequences. Generally, young children are just not "good eaters." They are picky, or they are playing a game of control with their parents and end up malnourished. Your pediatrician can recognize this immediately, as they plot your child on the CDC's Growth Chart (see Appendix B) during a checkup, and see that your child is failing to grow or "failing to thrive" as it is called in the medical industry. "Catching up" is critical—you never want to stunt a child's growth, for any reason. A registered dietitian is well equipped to put the child back on track to being a healthful eater, making a nutrition plan with the goal of taking in adequate calories and nutrients.

FACT

At least 10 percent of females in the United States suffer from an eating disorder. Eating disorder victims can range from as young as five- to eight-year-olds, to women in their fifties and sixties. Generally, there are two "types" of eating disorder patients: those who are in a very difficult phase of life, and with effective therapies can overcome the eating disorder and lead a normal life, and those who live forever with symptoms of their food issues, never living a normal life, some even succumbing to death.

The eating disorders anorexia nervosa and bulimia are mechanisms teens (and lately preteens) will use to maintain thinness. This is a serious psychological issue, with food being the symptom of a much larger problem. It is vital for you to get professional help for your children if you see "strange" eating habits, such as: pushing food around on their plate, skipping meals, eliminating "fats" or "carbs" completely from their diets, throwing up after a meal, or just eating very little. Do not pass this off as a stage or a "phase of life"—do seek psychological help from a therapist with eating disorder experience.

Top Ten "Musts" for Raising a Healthy Child

Use the following guidelines in your nutrition parenting. Take each one of these tips seriously, and introduce them as early as you possibly can in your child's life. There are plenty of wonderful food choices to be made, and lots of opportunities to teach moderation, too.

Number 1: Be the Very Best Role Model You Can Be

You may opt not to smoke or drink in front of your kids anymore, to discourage them from taking up these habits; so, do not load up on cheeseburgers and French fries from your local fast food restaurant three times a week either. Is there any better way for a child to learn what is acceptable or appropriate behavior than what they see at home? What if you really would like a doughnut before bed every night, however? Please wait until your child goes to bed first!

Number 2: Physical Activity Is Non-Negotiable

Forty percent of high schoolers spend three or more hours a day watching television or on their computers/phones/iPods, and at least 10 percent of children are completely sedentary, without any form of even moderate exercise. This has been a huge disaster for children, contributing to a generation of ill young people. Kids don't have to be marathon runners, but a team sport is wonderful for their physical bodies, their emotional well-being, their self-confidence levels, and establishing a habit of enjoying movement. Find them something early on in their lives that they will create a passion for—ice skating, dance classes, jump rope team, basketball, lacrosse, swimming, track and field, anything your child can feel good about participating in. Additionally, include regular activity with the children as a family, as soon as their little legs can move—bike ride together, play tennis, walk on the beach, snow ski—again, a message to the children that being physical will keep that heart of theirs strong, forever.

Number 3: Build in a Nutrition and Eating Structure Early

Do not allow eating as a type of "sport" in your home. Teach that there are appropriate eating times—breakfast, lunch, dinner, and snacks. As the children grow into their older teenage years, they may not need as many snacks as when they were going through their growth spurts. Curb those snacks in an effort to decrease the risk of overweight and obesity. Exception: teenage athletes, who need the additional calories, protein, and carbohydrates to perform.

ESSENTIAL

It is so important that after-school athletes take in a hearty snack before their game or workout. Each snack should contain a healthy carbohydrate and a source of protein, so their high energy lasts them for several hours: for example, a peanut butter sandwich and a glass of milk.

Number 4: Your Home Has to Be a Healthy Haven, Forever

What foodstuffs you bring into your home is the greatest message to your children. This does not mean that your favorites (or theirs) cannot appear in the kitchen pantry; however, the unhealthy favorites must be kept to a minimum. *Teaching the art of discipline and self-control is absolutely critical.* It is your job, as the parent, to initiate this concept, completely, and early.

Number 5: Teach Children Nutrition Independence

Give them options, within reason, and allow them to make their own decisions—on how much they would like to eat, whether they want to eat or not, and what they would like to have (knowing you have provided the acceptable healthy options). For example, keep them in the loop of what you are thinking of making for dinner—"Lisa, would you like to have pasta and meatballs, or chicken and a baked potato?" Allow them to assist in the decision-making process. When discussing how much they should eat during dinner, serve them a reasonable portion; if they claim they are still "hungry" after they are through, ask them to wait five to ten minutes, and if they continue to feel hunger, then they can have a second portion. These are fantastic behaviors, that when taught properly, teach brilliant self-confidence, self-control, and self-sufficiency.

Number 6: Never Lower the Bar

From the time children are babies, stick to healthful eating habits. Never let there be a time in which you throw in the towel and stock the house with our fattening favorites! If this is all your children know from a young age, they will not expect any different. Is it okay to have the occasional fast food meal? Sure. To share desserts in a restaurant? Absolutely. To eat Halloween candy? Why not (somewhat monitored, of course)? Please teach your child the healthy way, no matter what it takes.

Number 7: Take Your Children under Your Wing in the Grocery Store

Make the children a part of their own food lives. Allow them to pick and choose some items in the grocery store. Teach them while you are there, as they become old enough, to read a food label and ingredient list, and become familiar with what they are putting into their bodies. Remember to avoid high amounts of sugar and saturated fats, and to avoid the trans fats (partially hydrogenated vegetable oils) at all times. Look for foods, cereals, and breads that are higher in fiber, to ensure their intestinal health, promote heart health, and decrease their cancer risk.

FACT

At about the age of six, arteries begin to clog, especially when the high-fat, high-sugar foods arrive. According to the current research, early inflammation of the arteries from the high-fat food intake and possible dilation of the arteries from the high sugar intake is so very dangerous later in life.

Number 8: Talk to Your Children about Their Growing Bodies

You want your children to realize not only the significance of maintaining a healthy weight, but to learn their responsible part in preserving their healthy bodies, forever. Teach the kids what they truly are in control of. Obviously, their genes are their genes, however, there is so much they (and you) can do to be sure that they sustain their good health. Most importantly, afford them the high self-esteem and good feelings about themselves that they so deserve.

Number 9: Do Not Allow Your Children to Skip Meals

Recent studies promote the concept of "a one-letter-grade increase" in math, just by eating a healthful breakfast. In today's world, there may be limited time in the morning to have your child sit and eat scrambled eggs, English muffin, and fruit salad. But, everyone needs to find the time to eat some form of breakfast that includes a source of protein and healthy carbohydrate such as low-fat, low-sugar chocolate milk and a raisin bran muffin, or a container of yogurt and some whole wheat crackers, or cereal and milk, or a sandwich, or even a hard-boiled egg and a pita. Even if you have to eat breakfast on the run (or in the car) you, and your children need to eat it. Do whatever you must to get in that first meal of the day. Remember, just as adults feel weak and irritable after too many hours without food, kids are the same, if not worse, as their blood sugars begin to drop, and they still need to concentrate in school, or on homework, later in the day.

ALERT

"Children's menus" are generally filled with unhealthy choices. Take a look at the kid's menu when you go out to your next restaurant. Certainly, they are filled with the kids' favorites, but macaroni and cheese, pizza, chicken fingers, cheeseburgers, and corn dogs are far from the choices you want your children to make. So skip the children's menus in a restaurant.

Number 10: Teach Sensible Eating Behaviors in a Moderate Way

Before you know it, your toddler daughter is at a birthday party every weekend, your husband is taking your preadolescent son to the NBA basketball arena, and your children are vacationing with you on a cruise during the holiday break. Do you abandon your healthy habits during any or all of these events? No! Fun events like these come so often you'd never get back on track!

How to Handle Tough Situations

"Scenarios" will come up daily as your children begin to grow up: parties, family gatherings, vacations, holidays, and many other celebrations over their lifetime. The message here is to think ahead, plan ahead, and ready your child to make a decent decision, rather than choose foods because they are "starving"!

Parties

If you are unsure of the "meal" to be served at a birthday party, give your child a hearty snack before going to the party. Then, if the choices are chicken wings, French fries, potato chips, and chocolate kisses, she may not be so hungry as to eat *all* of those unhealthy choices. Encourage water over fruit juice or soda, whenever possible, and *never* refuse her a small piece of birthday cake! How would *your* daughter's birthday party look with the following choices: pizza or a long sub sandwich (preferably turkey or roast beef), baby carrots, baked Doritos or baked chips, and a birthday cake! Doesn't sound so terrible, does it? Her friends probably will not notice that the food is a little different.

Sporting Events

One of the things people love to do with their children is make them sports fans—whether your hometown teams are football, baseball, ice hockey, or basketball. The stadium setting has become a little healthier than in years past. Remember to order healthy as their parent, too—you can never give up being the role model.

At the sports stadiums, things have changed quite a bit—grilled chicken sandwiches, wraps, grilled hamburgers, frozen lemonade, peanuts, frozen yogurt, and the like—many of these items are now appearing across the country. Certainly aiming for better choices than the traditional foot-long hot dogs, fries, and nachos, professional stadiums are finally offering options that are more worthwhile and easier on the heart. If you will order the grilled chicken or the wrap, so will your son. Share a frozen lemonade, and the rest of the fun will come from the game itself!

Vacations

Finally, vacations are always a special part of growing up. Who doesn't remember many of their childhood vacations? The hope is that the activities and the sights are what we cherish, not so much the food! Once again, moms and dads have to take the lead, and order and choose in a manner in which the children will understand that our behaviors and habits in other destinations are similar to those we abide by at home. This does *not* mean that you avoid the high-fat wonderful specialty of the area, it means you *share* the famous strawberry milkshake or the Philly steak sandwich. Do attempt to keep the structure of meals, having three meals a day, and maybe a snack thrown in for the young ones. Again, restaurant menus today, in most every country, have some sort of healthier selections available. Please choose them.

"I Don't Mind Being a Healthy Eater Because . . ."

Being surrounded by children for much of my professional career, and now spending time teaching in a high school setting, I am bombarded with children's eating habits. As a nutritionist/teacher who is very interested in why young people acquire certain habits, I often take short "polls" from young people regarding the choices they make, why they make them, their thoughts about eating, and how they feel about their bodies.

Knowing many youngsters who truly do maintain healthful eating habits at home and outside of their home, the latest statement that I wanted them to answer was: "I don't mind being a healthy eater in my home because . . .", and the conclusions were priceless. Their parents did a *great* job in nutrition parenting, and it appears these children could be on their way to having learned one of the toughest jobs facing their lives today, keeping up their fitness and well-being. Here were some of their invaluable responses:

- "I really never knew any other way. This is just always the way my family ate, and it is really okay with me. I don't miss much."—Sara, age 9
- "When I think I am hungry, but I know I am really not, I have some other outlets to use instead of just eating—I'll take out my basketball or go out for a quick bike ride, then I'm not around the kitchen or the food at home."—Jason, age 13
- "I still have some great snack foods—even though it might not be regular ice cream or regular chips. My Mom has found me snacks that I

still love, so I really never feel deprived. And, of course, on occasion, she does bring in my favorite—powdered doughnuts."—Scott, age 7

- "We do not leave any food out on the kitchen counters which is a big help in my house. That is so hard to just pass up that leftover cake when it is sitting out on the counter—who wouldn't be tempted! We keep fruit in a big bowl, and that's just fine for me."—Erica, age 16
- "Mom and Dad have taught me the definition and the practice of 'moderation' in a lot of things I do, so I'm pretty good at it, and I have learned some control over what choices I make."—Ben, age 14

Make good use of this guide to assist your children in creating eating habits that will last them a lifetime.

CHAPTER 2

The Toddler Years—Those Veggies Really Aren't "Yucky"

Feta and Zucchini Zany Soufflé

A soft, colorful pudding that the little ones will enjoy—great for getting in the veggies, the protein, and the serving of dairy for those growing bones!

INGREDIENTS | SERVES 6

2 tablespoons trans-fat-free margarine
¼ cup flour
¼ teaspoon dry mustard
1 cup low-fat milk
¾ cup low-fat feta cheese, crumbled
3 tablespoons Parmesan cheese, grated
2 cups zucchini, shredded
2 whole eggs
4 egg whites
Nonstick cooking spray

Ever Met a Child Who Begs for Vegetables?

Please, Mom, more vegetables! Didn't think so. Cooking the recipes in this chapter is an easy way to persuade and enhance their veggie intake—truly one of the most important of the food groups they need to eat. There are fifty-five essential nutrients human bodies need on a daily basis. These vegetables make up so many of them.

1. Preheat oven to 375°F.

2. In a medium saucepan, melt margarine. Blend in flour and mustard, and add milk.

3. Bring to a boil, and cook for 2 to 3 minutes.

4. Remove from stove.

5. Stir in the cheeses and the shredded zucchini.

6. In individual bowls, separate the whole eggs into egg yolks and egg whites.

7. Beat egg yolks and add to the cheese and zucchini mixture.

8. Whip egg whites with electric mixer until foamy and peaks form.

9. Gently fold the egg whites into the zucchini mixture until well blended.

10. Coat 6 soufflé cups with cooking spray, and spoon mixture into the cups.

11. Bake for 20 to 25 minutes.

Colorful Vegetable Couscous

You can add in pine nuts to sneak in some healthy monounsaturated fats!

INGREDIENTS | SERVES 6

1½ cups couscous, dry
1 clove garlic, minced
1 scallion, chopped
1 cup broccoli, finely chopped
1½ tablespoons olive or canola oil
¼ cup balsamic vinegar

1. Cook couscous according to package directions.

2. Sauté garlic, scallions, and broccoli in olive or canola oil.

3. Mix together the couscous and the garlic and scallion mixture.

4. Add the balsamic vinegar, mix well.

5. Serve warm or at room temperature.

Crazy Cauliflower Smash

Serve to your toddler with some additional color in their entrée, starch, and/or fruit. This is an enticing dish, tasting almost like mashed potatoes!

INGREDIENTS | SERVES 4

1 pound cauliflower florets, chopped
1 clove of garlic, chopped
⅔ cup chicken broth
1 teaspoon salt
4 tablespoons whole milk
1 tablespoon trans-fat-free margarine

1. Simmer cauliflower, garlic, broth, and salt in a saucepan, covered, for 15 minutes, until tender.

2. Transfer cauliflower mixture to a food processor or blender. Add milk and margarine.

3. Blend until smooth.

Sweet Potato Soufflé

Substitute canned yams if you're short on time—use 4 cups canned yams (drained).

INGREDIENTS | SERVES 8

4 large sweet potatoes, peeled and cut in quarters

⅔ cup low-fat milk, scalded

2 teaspoons ground cinnamon

½ teaspoon ground nutmeg

Nonstick cooking spray

1 cup rolled oats

½ cup sugar-free pancake syrup

Sweet Potatoes Are Filled with Incredible Nutrients

Smile when *you* eat *your* sweet potatoes— you want your children to get the potassium, fiber, vitamin C, beta-carotene, and healthy carbohydrate that comes with eating the sweet potato, especially.

1. Preheat oven to 400°F.

2. Cook the potatoes in a pot of boiling water until very tender.

3. Drain the potatoes and transfer to a large mixing bowl.

4. Mash the potatoes, milk, 1 teaspoon cinnamon and the nutmeg.

5. Spray 9" × 13" casserole dish with nonstick cooking spray.

6. Pour the potato mixture into casserole dish and smooth with a spatula.

7. In a small bowl, toss the remaining cinnamon with the oats.

8. Spread evenly over the potatoes.

9. Bake for 35 to 40 minutes on top rack of oven, or until the topping appears brown and crispy.

10. Serve with sugar-free pancake syrup.

Broccoli Extraordinaire

This recipe tends to be one of the family favorites—you'll be making it often!

INGREDIENTS | SERVES 4–6

3 to 4 cups fresh broccoli, steamed, or 2 (10-ounce) packages frozen chopped broccoli

3 eggs

Salt and pepper to taste

1 tablespoon onion soup mix

½ cup light mayonnaise

Nonstick cooking spray

2 tablespoons flour

Vary the Veggies If You Like

Try this recipe with cauliflower or "broccoflower." Broccoli, however, is loaded with vitamin C, fiber, and potassium. Vitamin C is beneficial for healthy cells and prevention of colds; potassium is a terrific nutrient for healthy muscles and a healthy heart. Fiber, of course, keeps their tummies in good shape and gives kids a feeling of fullness.

1. Preheat oven to 350°F.

2. If using frozen, cook broccoli according to package directions.

3. Drain thoroughly and set aside.

4. In a mixing bowl, beat the eggs.

5. Add salt, pepper, and onion soup mix to the eggs.

6. Add the mayonnaise and continue mixing until well blended.

7. Stir in the cooked broccoli.

8. Spray a 7" × 11½" inch baking dish with the nonstick cooking spray.

9. Dust it lightly with 1 tablespoon flour.

10. Pour in the broccoli mixture and sprinkle with the remaining flour.

11. Bake for 40 to 50 minutes, until the top is golden brown.

Creamy Corn Pudding

This delicious recipe can be made ahead of time and reheated. It tastes even better on day two. And it is a big hit at the holiday dinner table!

INGREDIENTS | SERVES 6

½ cup sugar

3 tablespoons cornstarch

Salt and pepper to taste

1 (14.75-ounce) can creamed-style corn

1 (11-ounce) can corn niblets

3 eggs plus 4 egg whites, lightly beaten

⅓ cup low-fat milk

¼ cup trans-fat-free margarine, melted

Nonstick cooking spray

1. Preheat oven to 400°F.

2. In a small bowl, combine sugar, cornstarch, salt and pepper.

3. In a larger bowl, place creamed corn, corn niblets, and beaten eggs, and mix well.

4. Add previously combined dry ingredients and mix.

5. Stir in milk and melted margarine.

6. Place in medium casserole dish sprayed with nonstick cooking spray. Bake for 1 hour.

Creamy Vegetable Chicken Soup

A delicious vegetable soup—add any vegetables the children enjoy! Great for a winter snack or meal.

INGREDIENTS | SERVES 6–8

4 to 5 large carrots, chopped finely

10 ounces frozen green beans, thawed

1 small onion, chopped finely

¼ cup water

2 (11-ounce) cans low-fat cream of chicken soup (condensed)

2 cups low-fat milk

2 cups chicken breast, cooked, cubed

Salt and pepper to taste

1. In a large saucepan, combine carrots, green beans, onions, and water.

2. Cook on medium heat for 6 to 8 minutes.

3. Add cream of chicken soup, milk, chicken, and spices.

4. Cook on low heat for 30 to 60 minutes, until vegetables are tender.

Very Veggie Minestrone Soup

Everything in this recipe can be organized ahead, celery and carrots chopped.
Use a whole wheat noodle—no one will know the difference!

INGREDIENTS | SERVES 8–10

1 cup celery, chopped finely
2 cups carrots, chopped finely
¼ cup chopped garlic
Salt to taste
2 tablespoons olive oil
32 ounces vegetable or chicken broth
1 (14-ounce) can stewed tomatoes
1 (16-ounce) can red kidney beans
Pinch of basil and oregano
2 cups macaroni noodles (al dente)
Sprinkle of Parmesan cheese

1. Sauté celery, carrots, chopped garlic, and salt in olive oil.

2. Add broth, stewed tomatoes, kidney beans, basil, and oregano.

3. Simmer for at least 20 minutes.

4. If eating right away, add cooked macaroni and sprinkle of Parmesan.

5. If eating soup later, cool the soup, then add macaroni, and reheat until macaroni is cooked. Add Parmesan cheese.

Another Wonderful High-Fiber, Nutritious, Tasty Meal

Feel free to vary the vegetables and throw in what the children like to eat. Let's get them to eat beans early on in their lives, too, as beans are little powerhouses of health—including a great source of iron, vitamins, fiber, and potassium.

Cool Carrot Pie

One more way to camouflage essential vegetables—this is such a pretty dish on the table, too!

INGREDIENTS | SERVES 6–8

¾ cup trans-fat-free margarine

½ cup brown sugar

2 eggs

1 tablespoon lemon juice

1 tablespoon cold water

1 cup flour

½ teaspoon baking soda

½ teaspoon baking powder

3 to 4 large carrots, shredded

Pinch of salt

Nonstick cooking spray

1. Preheat oven to 350°F.

2. Combine all ingredients together in large mixing bowl. Mix well.

3. Spray a medium casserole dish with nonstick cooking spray.

4. Transfer mixture to casserole dish.

5. Bake for 45 minutes or until golden brown.

Great Eyesight Forever!

Crunchy, sweet, and orange—carrots are pretty much the winning favorite, if there is a favorite veggie! One of *the* greatest sources of beta-carotene, vitamin A (that's the one for the nighttime eyesight), fabulous vitamin C, potassium, and fiber. With such high beta-carotene, carrots are an excellent antioxidant, warding off cancer and heart disease. Be courageous, and have your children plant and grow them for a wonderful carrot garden!

Crunchy Green Beans

A wonderful combination—a great vegetable with great crunch!
The kids seem to enjoy the texture of this dish!

INGREDIENTS | SERVES 6

3 to 4 cups fresh string beans,
steamed, or 2 (10-ounce) boxes of
string beans, frozen
3 tablespoons trans-fat-free margarine
1 cup corn flake crumbs
Salt and pepper to taste

Green Veggies Rule

As babies, hopefully, your children were
offered the "green" baby food vegetables first, prior to tasting the "sweet,"
such as squash and sweet potato. That is
the general rule of thumb. If they will eat
and enjoy the green, not-so-sweet-and-
tasty vegetables, the sweet ones will be a
breeze. As they begin regular foods,
introduce them at the same time *you* are
eating them—they are more apt to follow
the "monkey-see, monkey-do" idea.

1. If using frozen beans, cook according to package directions. Drain. If using fresh green beans, place beans and ¼ cup water into a microwave-safe dish and cook 7 to 10 minutes or until desired doneness. Remove from microwave and drain.

2. Over low heat, brown the corn flake crumbs in the margarine.

3. Mix string beans with corn flake crumbs, and place in serving dish.

4. Add salt and pepper to taste.

Winter Squash Soup

Substitute fresh butternut squash if desired. Cook it and blend in a food processor or blender. Then follow directions below.

INGREDIENTS | **SERVES 10–12**

Nonstick cooking spray

1 medium onion, diced

3 (12- to 16-ounce) cans chicken soup or broth

6 (10-ounce) packages frozen winter squash, thawed

½ teaspoon garlic powder

Salt and pepper to taste

The Squash Glossary

Summer squash tend to be thin-skinned, yet firm, with more water content. Winter squash have hard skins or rinds; they are drier, and keep longer. Acorn squash are green, gold, or white in color, hard-skinned—this is one of the sweeter squash versions. Sweet potato squash are oblong and lemon-colored, the consistency and taste is between sweet potato and butternut squash. Spaghetti squash, or orangetti squash are pale and orange-fleshed; as it cooks, it shreds into spaghetti-like strands. It cooks like any other squash, but can be piled high like a serving of pasta!

1. Spray small pan with nonstick cooking spray and sauté onion in pan until it is transparent.

2. Place a large pot over medium heat. Add chicken soup, squash, and sautéed onions to the pot. Mix to combine.

3. Add garlic powder, salt and pepper to soup mixture.

4. Simmer 20 to 30 minutes. Cool. Soup will thicken as it stands.

5. Put soup through a blender if smoother consistency is desired.

Broccoli "Pie"

Broccoli is often a big hit, if offered early in the vegetable repertoire!
This recipe is a delicious way to introduce some of those greens!

INGREDIENTS | SERVES 8–10

3 eggs plus 2 egg whites

1 cup whole milk

1 cup low-fat milk

1 tablespoon flour

1 cup low-fat shredded Cheddar cheese

½ cup shredded Cheddar cheese

2 cups fresh broccoli florets

Salt and pepper to taste

3 to 4 tablespoons Parmesan cheese, grated

Nonstick cooking spray

1. Preheat oven to 325°F.

2. In a large mixing bowl, blend all ingredients except Parmesan cheese and cooking spray.

3. Spray pie pan with nonstick cooking spray.

4. Pour mixture into a medium pie pan.

5. Sprinkle Parmesan cheese on top.

6. Bake for 1 hour.

Spinach Pie in the Face

Children tend to enjoy the soft and smooth texture of a quiche. The type of vegetable
can be varied with this recipe, and it is perfect for any meal of the day.

INGREDIENTS | SERVES 8–12

Nonstick cooking spray

4 tablespoons onions, chopped finely

1 (12-ounce) package frozen spinach, cooked and drained

½ pound shredded mozzarella cheese

½ cup grated Parmesan cheese

½ cup low-fat ricotta cheese

3 eggs

1 cup 2% low-fat milk

Pepper to taste

1. Preheat oven to 350°F.

2. Spray a small skillet with nonstick cooking spray. Add onions and sauté until transparent and soft.

3. In a medium mixing bowl, combine sautéed onions, spinach, cheeses, eggs, milk, and pepper. Blend well.

4. Spray a medium pie pan with nonstick cooking spray.

5. Pour mixture into pan and bake for 30 minutes, until top is golden brown.

Pasta with String Beans and White Beans

All kinds of different textures thrown into this delicious pasta dish, all kinds of things to pick from! Filled with great vegetables and protein and iron-packed beans, too.

INGREDIENTS | SERVES 6–8

8 ounces penne or rotini pasta, uncooked

2 tablespoons pine nuts

2 tablespoons olive oil

1 medium red pepper, cut in thin strips

2 cloves garlic, minced

1½ pounds fresh string beans, washed and cut into bite-sized pieces

1 (15-ounce) can white beans (or black beans), drained

1 teaspoon salt

1 tablespoon dried basil

½ cup Parmesan cheese, grated

1. Prepare pasta as directed. Set aside.

2. In microwave-safe dish, cook pine nuts in microwave for 2 to 4 minutes, until golden.

3. Place olive oil in medium frying pan.

4. On medium heat, pan-fry peppers and garlic, until soft.

5. Stir in string beans, and continue cooking until tender. Add a little water if the pan is getting dry.

6. Stir in white beans, and mix well.

7. Cover, and allow to cook 2 to 3 minutes more.

8. Transfer pasta into a serving dish.

9. Toss pasta, string bean/white bean mixture, salt, basil, and Parmesan cheese.

10. Sprinkle with pine nuts and serve.

Oven-Baked Acorn Squash

Easy and delicious. This sweet, bright vegetable is usually a favorite for picky veggie eaters.

INGREDIENTS | **SERVES 4–8**

2 large acorn squash

Nonstick cooking spray

2 to 3 tablespoons trans-fat-free margarine

2 to 3 tablespoons brown sugar

2 to 3 tablespoons ground cinnamon

Yellow, Orange, and Red Fruits and Vegetables—a Must!

Years of research support the fact that these high-beta-carotene foods, rich in these colors will help to ward off cancer and heart disease. Critical antioxidants, it is suggested you get them primarily in foods, not supplement form. Keep offering these! They will eventually like them (or at least some of them)!

1. Preheat oven to 375°F.

2. Slice each acorn squash into 4 quarters.

3. Scoop out the seeds.

4. Spray a medium glass dish with nonstick cooking spray.

5. Place squash face down in dish.

6. Add water to the dish until it covers the squash about halfway.

7. Bake in the oven for 30 minutes.

8. Remove from oven and drain water.

9. Turn the squash pieces over, so they face up.

10. Place about 1 teaspoon margarine, sugar, and cinnamon on each piece. Spread well.

11. Return to oven for 10 to 15 minutes.

Root Vegetable Pancakes

*This is a wonderful way to get your toddlers to take in unique vegetables—
a fun pancake to serve with applesauce (or low-fat sour cream).*

INGREDIENTS | SERVES 10–20

2 cups white potatoes, unpeeled, uncooked and shredded

1 cup sweet potato, peeled, uncooked, and shredded

1 cup canned beets, drained, rinsed, and shredded

1 cup carrots, shredded

1 cup parsnips, shredded

2 eggs, beaten

¼ cup whole wheat flour

¼ cup flour

1 teaspoon salt

½ teaspoon pepper

3 to 4 tablespoons olive or canola oil

Applesauce or low-fat sour cream (optional)

1. Place shredded potatoes in a food processor with a steel blade.

2. Cover and pulse for 30 seconds to 1 minute or until smooth.

3. In a large mixing bowl, combine potatoes, carrots, beets, and parsnips.

4. Add beaten eggs, both flours, salt and pepper.

5. In a large frying pan, heat oil on low heat.

6. Using about ¼ cup mixture for each pancake, drop into pan and fry until golden brown, flip once. Pancake should take 3 to 4 minutes to cook.

7. Serve hot.

Camouflaging Vegetables Is Not a Crime!

Probably the number one problem feeding children today is how to get them to eat their veggies. Vegetables are a significant part of the diet—providing fiber, for one, regulating their bowels, and keeping everything moving in the system, marching to a little megaphone! Vegetables keep you feeling "full and satisfied" long after you have finished eating them. Additionally, the vitamin C, potassium, iron, vitamin A, and beta-carotene are all part of those essential veggies: good fuel for the muscles, and phytochemicals and antioxidants for long-term cancer prevention.

Sweet-ie Potato Pancakes

A light and heavenly side dish—filled with cancer-fighting nutrients, good for holidays or at any family meal.

INGREDIENTS | SERVES 8

2 pounds sweet potatoes, peeled (about 4 to 5 potatoes)
2 eggs, beaten
½ cup flour
1 tablespoon dark brown sugar
1 teaspoon salt
¾ teaspoon apple pie spice
3 tablespoons canola oil
Nonstick cooking spray

1. Shred peeled potatoes (should result in approximately 4½ to 5 cups of potatoes).

2. In food processor, puree 1 cup of the potatoes.

3. Place all of the potatoes in a large mixing bowl. Add eggs, flour, sugar, salt, and apple pie spice. Stir well.

4. Place oil in large skillet on low heat, and pan-fry pancakes until brown on each side.

5. If the pan becomes dry, spray with nonstick cooking spray, and continue frying.

Peter Piper Picked a Pumpkin Pudding

A sweet and delicious pudding that doesn't have to be saved for Thanksgiving.

INGREDIENTS | SERVES 8–10

2 (12-ounce) boxes frozen butternut squash
1 (15-ounce) can solid pumpkin
2 eggs, beaten
2 tablespoons sugar
½ teaspoon ginger
½ teaspoon cinnamon
1 teaspoon vanilla extract
Nonstick cooking spray

1. Preheat oven to 375°F.

2. Cook squash according to package directions.

3. In a medium mixing bowl, mix squash, pumpkin, eggs, sugar, seasonings, and vanilla extract.

4. Spray nonstick cooking spray into a medium pie pan.

5. Bake 45 minutes.

Black Bean and Veggie Lasagna

This is a unique blend of Italy and South America, coming together in one delicious dish!

INGREDIENTS | SERVES 12

Nonstick cooking spray

1 medium green bell pepper, cut in strips

1 medium red pepper, cut in strips

1 (16-ounce) can black beans, rinsed and drained

1 small onion, diced

1 (28-ounce) can crushed tomatoes

4 cloves garlic, minced

¼ cup cilantro leaves

1 tablespoon chili powder

2 teaspoons dried oregano

1 (16-ounce) can kernel corn

2 cups low-fat cottage cheese

8 ounces low-fat (2%) shredded Cheddar cheese

Pepper to taste

8 ounces oven-ready lasagna noodles

¼ cup grated Parmesan cheese

1. Preheat oven to 350°F.

2. Spray a small skillet with nonstick cooking spray. Sauté peppers and onions until tender.

3. In a large saucepan, place beans sautéed peppers and onions, canned tomatoes, garlic, cilantro, chili powder, and oregano. Simmer for 15 minutes.

4. Add corn, cottage cheese, shredded Cheddar cheese, and pepper to taste. Mix well.

5. Spray large (9½" × 14") baking dish with nonstick cooking spray.

6. Place a layer of oven-ready noodles on the bottom of the pan. Next, pour prepared sauce on top to cover the noodles. Layer noodles and sauce again.

7. Sprinkle with Parmesan cheese.

8. Bake for 45 to 50 minutes, until the top is golden brown.

The Story of the Bean

Beans seem to have become more popular these days—in soups such as lentil, black bean, split pea, white bean, and minestrone, and in bean dips, hummus, beans and rice, and even beans in a lasagna dish. Beans are a wonderful food—so start the kids early, adding beans to their diets in one, or several, of the above ways—incredible fiber, protein and iron; very few foods are packed with such power.

Cheese and Potato Pancakes

Have your children help prepare the pancakes—alternate flavors of cheeses, or even give a sweet potato pancake a chance! Those sweet potatoes are even healthier!

INGREDIENTS | SERVES 6–8

3 large potatoes, peeled and cubed

¼ cup low-fat milk

2 tablespoons trans-fat-free margarine

2 cloves garlic, minced

½ cup low-fat mozzarella cheese, shredded

Salt and pepper to taste

2 to 3 tablespoons canola or olive oil

1. In a large pot, bring sufficient water to a boil to cover potatoes.

2. Add potatoes, and cook until potatoes are tender, approximately 15 to 20 minutes.

3. Cool potatoes, shred them, and set aside.

4. In a medium saucepan, combine milk, margarine, and garlic. Bring to a boil for 1 minute.

5. Mix in the potatoes, and then blend in the cheese until even thickness.

6. In a large skillet, heat oil on low heat, and pan-fry pancakes until browned on both sides.

Chunky Homemade Baked Potato Chips

A very tasty version of fried potatoes—but baked! Looks and tastes just like a potato chip!

INGREDIENTS | SERVES 8

Nonstick cooking spray

4 tablespoons grated Parmesan cheese

1 teaspoon salt

1 teaspoon garlic powder

1 pound baking potatoes, scrubbed, and cut in thin slices

1. Preheat oven to 350°F.

2. Spray a baking sheet with nonstick cooking spray.

3. In a small bowl, mix cheese, salt, and garlic powder.

4. Place potatoes in a single layer on baking sheet. Sprinkle with cheese mixture.

5. Spray top of potatoes with nonstick cooking spray.

6. Bake for 30 to 45 minutes, until potatoes are tender.

Stringy Spaghetti Squash

Shhh—the children are sure they are eating spaghetti! Looks like spaghetti, but tastes even better!

INGREDIENTS | SERVES 3–4

1 large spaghetti squash, cleaned

1 tablespoon trans-fat-free margarine

3 to 4 tablespoons Parmesan cheese

1. Pierce the skin of the squash with a fork in about five to six places and microwave for 2 to 3 minutes.

2. Cut the squash in half (lengthwise) and scoop out the seeds.

3. Use fork to scrape into strands, and place in a small serving bowl.

4. Blend squash with margarine, and sprinkle with Parmesan cheese.

5. Serve immediately while still warm.

CHAPTER 3

From Toddlers to School-Age—Eating Breakfast for Better Grades

Great Grilled Cheese Sandwich

Purchase a whole grain bread that has a minimum of 5 grams of fiber in 2 slices. Today, you can find a whole grain/whole wheat bread that appears white in color. This is especially helpful if your children do not want to eat bread if it is "brown."

INGREDIENTS | SERVES 1

1 slice whole grain bread
1 to·2 slices low-fat American cheese
1 tablespoon trans-fat-free margarine

Make This a Complete Meal with Ease

Don't forget that glass of milk and a handful of grapes. With that, you have incorporated healthy carbohydrate (bread), protein (cheese and milk), calcium (cheese and milk) and fruit. That was easy. Of course, any fruit can be substituted—let them choose one of their favorites!

1. Set toaster oven to 300°F.

2. Spread margarine evenly on both sides of bread.

3. Place cheese on top of bread.

4. Bake for 5 minutes, or until cheese is melted.

5. Remove from toaster oven. Fold it to make a sandwich, and serve.

Quick Hot Oatmeal

Most oatmeal recipes call for using water. However, you can always substitute milk for a power breakfast with more protein and more calcium. If you are in a rush in the morning, feel free to use the microwave!

INGREDIENTS | SERVES 1

½ cup cooked oats, dry
1 cup low-fat milk
½ teaspoon vanilla extract
1 teaspoon sugar (optional)

Not a "Real" Breakfast Food Eater?

Try any sandwich in the morning, with a glass of low-fat milk and a piece of fruit—2 slices whole grain bread, and 2 to 3 slices turkey, roast beef, or ham, and 1 teaspoon of light mayonnaise or mustard if desired. That works just fine as breakfast.

1. Pour the oats into a microwave-safe bowl.

2. Add milk and vanilla extract.

3. Microwave for 1 minute 30 seconds, or until thick and creamy.

4. Sweeten with sugar if desired.

Stuffed French Toast Pudding

Serve with low-sugar pancake syrup and a low-fat glass of milk. It's divine!

INGREDIENTS | SERVES 6–8

1 (8-ounce) package low-fat cream cheese

7 slices whole wheat bread (cut the crust off)

Nonstick cooking spray

3 eggs plus 6 egg whites

1 cup low-fat milk

1 teaspoon vanilla extract

¼ cup low-sugar pancake syrup

Cinnamon and sugar to taste

Powdered sugar to garnish

1. Cut cream cheese and bread into 1-inch cubes.

2. Spray 9" × 11" pan with nonstick cooking spray.

3. Spread cubes of cream cheese and bread around the bottom of the pan.

4. In a blender mix eggs, egg whites, milk, vanilla, and syrup.

5. Pour over bread and cream cheese mixture.

6. Cover and refrigerate overnight. Or if you want to serve that morning, allow liquid mixture to set into bread/cream cheese for 2 hours.

7. Preheat oven to 350°F.

8. Sprinkle top with cinnamon and sugar. Bake 45 to 50 minutes.

9. Before serving, garnish with a sprinkle of powdered sugar.

Egg-cellent Sandwich with Cheese

To expedite the morning breakfast process, feel free to scramble the eggs the night before and just place in the refrigerator! Then in the morning just place the cheese and eggs onto the muffin, put the sandwich in the microwave and heat it and go.

INGREDIENTS | SERVES 1

1 to 2 eggs
Nonstick cooking spray
1 to 2 slices low-fat Cheddar cheese
1 whole wheat English muffin or whole grain roll

1. Spray a small frying pan with nonstick cooking spray.

2. Scramble eggs in frying pan.

3. Assemble sandwich with eggs and slice(s) of cheese.

Spicy Breakfast Wrap

Choose your own level of salsa! Mild or hot, this is a fun and unique portable breakfast!

INGREDIENTS | SERVES 1

1 to 2 eggs
Nonstick cooking spray
1 whole wheat tortilla
3 tablespoons salsa

1. Spray a small frying pan with nonstick cooking spray.

2. Scramble the eggs in the pan.

3. Lay tortilla flat and place scrambled eggs down the center. Top eggs with salsa. Roll tortilla up and serve.

Talk about Quick and Easy!

With the protein of eggs, and the tomato salsa for kick (and even a little bit of vitamin C and antioxidants), add in the fiber of the wrap or tortilla, and a glass of milk, and the nutrients in the morning do not get any better than this. It takes moments to prepare, and just a few minutes to eat, but the children will have a nutritious breakfast, which will absolutely improve their performance on that school day!

Weekend Grilled French Toast

Kick back on the weekend, and make something family friendly. This will be a grilled or pan-fried dish, fairly healthy—and once again, won't keep you in the kitchen for too long.

INGREDIENTS | SERVES 3–4

Nonstick cooking spray
2 eggs
1 cup low-fat milk
1 teaspoon vanilla extract
4 to 6 slices whole grain bread
Sugar-free pancake syrup, to taste

1. Spray nonstick cooking spray into frying pan. Place on low heat.

2. Whip eggs, milk, and vanilla extract with a wire whisk.

3. Place in a large shallow bowl (large enough to dip the bread into).

4. Dip each slice of bread into the egg-milk mixture.

5. Carefully transfer the bread into the frying pan. Cook on each side until golden brown.

6. Serve with sugar-free pancake syrup.

Split-Second Yogurt Sundae

A perfect on-the-run morning breakfast—any modification can happen: assorted flavors of yogurt, and different fruits and cereals.

INGREDIENTS | SERVES 1

4 ounces light canned peach or pear slices, drained
1 cup vanilla low-fat yogurt
½ cup favorite cereal (e.g., Raisin Bran or Cheerios)

1. Place ½ cup of yogurt in a glass.

2. Layer peaches or pears, then the remaining yogurt. Top with cereal.

3. Serve immediately or cover and refrigerate until ready to eat.

Speedy Is Important

In your children's generation, school starts very early in the morning, and is a very long day. Breakfast is so critical to the day—but so many children find it easier to just run out of the house without eating, and suffer the consequences of feeling hungry later on. Don't let them out of the house without something to eat.

Banana Muffins and Milk

A delicious treat—a little sweet fun, and served with an 8-ounce glass of milk, it's a perfect way to get ⅓ of their calcium requirement for the day!

INGREDIENTS | SERVES 6–12

1 teaspoon baking soda
4 tablespoons low-fat sour cream
Nonstick cooking spray
1¼ cups sugar
½ cup canola oil
2 eggs
1 cup mashed, ripe bananas
1 cup all-purpose flour
½ cup whole wheat flour
1 teaspoon vanilla
¼ teaspoon salt

1. In a small dish, add baking soda to low-fat sour cream and set aside.

2. Preheat oven to 350°F.

3. Spray muffin tin with nonstick cooking spray (or use baking cups).

4. With an electric mixer, cream together the sugar, oil, and eggs.

5. Add the baking soda and sour cream mixture, and blend well.

6. Add bananas, flours, vanilla, and salt, and stir until smooth.

7. Pour into muffin tins. Fill each about halfway with batter.

8. Bake 45 minutes or until toothpick comes out dry.

Egg and Potato Volcano

An innovative and unique breakfast the kids will love—great for the weekend!

INGREDIENTS | SERVES 4

3 medium potatoes, Yukon Gold (preferably)

2 to 3 tablespoons trans-fat-free margarine

½ teaspoon salt

Black pepper, to taste

4 to 5 slices turkey bacon, cooked, chopped

Nonstick cooking spray

4 large eggs

4 tablespoons Parmesan cheese

2 teaspoons fresh parsley, chopped (garnish)

1. Preheat oven to 400°F.

2. Clean potatoes and create several holes in each potato with a fork.

3. Put potatoes on a paper towel and place in the microwave. Microwave on high power for 7 to 10 minutes, until soft.

4. Mash the potatoes, and add margarine, salt, and pepper.

5. Add the chopped turkey bacon to this mixture.

6. In a muffin pan, spray nonstick cooking spray in 4 of the muffin cups.

7. Place about ¾ cup of the potato mixture into each of the muffin cups.

8. Make a well in the center of the potato mixture, and crack an egg into each.

9. Sprinkle each with 1 tablespoon Parmesan cheese.

10. Bake for 12 to 15 minutes.

11. Garnish with parsley and serve.

Dutch Baked Apple Pancake

Worth the work—and fun for the whole family!

INGREDIENTS | SERVES 3–4

Apple filling:

2 tablespoons trans-fat-free margarine

3 to 4 Granny Smith apples, peeled, cored, and sliced thinly

6 tablespoons sugar

1 teaspoon cinnamon

Pancake batter:

3 eggs

½ cup flour

½ cup low-fat milk

1 tablespoon low-fat plain yogurt

1 teaspoon lemon zest, grated

Powdered sugar, to garnish

A Fun Breakfast—Loaded with Vitamin C

Add either an 8-ounce container of any flavored low-fat yogurt, or a glass of low-fat milk, and some fresh fruit salad, and this becomes a perfect well-rounded breakfast for all.

1. Preheat oven to 400°F.

2. In a skillet, melt the margarine.

3. Add sliced apples, cinnamon, and sugar. Sauté, continue stirring, until apples are soft. Remove from heat, transfer apples to a large round pie pan and set aside.

4. Mix eggs until foamy.

5. Add flour, milk, yogurt, and lemon zest, and beat until smooth.

6. Pour pancake batter over apples.

7. Place in the oven for 25 minutes, until puffy and golden brown.

8. Using a sieve, dust powdered sugar over the top before serving.

The Traditional Belgian Waffle

Lots of topping options including: fresh berries, raisins, jam, a few mini-chocolate chips, low-sugar pancake syrup, powdered sugar.

INGREDIENTS | SERVES 8

2 cups all-purpose flour
2 teaspoons baking powder
3 tablespoons confectioners' sugar
1 tablespoon canola oil
2 cups low-fat milk
3 eggs, separated
2 teaspoons vanilla extract
Pinch of salt
Nonstick cooking spray

1. Combine flour, baking powder, confectioners' sugar, oil, milk, egg yolks, vanilla, and salt. Mix well.

2. Beat the egg whites until stiff and fold into batter.

3. Spray waffle iron with cooking spray.

4. Using a 4-ounce measuring cup, fill the measuring cup and pour batter into waffle iron.

5. Bake about 2 to 3 minutes, or until light golden brown.

6. Top with fruit or your favorite topping.

Round Out This Easy Breakfast

Add a serving of protein, e.g., scrambled eggs, low-fat cottage cheese, or a glass of low-sugar chocolate milk for a fast and complete breakfast.

PB and B Wrap

Tip: Prepare this quick-and-easy wrap first thing in the morning.
If prepared the night before, it is going to be soggy!

INGREDIENTS | SERVES 1

1 whole wheat wrap
2 tablespoons trans-fat-free peanut butter
2 teaspoons honey
Small ripe banana

1. Spread peanut butter and honey onto wrap.

2. Mash banana. Spread onto wrap.

3. Pull up one side of the wrap about ⅓ of the way and fold over.

4. Wrap both sides in, and close the top.

A High-Energy Way to Start the Day

Whole wheat wrap, peanut butter, and banana—hits all of those necessary groups of food first thing in the morning. Those first few classes of the day will have students' ultimate concentration! Whole wheat bread or a whole wheat roll can always be interchanged for the warp.

Fruit Salad and Yogurt Parfait

Allow your child to choose his favorite low-fat yogurt flavor, and his favorite fruits, and this becomes a delightful morning meal. Serve with a whole grain English muffin or small whole wheat pita.

INGREDIENTS | SERVES 2

1 to 1½ cups fresh fruit chunks (cantaloupe, honeydew, watermelon, grapes)
1 small apple, cored and sliced
1 to 2 cups flavored low-fat yogurt
4 tablespoons raisins (optional)
4 tablespoons low-fat granola (or other favorite high-fiber cereal)

1. In a parfait glass or a stemmed glass, place half the fruit at the bottom.

2. Layer with ½ cup yogurt and raisins. Layer once again with fruit, and then yogurt.

3. Top with granola or other cereal.

Don't Let Kids Skip Breakfast

If there were a meal of the day to be chosen as the "leading role," it would undoubtedly be the breakfast meal. Remember the prior meal (dinner) was eaten at least 9 hours before, so if kids skip breakfast and wait until lunch, that leaves 13 to 15 hours without replenishing any energy. Remind yourself, as their parent, how you feel after that many hours without food!

Bunny's Favorite Carrot Raisin Bread

*With a nice cold glass of milk, or container of low-fat yogurt, this makes
for a quick and tasty breakfast—weekday or weekend.*

INGREDIENTS | SERVES 10–12

1 cup sugar

¼ teaspoon baking powder

1 teaspoon baking soda

½ teaspoon salt

1 teaspoon cinnamon

½ teaspoon ground nutmeg

1⅔ cups flour

½ cup canola oil

1 teaspoon vanilla extract

½ cup water

1 cup cooked mashed carrots, cooled

2 eggs

½ cup raisins

Nonstick cooking spray

1. Preheat oven to 325°F.

2. Combine sugar, baking powder, baking soda, salt, and spices.

3. Add flour, oil, vanilla, water, carrots, eggs, and raisins.

4. Mix until well blended.

5. Spray loaf pan with nonstick cooking spray.

6. Pour batter into loaf pan, and bake 1 hour and 30 minutes, until toothpick comes out dry.

Fruits and Veggies Do Count, Even When Out of Sight

This recipe is a pleasant way to offer sweet carrots and raisins. The ultimate goal will be for your children to try a variety of fruits and vegetables, and then pick out those they will continue to make a regular part of their diet (for now—remember that changes over time). Do not panic when cauliflower is their favorite one week, and they won't touch it the next! That's normal!

Blockbuster Cheese "Pot Stickers"

Serve with fresh fruit, pie fillings, low-fat sour cream, or applesauce, or all of it! Low-fat cottage cheese, or even goat cheese will change the flavor and make these pot stickers something unusual.

INGREDIENTS | SERVES 6–12

Batter:

½ cup flour

½ teaspoon salt

2 eggs, well beaten

⅔ cup low-fat milk

1 tablespoon trans-fat-free margarine, melted

Filling:

½ pound part-skim farmer's cheese

½ pound whipped cream cheese

1 egg, well beaten

2 tablespoons sugar

2 tablespoons trans-fat-free margarine, melted

¼ teaspoon cinnamon

Nonstick cooking spray

1. In a small bowl, sift flour. Add salt.

2. In a medium bowl, combine eggs, milk, and margarine.

3. Add flour slowly to egg batter and beat until smooth. Set aside.

4. Prepare the filling in a separate bowl. Mix the farmer's cheese and cream cheese together.

5. Add beaten egg to the cheese mixture. Add sugar, melted margarine and cinnamon. Blend well. Set aside.

6. Spray a small skillet with nonstick cooking spray, and heat on low heat.

7. Pour the batter mixture into heated skillet, just enough to cover the bottom of the skillet.

8. Cook until firm and slightly browned on one side.

9. On a large piece of wax paper, place the completed crepe.

10. When all the batter is used up, fill each crepe with about 2 tablespoons of cheese filling.

11. Place the filling on the center of the browned side of the crepe and fold over the 2 opposite sides to close the crepe.

12. Roll up the remaining sides to enclose the filling in the crepe.

13. Spray cooking spray into skillet once again, and heat. Brown crepe just before serving.

Breakfast Crepes

Worth the time—here's another one the kids can be hands-on with in the kitchen. A wonderful Sunday brunch item.

INGREDIENTS | SERVES 8

1 cup all-purpose flour
2 eggs
½ cup low-fat milk
½ cup water
¼ teaspoon salt
2 tablespoons trans-fat-free margarine, melted
1 to 2 tablespoons canola oil

Fillings for Breakfast Crepes

Berries and yogurt: fill crepes with low-fat flavored or vanilla yogurt and fresh berries. Roll crepes and dust with powdered sugar. Dessert Crepes: Using above batter, spread crepes with low-fat frozen yogurt and sliced bananas. Roll crepes and dust with powdered sugar. This batter is so adaptable and delicious that you may fill the crepes with just about any combination of foods, just fill, roll, and enjoy.

1. In a large mixing bowl, mix together the flour and the eggs.

2. Gradually add in the milk and water, stirring until smooth.

3. Add the salt and melted margarine. Beat until smooth.

4. Heat a lightly oiled frying pan over low heat.

5. Pour the batter into the frying pan, using approximately ¼ cup for each crepe.

6. Tilt pan in a circular motion, so that the batter coats the surface evenly.

7. Cook the crepe for about 2 minutes, until the bottom is light brown.

8. Loosen with a spatula; turn and cook the other side.

9. Fill as desired and serve.

Beautiful Baked Omelet

You may choose to try different cheese selections, and certainly opt to add the kids' favorite veggies.

INGREDIENTS | SERVES 6

Nonstick cooking spray
6 eggs
1 cup low-fat milk
½ cup all-purpose flour
½ teaspoon salt
¼ teaspoon ground black pepper
1 cup low-fat Cheddar cheese, shredded

1. Preheat oven to 450°F.

2. Spray a 9" × 13" pan with nonstick cooking spray.

3. Whisk together eggs, milk, flour, salt, and pepper until smooth.

4. Pour mixture into pan.

5. Bake about 20 minutes, until set.

6. Remove from oven and sprinkle with cheese.

7. Cut omelet in 6 pieces, place on separate dishes, and carefully roll up each omelet, cheese-side in. Cheese will melt.

8. Serve with whole grain roll.

Peanut Butter Monster Muffins

A perfect school breakfast, quick, and full of those nutrients that will keep the brain running until lunchtime—do include a glass of low-fat milk, a slice of low-fat cheese, or a container of low-fat flavored yogurt, and a piece of fruit, to complete this meal. Nice for a change.

INGREDIENTS | **SERVES 12**

2 eggs
1 cup low-fat milk
1 medium banana, mashed
¼ cup trans-fat-free peanut butter
⅓ cup canola oil
¼ cup frozen apple juice concentrate, thawed completely
¼ cup nonfat dry milk
2¼ cups flour
1½ teaspoons baking powder
1 teaspoon baking soda

1. Preheat oven to 350°F.

2. In a small bowl, beat eggs. Set aside.

3. In a large bowl, combine the milk, mashed banana, peanut butter, oil, apple juice, and dry milk.

4. Add the eggs to the large bowl. Mix until creamy and smooth.

5. Combine the flour, baking powder, and baking soda, and add into the large bowl. Mix again until smooth.

6. Line a muffin tin with paper liners (or lightly spray with nonstick spray).

7. Fill each muffin cup about ⅔ full.

8. Bake for about 12 to 15 minutes.

Breakfast Banana Bars

Another on-the-run breakfast. Needs a glass of milk or a hard-boiled egg to go with it, and the kids are good to go.

INGREDIENTS | SERVES 24–36

Nonstick cooking spray
½ cup brown sugar
1 (10-ounce) jar low-sugar apricot preserves
½ cup trans-fat-free margarine
1 teaspoon vanilla
2 eggs
1 cup all-purpose flour
¾ cup whole wheat flour
½ teaspoon baking powder
½ teaspoon baking soda
3 medium bananas, mashed

1. Preheat oven to 350°F.

2. Spray 13" × 9" pan with nonstick cooking spray.

3. In a medium mixing bowl, combine sugar, preserves, margarine, vanilla, and eggs. Blend well.

4. Stir in by hand the flours, baking powder, baking soda, and bananas. Stir until moistened.

5. Pour into baking pan. Bake 30 to 40 minutes until toothpick inserted in center comes out clean.

Little Johnny's Johnnycakes

An old ethnic favorite, made a little more healthfully. Scramble a few eggs and serve with melon slices, and a wonderful and unique little breakfast has arrived.

INGREDIENTS | SERVES 10

2 cups cornmeal
1 teaspoon salt
4 tablespoons trans-fat-free margarine, melted
1 cup low-fat milk
2 tablespoons boiling water (approximately)
Nonstick cooking spray

1. In a medium mixing bowl, blend the cornmeal, salt, and margarine together.

2. Add the milk and enough boiling water to make a moist but firm batter. Continue mixing until well blended.

3. Spray a large skillet with nonstick cooking spray. On low heat, drop batter by tablespoon-size spoonfuls.

4. Compress slightly with the back of the spoon, forming a thick pancake.

5. When brown, turn and cook the other side, until golden brown.

Oatmeal Strawberry Bread

This recipe requires a bread machine. Follow the directions per your particular model of brea...

INGREDIENTS | SERVES 10

⅓ cup low-fat milk
⅓ cup fresh strawberries, mashed
⅓ cup whipped cream cheese
1 tablespoon trans-fat-free margarine
1 teaspoon vanilla extract
2 tablespoons honey
½ cup rolled oats
1½ cups bread flour
1½ teaspoons active dry yeast

1. Place ingredients in the container/pan of the bread machine in the order suggested.

2. Bake as instructed by your machine.

Fun Fruit and Yogurt Kabobs

You could make these with any type of fruit, any type of low-fat cheese, and any flavor yogurt. If using grapes, remember to cut them in half for children under five to prevent choking.

INGREDIENTS | SERVES 4

½ medium cantaloupe, cut in small chunks
20 to 25 seedless grapes
1½ cups fresh pineapple chunks
4 low-fat string cheeses, cut in small chunks
4 popsicle sticks or skewers
2 cups low-fat yogurt

1. Get all tools and ingredients ready: the fruit, the cheese, and the sticks/skewers.

2. Alternate the cantaloupe, grapes, pineapple, and cheese on the stick/skewer.

3. Use ½ cup yogurt and dip your stick or skewer in for a refreshing snack!

A Fun, Child-Friendly Way to Serve Colorful Fruits

The more they see them, the more likely they are to eat them. A great idea to add in a little protein and calcium (the cheese), and a favorite yogurt flavor for dipping. Vary the fruits and the yogurt flavors for a cool breakfast, or a snack. Remember, let the kids make this one!

Warm Apple Pie Waffles

Prepare the night before, and the kids will love this sweet waffle—don't forget the protein source to go with it, either that glass of milk, eggs, or container of low-fat cottage cheese. Remember to substitute different fruits if desired.

INGREDIENTS | SERVES 4

1 cup whole wheat flour

¾ cup refined flour

½ teaspoon salt

1 teaspoon apple pie spice

¾ cups warm water

1 teaspoon honey

2 teaspoons active dry yeast

2 medium apples, peeled and grated

3 tablespoons unsweetened applesauce

1 cup low-fat milk

2 egg whites

Nonstick cooking spray

1. In a large mixing bowl, stir together the flours, salt, and apple pie spice. Place aside.

2. In a separate medium mixing bowl, stir together the water and honey. Sprinkle the yeast over the surface of the water/honey mixture. Let this stand for about 5 minutes, in order to dissolve.

3. When the yeast has dissolved, stir in the apples, applesauce, milk, and egg whites until well blended.

4. Stir this mixture into the dry ingredients. Cover and let sit for 15 to 20 minutes.

5. Heat a waffle iron, and coat with nonstick cooking spray.

6. Spoon the waffle batter into the waffle iron (about 3 to 4 heaping tablespoons). Close the iron.

7. Cook waffle for about 6 to 7 minutes, or until the steam stops coming out and the waffle can be easily removed.

8. Continue with remaining batter to create delicious waffles.

"Bran New" Cranberry Muffins

Muffins are such an easy way to get in healthful carbohydrate for that morning brain function. Once more, as long as there is a quick source of protein to go along with it, a hard boiled egg, or a slice of low-fat cheese, they're good to go until lunchtime.

INGREDIENTS | SERVES 12

Nonstick cooking spray
1 cup whole wheat flour
1 cup refined flour
2 teaspoons baking powder
2 teaspoons baking soda
1 tablespoon barley malt flour
3 tablespoons canola oil
⅔ cup honey
1¼ cups low-fat milk
1 cup low-fat plain yogurt
1 teaspoon vanilla extract
2 eggs, beaten
1 cup "cranraisins" or dried cranberries

1. Preheat oven to 350°F.

2. Spray 12-cup muffin pan with nonstick cooking spray, or use paper liners.

3. In a medium bowl, mix flours, baking powder, baking soda, and barley malt flour.

4. In a separate medium bowl, thoroughly blend oil, honey, milk, yogurt, vanilla extract and eggs.

5. Gradually blend liquid mixture into the flour mixture until well moistened.

6. Add in the cranraisins/dried cranberries, and mix well.

7. Spoon into the prepared muffin pan.

8. Bake 20 to 25 minutes, until a toothpick inserted in the center of a muffin comes out clean.

CHAPTER 4

Packing Those Healthy (Not Traded!) School Lunches

Chicken Salad Pita Sandwich

Purchase the best whole grain bread—the first label on the ingredient list should be "whole wheat flour," not "enriched wheat flour." Look for anywhere from 3 to 5 grams of fiber per slice of bread.

INGREDIENTS | SERVES 1

3 ounces solid white chicken

1 to 2 tablespoons low-fat mayonnaise

1 teaspoon celery salt (optional)

1 teaspoon garlic powder (optional)

1 medium whole wheat pita

1. Mash chicken with low-fat mayonnaise. Add spices, if desired. Put in pita bread and serve.

They Won't Be Sharing with Their Classmates

The rest of the lunch box should include: ½ to 1 cup of berries or a small banana; you can add a little chopped lettuce and tomato to the sandwich, for the older kids; a smart snack, such as pretzels or low-fat popcorn (for children older than 5 to 6 years old). Your kids won't trade this lunch.

Happy Hour Tapas for Kids

An easy, two-minute packing job—the crunch is just great; it sure feels like a cocktail party!

INGREDIENTS | SERVES 1

2 to 3 low-fat string cheeses

1 serving whole grain crackers (about 8)

½ cucumber, sliced

1 large carrot, sliced

1 celery stalk, sliced

1. Cut string cheese into chunks and place in a plastic sandwich bag with the crackers.

2. Cut up the vegetables, and place in a plastic sandwich bag.

A Great "Finger Food" Idea

Just what you're looking for: easy, and the kids seem to like the variety of foods. Remember to add a 100-calorie pack of healthier cookies, and their favorite fruit to their lunch box. Avoid packing juice or juice boxes—encourage your kids to be great water drinkers. Juice is full of sugar, and eating the fruit is a much better idea!

Rice and Beans with Flair

The rice and beans can be served at room temperature, or if they have access to a microwave, feel free to let them warm it up!

INGREDIENTS | SERVES 1

Nonstick cooking spray
½ teaspoon minced garlic
1 tablespoon onions, finely chopped
½ to 1 cup canned black beans
½ to 1 cup brown rice

Color Is Important When Packing Children's Lunches

Make lunch more palatable by packing different colored items, too. Consider sliced colored peppers, or black olives; add a serving of pretzels, a serving of graham or animal crackers, a sliced peach or ½ cup strawberries in a plastic container. Don't forget a drink—the best choice is a bottle of water.

1. Spray nonstick cooking spray into a frying pan. Over low heat, sauté garlic and onion until soft.

2. In a small pot, warm beans on top of stove, adding the garlic and onion.

3. Cook rice according to directions (consider adding a bouillon cube into the boiling water for more flavor).

4. Mix the rice and beans together. Place in a plastic container.

Left-Over Weekend Chili

Substitutions can be made to this recipe, for instance, using ground turkey breast or ground veal for lower saturated fat content; you can also use black beans or white beans.

INGREDIENTS | SERVES 10–12

2 medium onions, chopped

2 garlic cloves, chopped

1 green bell pepper, chopped

Nonstick cooking spray

3 pounds ground sirloin

1 small package chili spice mix

1 (24-ounce) jar tomato sauce

1 (6-ounce) can tomato purée

½ cup ketchup

1 (15-ounce) can kidney beans

1 square Baker's chocolate

Salt and pepper to taste

1. Sauté onions, garlic, and pepper in cooking spray on low heat, until transparent.

2. Add ground sirloin, browning until done. Stir continuously.

3. Add chili mix, tomato sauce, purée, ketchup, and beans. Simmer for 10 to 15 minutes.

4. Add chocolate square and continue to simmer until ready to serve, a minimum of 30 minutes. Salt and pepper to taste.

A Wonderful Warm School Lunch

This one they won't give up either! For a cold winter day, send the chili in a plastic container, along with a bunch of baby carrots, some whole-grain crackers, a healthy snack, and a fresh peach or pear—there won't be any leftovers!

Weekend Sail (Tuna) Boat

If you can encourage your kids to eat fish at an early age—that habit is priceless! Offer the solid white tuna no more than once per week, due to higher mercury levels; however, levels in chunk light tuna are lower—kids can have this type of tuna more often.

INGREDIENTS | SERVES 4

2 white baking potatoes

12 ounces tuna packed in water

3 to 4 tablespoons low-fat mayonnaise

1 to 2 stalks celery

Pepper, onion powder, and garlic powder to taste

4 pretzel rods

4 (1-inch) chunks of cheese, cut in a triangle shape

School Lunches—a Dilemma for Generations

Most schools in the United States are far behind in providing a healthful lunch—that children will eat. Additionally, as long as the chicken fingers or pizza are still available on the same day the grilled chicken sandwich is offered, what do you think kids will pick? Therefore, until the school budgets can afford to serve healthy items—across the board—this will not be the venue for children to create healthful habits. So, when packing a fun and healthy school lunch, it should contain the following items: Sandwich or entrée with protein, some form of crunchy vegetable in a zip-top bag, a fun/healthy snack or two, a fruit serving, and a bottle of water.

1. Wash potatoes, and poke with a fork in 6 different areas of the potato.

2. To cook the potato in the microwave, place paper towel inside microwave. Place potatoes on the paper towel. Cook on high power for 5 to 7 minutes, until potatoes are soft.

3. Allow potatoes to cool, and then slice them lengthwise in half.

4. Hollow out most of the potato. Reserve the inside of the potato for another dish.

5. Prepare tuna in a small mixing bowl, mashing, adding mayonnaise, celery, and seasonings.

6. Fill the potato with tuna salad.

7. To finish the boat, place the pretzel rod at one end of the potato. Place chunk of triangle cheese toward the back of the potato, and lean the pretzel rod against the cheese, forming a "sail."

The Cool Kids' Greek Salad

Prepare the salad ahead of time, pack in a plastic container, with the salad dressing on the side, otherwise the salad is just too soggy to enjoy! Remove or add favorite ingredients.

INGREDIENTS | SERVES 4

1 medium bunch of romaine lettuce leaves, cleaned well

1 (14-ounce) can pitted black olives

1 pound crumbled low-fat feta cheese

1 large tomato, cut in small chunks

1 large cucumber, peeled and sliced in quarters

2 tablespoons olive oil

2 tablespoons lemon juice

Oregano and pepper to taste

1. Chop romaine lettuce and place in a mixing bowl.

2. Add olives, feta, tomato, and cucumber.

3. Prepare salad dressing by blending oil, lemon juice, and seasonings.

Chillin' Chinese Salad

This is a fantastic Asian salad—add a protein source to make it a complete meal—sliced chicken breast, grilled shrimp, sliced flank steak.

INGREDIENTS | SERVES 4

Salad:

1 (12-ounce) bag prepared coleslaw

4 scallions, chopped finely

1 (14-ounce) can mandarin oranges

½ cup sliced almonds (optional)

½ cup rice noodles (optional)

Dressing:

4 tablespoons balsamic vinegar

¼ cup olive oil

2 tablespoons sugar

1 teaspoon pepper

2 teaspoons ginger powder

1 teaspoon poppy seeds

1. In a medium mixing bowl, combine coleslaw, scallions, and mandarin oranges.

2. Blend all dressing ingredients. Drizzle dressing on salad.

3. Add optional rice noodles and almonds on top.

Marvelous Mango Salad with Grilled Chicken

A wonderful summer salad, with sweet, bright-colored mango—
encourage their eating of this extremely healthy fruit.

INGREDIENTS | SERVES 8

3 large ripe mangos

1½ tablespoons salt

½ cup chopped cilantro

¼ cup chopped scallions

1 teaspoon sesame oil

1 tablespoon olive oil

2 teaspoons apple cider vinegar

4 medium limes

2 bags pre-shredded coleslaw (with carrots)

4 large chicken breasts, cooked, cut in strips

1. Cut mangos into small chunks.

2. In a blender, mix salt, ¼ cup of the cilantro, chopped scallions, sesame oil, olive oil, chunks from 1 mango, and vinegar until smooth. Set dressing aside.

3. Juice all of the limes and place in a mixing bowl with coleslaw, the remaining ¼ cup cilantro, and prepared mango dressing.

4. Mix coleslaw with chicken breasts, add additional mango chunks and toss until well blended.

5. Chill 15 minutes and serve.

Early Introduction Makes for Great Salad Eaters!

Toddlers enjoy color and texture—just like play-doh and colored blocks. After age one, it is acceptable to present all of the different vegetables (avoid spinach, beans, beets, nuts, soy, and other "high-oxalate" foods before the age of one)— from puréed to the fresh. These are perfect finger foods; for instance, chopped pieces of tomato, soft-cooked broccoli and cauliflower, and well-cooked carrots, chopped to prevent choking.

Light and Flaky Tuna Melt

A great weekend family recipe—or if the children have a microwave in school—re-zap their melt for an unusual "sandwich."

Healthier Options on the Cafeteria Lunch Line

Entrees: grilled chicken breast, grilled chicken breast sandwiches, pasta with marinara sauce and Parmesan cheese, ham and cheese sandwich/whole wheat bread, peanut butter and jelly sandwich/whole wheat bread, tuna salad on a whole grain bun. Vegetables: corn on the cob/corn kernels, baked potatoes, whole wheat pasta, green beans, green peas, carrots, small green salad. Desserts: fresh fruit, canned fruit (in own juices). Beverages: water, low-fat milk, low-fat chocolate milk, 100% fruit juice (teach moderation here).

1. Preheat oven to 375°F.

2. In medium bowl, combine mayonnaise, mustard, onion, and celery salt.

3. Stir in tuna and chopped eggs.

4. Unroll dough into 2 long rectangles. Place on ungreased cookie sheet with long sides overlapping ½ inch. Firmly press together the two rectangles' edges and perforations to seal. Mold to form 14" × 9" rectangle.

5. Spoon tuna mixture into dough. Sprinkle ½ cup cheese over filling. Close up dough to cover tuna filling.

6. Bake for 15 to 20 minutes, until golden brown. Remove from oven, and sprinkle with remaining ½ cup cheese and sesame seeds.

7. Return to oven and bake until cheese melts, about 2 to 3 minutes.

8. Cool 5 minutes before serving.

Cheesy Chowder

*On that freezing winter day, serve this hot and delicious vegetable soup,
giving the kids protein and calcium while they are warming up!*

INGREDIENTS | SERVES 16

3 cups water

6 cubes of chicken bouillon

3 white potatoes, cubed

1 clove garlic, minced

1 small onion, chopped fine

3 to 4 celery stalks, chopped fine

6 large fresh carrots, chopped

2 (15-ounce) cans corn kernels, drained

2 cups fresh green beans, chopped

¼ cup trans-fat-free margarine

¼ cup all-purpose flour

1½ cups low-fat milk

8 ounces low-fat mozzarella cheese, shredded

1. In a large pot, combine water, bouillon, potatoes, and garlic.

2. Bring to a boil, and cook until potatoes are somewhat tender, about 30 minutes.

3. Add onion, celery, and carrots, and simmer, covered, for 15 minutes.

4. Stir in corn and green beans, and continue to simmer.

5. In a small skillet, melt margarine.

6. Stir in flour, slowly, until well blended and thickened.

7. Whisk in milk, until well blended.

8. Stir cheese into milk mixture until it melts.

9. Add the milk and cheese mixture to the large pot of soup. Stir to mix. Let cook for 3 to 5 minutes and serve.

Super Sloppy Joes

An easy family favorite—this can be made the night before, and packed in their insulated lunch boxes. Certainly a terrific weekend option, too!

INGREDIENTS | SERVES 6

Nonstick cooking spray
1 small onion, chopped finely
½ cup green and red pepper, chopped
1 pound lean ground sirloin
¾ cup barbecue sauce
½ cup canned corn
¼ teaspoon salt
⅛ teaspoon pepper
6 whole wheat buns

1. Spray nonstick cooking spray into a large skillet. Over low heat, sauté onions and peppers until soft.

2. Add ground beef to pan and cook through. Drain off the fat from the beef.

3. Add barbecue sauce, corn, salt, and pepper; heat thoroughly. Simmer for 10 minutes.

4. Serve on buns.

Terrific Teriyaki Tofu

When pan-fried, this tofu is quite flavorful. This is a great way to introduce your children to a very healthy option, for lunch, or anytime.

INGREDIENTS | SERVES 4–6

1 tablespoon canola or olive oil
1 tablespoon water
2 teaspoons low-sodium soy sauce
1 egg, beaten
1 teaspoon minced garlic
1 pound medium tofu, cut into 2-inch long strips

1. In a large skillet, heat oil over low heat.

2. In a shallow mixing bowl, add water, soy sauce, egg, and garlic. Mix well.

3. Dip tofu pieces into above mixture.

4. Pan fry pieces in skillet until golden brown, about 5 to 7 minutes.

Tomato Tortellini Soup and a Sandwich

Soup and sandwich—a perfect combination for a refreshing weekend lunch, with a great burst of vitamin C. Feel free to substitute your favorite sandwich.

INGREDIENTS | SERVES 4

Soup:

1 (10-ounce) can condensed tomato soup

1 (9-ounce) package refrigerated low-fat cheese tortellini

½ cup grated Parmesan cheese

Sandwich:

Small whole grain baguette

2 to 3 slices fresh turkey or chicken

1 teaspoon mustard (optional)

1. In a large saucepan, place soup and 1 can full of water, and heat as directed on can.

2. Add the tortellini and heat over medium heat until the soup boils, stirring frequently.

3. Reduce heat and simmer for 2 to 3 minutes.

4. Sprinkle Parmesan cheese before serving.

5. Prepare sandwich and enjoy.

Soft Chicken Tacos

Another favorite lunch the kids won't trade. It's doubtful any of their friends will have anything so unique. Remember there are many lunches to pack over the years—you have to stay creative!

INGREDIENTS | SERVES 4

2 cups roasted skinless, boneless chicken breast, shredded

½ cup bottled salsa (choose spice level as desired)

8 (6-inch) corn or whole wheat tortillas

½ cup shredded romaine lettuce

1 cup chopped tomato

½ cup low-fat Cheddar cheese, shredded

1. In a medium mixing bowl, combine chicken and salsa, tossing well.

2. Spoon about ⅓ cup chicken mixture into each tortilla.

3. Add lettuce, tomatoes, and shredded cheese to each one. Fold in half and serve.

Ham, Egg, and Cheese "Muffin" Cups

Another breakfast to be able to prepare the night before—one the kids can grab and run with. Substitute any lean meat for the ham, and alternate cheeses if desired.

INGREDIENTS | SERVES 6

6 (1-ounce) thin ham slices
1 tablespoon olive oil
1 small onion, finely chopped
1 small red pepper, finely chopped
2 cups part-skim mozzarella cheese, shredded
6 eggs
4 egg whites
¾ cup low-fat plain yogurt
2 tablespoons Dijon mustard
Nonstick cooking spray

1. Preheat oven to 350°F. Grease six muffin cups, or use paper liners.

2. Place one slice of ham in each muffin cup, pressing down gently to line cups, letting any extra ham drape over sides.

3. In a small skillet, pour olive oil, and on low heat, lightly sauté chopped onion and red pepper, until soft.

4. Equally divide pepper and onion mixture among muffin cups. Top with half of the shredded cheese.

5. In a small mixing bowl, beat together eggs, egg whites, yogurt, and mustard until combined.

6. Pour over cheese and onion mixture in each cup. Top with remaining cheese.

7. Bake for 25 to 30 minutes, or until eggs are set and thoroughly cooked.

Tantalizing Taco Salad Wrap

This is a really fun "mish-mosh" salad with many new flavors for the children. Depending on their "spice-target," you can heat it up or mild it down. Try different types of beans and vegetables, and see what they like the most.

INGREDIENTS | SERVES 4

1 pound lean ground beef

1 (16-ounce) can kidney beans, rinsed and drained

1 teaspoon chili powder (optional)

1 teaspoon garlic powder

8 whole wheat flour or corn tortillas

½ head romaine lettuce, chopped finely

2 medium ripe tomatoes, chopped finely

1 cup black olives, chopped

1 (10-ounce) jar mild taco sauce (optional)

1. In a medium skillet, cook ground beef until cooked through. Drain fat from meat.

2. In a medium mixing bowl, combine beef, beans, chili powder, and garlic powder.

3. Wipe the skillet with a paper towel and then warm each tortilla in the skillet for 1 to 2 minutes.

4. On a plate, divide the meat and bean mixture equally over the tortillas.

5. Divide the salad greens, vegetables, and olives over each tortilla.

6. Top each with 2 tablespoons of taco sauce, if desired.

7. Fold tortilla over and wrap.

Turkey Burgers with Chipotle Ketchup

Maybe the burgers need to be made the night before, but the children will find this to be a really "different" kind of lunch—it's sure not your typical turkey sandwich!

INGREDIENTS | SERVES 4

1 pound ground turkey breast

⅓ cup seasoned bread crumbs

¼ cup minced fresh cilantro

¼ cup Parmesan cheese, shredded

¼ teaspoon salt

¼ teaspoon pepper

1 to 2 tablespoons olive or canola oil

1 (7-ounce) can chipotle chilies in adobo sauce

¼ cup ketchup

4 whole wheat hamburger buns or rolls

4 leaves romaine or Bibb lettuce

1. In a large mixing bowl, combine turkey breast with the bread crumbs, cilantro, Parmesan cheese, salt and pepper. Mix well.

2. Divide turkey mixture into 4 burger-size patties.

3. Heat oil in a large skillet over low heat. Add turkey patties and cook 5 to 7 minutes on each side, until at least medium doneness.

4. Remove 1 chili and 1 teaspoon adobo sauce from can. Reserve remaining chilies and sauce for another use. Finely chop chili.

5. Combine chili, adobo sauce, and ketchup in a small bowl.

6. Assemble turkey burgers on buns with lettuce leaf and chili sauce.

Chicken Parmesan—The Weekender

A great family weekend lunch for after those morning activities. Get together and have a nice warm lunch; serve with a side Caesar salad (with low-fat dressing) and a fruit and berry salad.

INGREDIENTS | SERVES 4

Nonstick cooking spray

½ cup seasoned bread crumbs

4 tablespoons grated Parmesan cheese, divided

¾ teaspoon diced rosemary

¼ teaspoon paprika

3 egg whites

4 skinless, boneless chicken breast halves (4 ounces each)

Sauce:

¾ cup tomato sauce

1 clove garlic, minced

¼ cup chopped fresh parsley

1 teaspoon dried basil

1. Preheat oven to 400°F. Line a baking sheet with aluminum foil and spray it with nonstick cooking spray.

2. On a large plate, combine bread crumbs, 2 tablespoons Parmesan cheese, rosemary, and paprika. Blend well.

3. In a shallow bowl, lightly beat egg whites.

4. Dip each piece of chicken into egg whites, then into bread crumb mixture. Coat both sides of chicken. Place chicken on baking sheet.

5. Bake for 20 minutes on one side and then turn chicken. Bake for another 10 minutes or so, until chicken is cooked through and crisp on the outside.

6. While chicken is baking, prepare the sauce. In a small saucepan, combine tomato sauce, garlic, parsley, and basil over medium heat for 5 minutes.

7. Remove sauce from heat.

8. Place chicken on a serving plate, and top with tomato sauce and remaining 2 tablespoons Parmesan cheese.

CHAPTER 5

I'm Starving—That Required
After-School Snack

Super-Charged Strawberry Smoothie

There is no doubt that when the kids arrive home from school, they are ready to raid the refrigerator. Try and have this terrific smoothie ready for them . . . it will recharge them for the afternoon.

INGREDIENTS | **SERVES 1–2**

1 cup low-fat milk

1 cup strawberries, sliced mango, or small banana

1 teaspoon sugar (or 1 teaspoon Splenda for the child older than 10)

1 teaspoon vanilla extract

3 to 4 ice cubes

1. Mix all ingredients in a blender, adding the ice slowly.

2. Blend until smooth.

Awesome Apple-Banana Smoothie

Another version of a healthy milkshake. Feel free to alternate fruits such as mango, melon or berries.

INGREDIENTS | **SERVES 2**

1 cup low-fat milk

½ cup no-sugar-added apple juice

1 teaspoon vanilla extract

1 medium banana, ripened

6 to 8 ice cubes

1. Mix all ingredients in a blender, adding the ice slowly.

2. Blend until smooth.

A Word about Your Children's Protein Needs

For the most part, people in the United States are *not* protein deprived. In many cases, due to the emphasis on higher protein diets today, Americans take in more than they need. It is quite unnecessary for children to increase their protein intake for any reason, unless recommended by a registered dietitian/nutrition-ist, or pediatrician—especially those athletes who think their muscles will be stronger if they keep eating protein. Too much protein puts great strain on kidneys.

Cheesy Easy Baked Potato

Sound unconventional? A great snack for the kids—stick a baking potato in the microwave, add some ever-important calcium, and it's a nice warm change to that typical after-school snack!

INGREDIENTS | SERVES 1

1 medium baking potato
2 to 3 ounces low-fat Cheddar cheese
1 tablespoon trans-fat-free margarine

Potato: White or Sweet—a Nutrient-Packed Tuber

Potatoes can be made in so many different ways—baked French fries, mashed, baked wedges, or boiled. Leave the skin on and encourage the kids to eat the skin. However you slice them, they are a wonderful source of vitamin C, vitamin A, potassium, fiber, and beta-carotene. Not too many foods can pack in that punch!

1. Wash potato skin well. With a fork, poke the skin in about 8 to 10 places. Place a paper towel on the bottom of the microwave, and place potato in the microwave. Cook for 3 to 4 minutes, or until soft.

2. Remove baked potato from microwave, and split open. Sprinkle Cheddar cheese on top.

3. Return to microwave for 30 to 45 seconds, or until cheese is melted.

4. Add melted margarine and serve.

Row Your Peanut Butter Boat

A fun little activity—let the kids prepare this one! Get in a little vegetable, fruit, and healthy nut protein.

INGREDIENTS | SERVES 2

2 to 3 celery stalks

2 to 3 tablespoons trans-fat-free peanut butter

2 to 3 tablespoons raisins (optional)

1. Wash the celery stalks and cut each in half.

2. Spread peanut butter in the hollow of the celery.

3. Top with raisins, if desired.

Pizza Muffins

This snack can be made right in the toaster oven, quickly, for a hungry child.

INGREDIENTS | SERVES 1

1 whole wheat English muffin

2 to 3 ounces part-skim mozzarella cheese

¼ cup tomato sauce

1. Slice English muffin in half.

2. Spread tomato sauce on top of each half. Sprinkle cheese on top of sauce.

3. Place in toaster oven for 3 to 4 minutes, or until cheese is melted.

A Picture Perfect Pizza

Pizza is generally a high-saturated-fatty food, with a white flour crust. However, pizza still holds a great source of calcium, vitamin C, and vitamin A (beta-carotene), and even more nutrients if you can sneak some vegetables onto the pizza. Make it the occasional meal *outside* your home, though now there are whole wheat crusts and low-fat cheeses in your grocery store with which you and the children may create a homemade favorite for the whole family. Homemade pizzas are so much better for us!

Peanut Butter–Chocolate Splurge

Let's splurge just a little. This snack will still give your children a whole grain, protein and iron, fresh fruit, with a little chocolate surprise thrown in.

INGREDIENTS | SERVES 4

4 flour tortillas (whole wheat preferably)

8 tablespoons trans-fat-free peanut butter

2 medium bananas, sliced thinly

4 tablespoons chocolate chip mini-morsels (preferably dark chocolate)

1. Spread 2 tablespoons of peanut butter on each tortilla.

2. Spread ½ sliced banana on each tortilla.

3. Sprinkle with mini-morsels.

4. Roll tortilla until it forms a wrap.

Be Sure to Insist on "Moderation"

No question, this is a snack item with a few extra calories and extra fat. It is important, however, to teach children early that "there is no food that is off limits." You must teach them that moderation is the absolute key to a long and healthy life—every nutrient is important to their good health—even if it means a little chocolate once in a while!

Take-Along Trail Mix

Trail mix is so versatile you can create your own versions, too. Try adding some yogurt-covered raisins, dry cereal, fish crackers, chocolate-coated candies, or even popcorn.

INGREDIENTS | MAKES 2 CUPS OF TRAIL MIX

½ cup small pretzel sticks or twists

½ cup raisins

½ cup peanuts

¼ cup sunflower seeds

¼ cup chocolate chips

In a large bowl, combine all ingredients together. Store in an airtight container or resealable bag.

Why Does Popcorn Pop?

Each popcorn kernel contains a small drop of water stored inside. When the kernel gets heated, the water inside turns to steam. The kernel then begins to expand as pressure starts to develop inside the hard shell. As a result, the kernel splits open and the popcorn explodes, popping the popcorn and releasing the steam. (Popcorn is a special breed of corn. You cannot take a regular corn kernel and make it pop.)

Apple Fondue and Rice Cakes

When the hungry ones come home from school, in a matter of a few minutes, they have a tasty and crunchy snack—substitute their favorite fruits and favorite cheeses.

INGREDIENTS | SERVES 2

½ cup whipped cream cheese

1 tablespoon honey

½ teaspoon ground cinnamon

4 rice cakes

1 medium apple, sliced (do not remove skin)

1 cup low-fat Cheddar cheese, shredded

1. Turn on oven broiler.

2. Blend cream cheese, honey, and cinnamon. Spread on the rice cakes.

3. Assemble apple slices on top of cream cheese mixture. Sprinkle with Cheddar cheese.

4. Heat 5 inches from the broiler, and broil 1 to 2 minutes or until Cheddar cheese is melted. Watch carefully, as it cooks quickly.

Homemade Pita Chips

*Add hummus, trans-fat-free peanut butter, or a spreadable low-fat cheese,
and this makes a crunchy little after-school snack the kids will love!*

INGREDIENTS | **SERVES 15–20**

1 package pita bread, preferably whole wheat

¼ cup olive oil

1 clove garlic, crushed

3 to 4 tablespoons Parmesan cheese

Salt to taste

Other Great Ideas for Snacks

100-calorie snack pack plus 1 cup low-fat milk; ½ turkey or ham sandwich plus a piece of fruit; ½ sandwich plus 1 cup low-fat milk; 3 cups low-fat microwave popcorn plus 8 ounces low-fat yogurt; 2 slices or 2 ounces low-fat cheese and handful whole grain crackers; 1 cup high-fiber cereal and 8 ounces low-fat milk.

1. Preheat oven to 350°F.

2. Cut the pita in half horizontally, creating 2 circles of pita.

3. Combine the olive oil and garlic in a small bowl. Brush on to the pita halves.

4. Sprinkle with Parmesan cheese and salt.

5. Place the pitas one on top of another, and slice into quarters.

6. Separate the pita pieces and arrange them on a baking sheet. Spray the pieces with cooking spray.

7. Bake 20 minutes, turning once.

Zany Zucchini Bread

One way to get in a sweet snack, with a little vegetable thrown in.

INGREDIENTS | SERVES 10–14

2 cups sugar

½ cup sugar (or ½ cup Splenda for children over 10)

3 cups all-purpose flour

1 teaspoon salt

1 teaspoon baking soda

½ teaspoon baking powder

2 teaspoons cinnamon

3 eggs

1 cup canola oil

2 to 3 cups grated zucchini

Nonstick cooking spray

1. Preheat oven to 350°F.

2. In a medium bowl mix together the sugar, (or Splenda), flour, salt, baking soda, baking powder, cinnamon.

3. In a separate bowl beat the eggs together.

4. Add oil and zucchini to the eggs.

5. Add dry ingredient mixture slowly, until well blended.

6. Spray cooking spray into 2 to 3 loaf pans. Add batter.

7. Bake breads for 1 hour.

Be a Food Role Model

Monkey-see, monkey-do is the traditional comment when raising children. That goes for positive modeling too! If the children don't see their parents eating vegetables, then they don't believe there is a real purpose in including vegetables in their diet either. If you allow yourself to eat French fries as your primary vegetable, it must be acceptable for the kids, too. You are the final role model throughout their childhood.

Fabulous Fruity Muffins

This is so easy to make—and a wonderful high-fiber, sweet snack. Add container of low-fat yogurt or low-fat, low-sugar chocolate milk for a perfect after-school snack.

INGREDIENTS | **SERVES 12**

Nonstick cooking spray
½ cup sugar
3 eggs
½ cup shredded coconut
½ cup chopped dates
½ cup raisins
½ cup dried cranberries
½ cup chopped apricots
½ cup finely chopped walnuts

Dried Fruits—Incredible Sources of Nutrients and Fiber

These muffins are flourless, chock full of wonderful sweet dried fruits, and delicious. Mega amounts of fiber, "good fats" from the nuts, and the more color in the fruits, the more nutrient-packed they are—so apricots, cranberries, dates, and raisins are perfect. Add a glass of low-fat milk, or smear some trans-fat-free peanut butter on the muffins—a totally fulfilling after-school snack.

1. Preheat oven to 350°F.

2. Spray muffin pan with cooking spray.

3. Beat eggs in a small bowl.

4. In a separate bowl, mix together the remaining ingredients.

5. Add eggs to mixture.

6. Pour batter into muffin pan.

7. Bake for 30 minutes.

Rice-A-Rolly

Another child-friendly experience—this can be a fun activity to do after school, and can be served at parties, holidays, or just for dinner; they are so easy.

INGREDIENTS | SERVES 8–10

1½ cups white rice, cooked

1½ cups brown rice, cooked

1 cup low-fat mozzarella cheese, shredded

4 tablespoons Parmesan cheese, grated

1 egg

¼ teaspoon oregano

¼ teaspoon basil

Salt and pepper to taste

Nonstick cooking spray

Getting In That Extra Fiber

Who would have ever thought that brown rice would be yummy to a young child? However, this recipe, which is fun for the kids to prepare, is a great way to influence good eating habits right from the start. Perhaps in the future, this dish can be made solely with brown rice, and the kids will enjoy it just as much.

1. Preheat oven to 350°F. Cook rice according to package directions.

2. In a medium mixing bowl, stir cooked white and brown rice together.

3. Add mozzarella cheese, Parmesan cheese, and egg.

4. Add seasonings, and mix well.

5. Spray nonstick cooking spray onto a baking sheet.

6. Wet hands with a small amount of water. Roll rice mixture into 1½-inch balls. Place them on the baking sheets, not allowing them to touch.

7. Bake 20 to 30 minutes, until firm.

Mimi's Famous Black Bean Soup

A perfect high-iron, high-fiber snack for a cold winter's day. Crumble a few whole grain crackers into the soup, and it's a wonderfully delicious "little meal."

INGREDIENTS | SERVES 12–15

1 bag of black beans, dry
1 medium onion, chopped
1 green bell pepper, chopped
3 garlic cloves, crushed
2 teaspoons salt
1 tablespoon olive oil
¼ cup apple cider vinegar
2 tablespoons sugar

They're Hungry—Perfect Time for Great Healthy Snacks!

Kids have a long day. Breakfast begins the day quite early, followed by lunch at school—just enough time to get it down; by the time children get home in the late afternoon, they are famished. It is the perfect opportunity to give them a snack that will help boost their energy for that homework hour, and give them that extra iron, supplying more oxygen to their cells, more energy, and nutrients for further growth and development.

1. Either the night before, or the day of cooking, soak beans in a large pot with water (for several hours).

2. Wash the beans off and place into a pressure cooker with enough water to cover the beans.

3. Add ½ the chopped onion, ½ of the green pepper, and the garlic.

4. Close pressure cooker. Add the locking piece. Turn pressure cooker on high until it begins to whistle about 5 minutes.

5. Lower temperature to medium for 20 minutes.

6. Carefully open the lid of the pressure cooker and add salt, and cook for 6 to 10 more minutes.

7. Open the lid of the pressure cooker carefully; you need to run some cold water over the top until the button decreases.

8. In a small saucepan, add 1 tablespoon of olive oil and sauté remaining onion and pepper until soft.

9. Add sautéed onions and peppers, sugar, and vinegar, and mix. Cook 5 more minutes and serve.

Hot Diggity Mouse

*The cutest snack ever! Great for after-school, parties, or even to prepare
a snack on a rainy day as a family. So lip-smacking and creative.*

INGREDIENTS | **SERVES 1**

1 whole wheat hot dog bun
2 to 3 tablespoons trans-fat-free
peanut butter
1 small ripe banana
2 maraschino cherries
1 large jelly bean
2 long strands red shoestring licorice
¼ cup shredded coconut

1. Spread peanut butter inside the hot dog bun.

2. Place whole banana on top of peanut butter.

3. Place cherries on the banana as a set of eyes. Place jelly bean for the nose.

4. On either side of the jelly bean, stick small strands of red licorice for the whiskers.

5. Lastly, sprinkle shredded coconut as fur for your mouse.

Quick Cheese Quesadilla

*Doesn't get any easier than this—less than 5 minutes, and a great tasty snack
for ravenous kids. Fast in the toaster oven, even faster in the microwave!*

INGREDIENTS | **SERVES 1**

1 flour or corn tortilla
1 to 2 slices low-fat cheese

1. Preheat toaster oven to 350°F.

2. Place cheese slices on tortilla.

3. Place tortilla in toaster oven.

4. Bake until cheese is melted. Cut tortilla into wedges or strips as desired.

Make-Ahead Banana French Toast

A dish to make the night before—so when the children return from school the next day, a quick 20 minutes in the oven for this delicious French toast, and they are ready for their afternoon schedule.

INGREDIENTS | SERVES 4

2 ripe medium bananas, sliced

1 tablespoon lemon juice

Nonstick cooking spray

8 slices whole grain bread

¼ cup mini dark chocolate morsels

2 eggs, beaten

¾ cup low-fat milk

2 tablespoons honey

1 teaspoon vanilla extract

1 teaspoon ground cinnamon

1 teaspoon sugar

Low-sugar pancake syrup (optional)

1. In a small bowl, place sliced bananas and lemon juice.

2. In a 9½" × 11" glass baking dish, spray nonstick cooking spray.

3. Layer half the bread slices on the bottom of the dish.

4. Top the bread with a layer of the bananas and chocolate morsels.

5. Layer remaining bread slices on top.

6. In a small mixing bowl, combine eggs, milk, honey, vanilla extract, and ½ teaspoon cinnamon, and mix well. Pour slowly over the bread to coat evenly.

7. Cover and place in refrigerator until ready to prepare.

8. When ready to prepare, preheat oven to 425°F. Uncover the Pyrex dish.

9. Sprinkle with ½ teaspoon cinnamon and 1 teaspoon sugar.

10. Bake for 5 minutes at this temperature.

11. Reduce oven temperature to 325°F. Bake 20 to 25 additional minutes until top of French toast is browned and inserted knife comes out dry.

12. Serve with low-sugar syrup, if desired.

Tyler the Turtle Sandwich

An easy after-school snack that the kids can construct themselves in just a few minutes—they can choose different deli slices and different vegetables (e.g., celery stalks or long carrots for limbs).

Sandwiches—an Ideal After-School Snack

Sounds like it could be a meal; however, sandwiches, made on whole wheat, rye bread, or a whole wheat pita pocket can be a terrific and nutritious snack. When the children are younger and still in their primary growing stages, give them a full sandwich. If they participate in after-school activities or sports, certainly enrich their afternoon with a sandwich. As the children slow down their growth, or are at risk for a weight issue, offer a half of a sandwich with a piece of fruit, or a ½ cup fruit smoothie.

1. Stuff pita pocket with the roast beef.

2. Cut green pepper into 5 thick slices, and 1 thin slice.

3. Cut open the pita pocket. Place two peppers at the open bottom and two at the top/side for feet. Place the thin slice at one end for the tail. Place the last pepper in the top opening for the head.

4. Slice cheese into 4 to 6 strips, and create 2 small "balls" for eyes with a small bit of the cheese. Place cheese strips diagonally on the top of the pita. Place small cheese balls on top of the "head" pepper for the eyes.

Sam's Silly Tuna Face Sandwich

Another easy and fun snack—full of crunch.

INGREDIENTS | SERVES 1

3 ounces canned tuna in water, drained

1 tablespoon low-fat mayonnaise

1 teaspoon garlic powder

½ small onion, chopped finely

1 teaspoon celery salt

1 whole wheat hamburger bun

½ cup shredded carrots

1 large pickle, sliced lengthwise

2 large black olives

Fish May Be the Number One Food to Eat

Strong studies have supported that provide fish, of all kinds, one of the best anti-inflammatory foods around. What is found in fish is the very healthy omega-3 fatty acids, reducing inflammation everywhere in the body, at any time. Nutritionists and pediatricians are recommending fish, even in supplement form. Caution: some fish contain higher levels of mercury, so don't offer white tuna more than once or twice a week, but certainly the light chunk tunas are just perfect.

1. In a small bowl, combine tuna, mayonnaise, garlic powder, onion, and celery salt.

2. Mash well, until ingredients are well blended.

3. Scoop tuna onto hamburger bun and cover with top of bun.

4. Use carrots to make hair. Use pickle for a nose and olives for eyes.

Orange Cream Creamsicles

Fun to make and even more fun to eat! Substitute different flavors of yogurt and even different types of juices (e.g., pineapple juice or white grape juice).

INGREDIENTS | SERVES 4–6

½ cup water
1 cup orange juice
½ teaspoon vanilla extract
1 cup low-fat vanilla yogurt
Popsicle sticks

1. In a small mixing bowl, combine all ingredients.

2. Using ice trays, fill about ¾ full with creamsicle mixture.

3. Place in freezer for 20 to 30 minutes.

4. Remove from freezer, and stick popsicle sticks in each popsicle.

5. Return to freezer and allow several hours to freeze completely.

Strawberry Yogurt Squares

The kids will love this sweet snack, light and fluffy. Let them change the flavors of the yogurt and the fruits—mango, pineapple, blueberry, raspberry.

INGREDIENTS | SERVES 9–12

1 cup Honey Bunches of Oats Cereal
3 cups low-fat strawberry yogurt
1 (10-ounce) bag frozen strawberries, unsweetened
1 cup fat-free condensed milk
1 teaspoon vanilla extract
1 cup lite whipped topping

1. Place tin foil at the bottom of an 8" × 8" square pan.

2. Sprinkle the cereal at the bottom of the pan evenly.

3. In a blender or food processor, place yogurt, strawberries, condensed milk, vanilla extract, and whipped topping. Blend until smooth.

4. Pour evenly over the cereal layer.

5. Cover with tin foil and place in the freezer.

6. Allow to freeze for 6 hours. Cut into squares and serve.

Cinnamon Quesadilla

This scrumptious ethnic twist and a glass of low-fat, low-sugar chocolate milk makes a perfect little after-school snack—your preschoolers can even help make this one.

INGREDIENTS | SERVES 2

3 tablespoons low-fat cream cheese

4 (8-inch) whole wheat flour tortillas

2 tablespoons sugar

1 teaspoon of cinnamon

2 teaspoons trans-fat-free margarine

1. Spread 1½ tablespoons cream cheese in an even layer over one of the tortillas.

2. Sprinkle with ½ the sugar and cinnamon. Top with the second tortilla to form a sandwich.

3. Melt the margarine in a small frying pan over low heat.

4. Cook the quesadilla until golden brown. Flip and brown the other side. Repeat with remaining tortillas and ingredients.

5. Slice each sandwich into quarters. Serve immediately.

Down-Home Cornbread

The mild, down-home taste of cornbread goes great with favorite comfort foods like chili and tomato soup.

INGREDIENTS | MAKES 16 PIECES

¾ cup cornmeal

1½ cups flour

1 cup sugar

2 tablespoon milk

1 tablespoon baking powder

½ teaspoon salt

1 egg

½ cup warm water

4 tablespoons butter, melted

1. Preheat the oven to 400°F. Spray an 8-inch square pan with cooking spray.

2. In a large bowl, combine the cornmeal, flour, sugar, milk, baking powder, and salt.

3. In another bowl, beat the egg. Add the water and melted butter to the egg, and mix well.

4. Combine the two mixtures and blend together. Pour the cornbread batter into the prepared baking pan, using a rubber spatula to clear the batter from the bowl.

5. Bake 20 to 25 minutes, or until golden brown.

Thai Tenderloin Salad

It's okay—let them have a salad for a snack. Infuse it with delicious steak, and it may turn out to be one of their favorites. Serve with a piece of fresh fruit or some baked chips. Alternate with flank steak or London broil for a less expensive cut of meat.

INGREDIENTS | SERVES 4

1 pound beef tenderloin, trimmed
Nonstick cooking spray
3 tablespoons lime juice
1 teaspoon sugar
6 cups chopped romaine lettuce
1 cup thinly sliced red bell pepper
1 cup thinly sliced peeled cucumber

1. Turn on oven broiler.

2. Place beef on broiler pan coated with nonstick cooking spray.

3. Broil 6 to 8 minutes on each side, until meat is cooked to medium doneness.

4. Remove from oven, cover, and let stand 10 to 15 minutes.

5. Cut beef diagonally across the grain into thin slices.

6. In a large mixing bowl, combine lime juice and sugar.

7. Add the beef, lettuce, pepper, and cucumber to the juice/sugar mixture, and toss well.

CHAPTER 6

On to Sports Practice—What Will Give Them That Burst of Energy?

Hearty Hummus and Pita Triangles

A great "sport nutrient" is the protein in beans; couple that with power-packed, healthy-carb pita, and your athlete is ready for that afternoon game.

INGREDIENTS | SERVES 3–4

1 can chickpeas, drained and liquid reserved

1 clove garlic, crushed

1 teaspoon salt

1 tablespoon olive oil

Juice of one lemon

Whole wheat pita triangles (3 medium pitas, cut up)

Assorted fresh vegetables (optional)

1. Place all ingredients (except pita) in a blender and purée.

2. Add a few tablespoons of the reserved chickpea liquid and mix. It should be a thick dip texture.

3. Serve hummus with pita triangles and fresh vegetables!

Time for an Energy Boost

Unfortunately, in today's world, it is not traditional anymore to offer just play time outside with friends. Most kids are signed up for at least one, if not several, after-school activities. The valuable part to this, when sports are the chosen extra-curricular activity, is getting in the physical activity that is so significant in a growing child's life. Give your student athletes the afternoon energy to perform their best. For teenage athletes, a smoothie made with low-fat milk and a large wedge of watermelon, in addition to the above, rounds out the snack for more heavy-duty workouts.

Banana Berry Energy Smoothie

Yet another quick and easy after-school pre-workout recipe; teenagers can prepare this themselves; they'll certainly feel that energy boost!

INGREDIENTS | SERVES 2–3

1 cup low-fat frozen yogurt
1 medium banana, ripened
1 cup fresh strawberries
½ cup lite cranberry juice

1. Combine all ingredients in blender.

2. Mix well until desired smoothie consistency.

A Word about Commercial Energy Drinks

Beware, popular energy drinks such as Red Bull, Monster, and Full Throttle are not intended for youth and teenagers—and the caffeine and sugar content is quite dangerous to a young athlete. The caffeine is a dehydrating factor, and the sugar will only provide an hour of quick energy, if that, prior to the energy crash that is sure to follow. Encourage high-energy food and drink products that will give your children some *good* nutrition.

Rod and Turkey Reel

Serve the rods and reels with a cup of fresh berries—and off to the races they go! Filled with protein and a carbohydrate to give children that extra vigor.

INGREDIENTS | SERVES 3–4

6 pretzel rods
12 slices turkey breast

1. Roll 2 to 3 turkey slices around each pretzel rod.

2. Serve with fresh fruit.

Absolute Apple Muffins

A great way to incorporate a little fruit into that snack—and grab a handful of nuts or eat an 8-ounce container of low-fat yogurt with this moist and delicious muffin—another well-rounded, power-filled snack. For that teenage athlete, give them two muffins!

INGREDIENTS | SERVES 6–12

Nonstick cooking spray
½ cup canola oil
¾ cup sugar
½ cup low-fat milk
1 teaspoon vanilla
1 egg
1 cup finely chopped, skinless apples
2½ cups all-purpose flour
1 teaspoon baking soda
¼ teaspoon salt
1 teaspoon cinnamon

1. Preheat oven to 350°F. Spray muffin pan with nonstick cooking spray.

2. Combine oil, sugar, milk, vanilla, and egg in a large bowl until well blended.

3. Add apples and stir.

4. In a separate bowl, mix together flour, baking soda, salt, and cinnamon.

5. Add the wet mixture to the dry.

6. Pour combined batter into muffin cups, filling half way.

7. Bake for 40 to 50 minutes.

Black Bean and Corn Salsa Baked Nachos

An all-in-one great sport snack! Prepare the bean "dip" ahead of time to avoid being late to practice.

INGREDIENTS | SERVES 4

1 (15-ounce) can black beans, rinsed and drained

1 (14½-ounce) can salsa-style chunky tomatoes

1 (7-ounce) can whole-kernel corn, drained

1 teaspoon hot chili powder (optional)

4 servings of baked tortilla chips

1 (16-ounce) package part-skim mozzarella cheese

1. Preheat oven to 350°F.

2. Blend beans and tomatoes in a food processor or blender until finely chopped.

3. Mix in corn and chili powder.

4. Spread baked tortilla chips on a cookie sheet. Sprinkle mozzarella cheese evenly over chips.

5. Bake for 5 to 10 minutes, or until cheese is melted. Remove chips from oven, and enjoy with the bean dip.

Serve the Team a Great Snack

This is a unique way to offer high protein (beans and cheese) plus that high carb for that afternoon practice. It should hold them well as they compete for first place!

Monkey Mango Bread

Just the smell will have them racing! Again, encourage 1 to 2 slices of cheese or a glass of milk with a nice-size slice of this tasty bread—they're sure to win their competition!

INGREDIENTS | SERVES 8–12

1 cup sifted all-purpose flour

1 cup sifted whole wheat flour

3 teaspoons cinnamon

Dash of nutmeg

2 teaspoons baking soda

½ teaspoon salt

¾ cup sugar

¼ cup brown sugar

3 eggs

½ cup canola oil

3 cups mango, finely chopped

1 teaspoon lemon juice

Nonstick cooking spray

1. Preheat oven to 350°F.

2. Mix together the flours, cinnamon, nutmeg, baking soda, salt, and sugars.

3. In a separate bowl, beat together eggs and oil.

4. Add wet mixture to dry mixture.

5. Add mango and lemon juice to the combined batter.

6. Spray 2 loaf pans with nonstick cooking spray. Pour batter into loaf pans. Bake for 1 hour.

Mango—an Extraordinary Fruit

Known today as a "superfruit" (because of the many potential health benefits), mango is known for its sweet flavor, delectable juices, awesome fragrance, and color. It is one of the most nutritious fruits around—just loaded with cancer-fighting antioxidants, beta-carotene, vitamin C, potassium, and fiber. In a smoothie, a muffin, or chopped in a salad, encourage your children to enjoy mango.

Franks, Beans, and Baseball

Double this recipe—add a chopped green salad and make an easy family meal.

INGREDIENTS | SERVES 2

4 reduced-fat hot dogs

1 (15-ounce) can vegetarian baked beans

1 medium apple, sliced

1. Boil or microwave hot dogs according to package directions.

2. Boil or microwave baked beans until heated.

3. Combine the hot dogs and beans.

4. Slice the "baseball" apple and enjoy!

Hot Dogs—Even with All That Salt?

Let's talk about salt, or sodium, for a moment. Sodium is a necessary nutrient for normal body function. Unfortunately, most Americans consume much more than the "daily requirement." It is essential that people with high blood pressure, diabetes, or kidney disease limit their salt intake. A low-fat hot dog, as an occasional meal or snack, is perfectly appropriate for those without these health issues. Kids love hot dogs! Just get them accustomed to eating them at home, where we can purchase them with lower fat and lower salt.

Peanut Butter and Banana Loaf

A high-protein snack for high energy on the field!

INGREDIENTS | SERVES 4

2 egg whites
2 ounces low-fat vanilla yogurt
2 tablespoons dry oatmeal
½ cup sugar
1 cup mashed ripe banana
2 tablespoons trans-fat-free peanut butter
1 teaspoon baking powder
Nonstick cooking spray

1. Preheat oven to 400°F.

2. Combine all ingredients in a medium bowl and mix well.

3. Spray loaf pan with cooking spray. Pour batter into pan. Bake for 45 minutes.

It's Not *Just* about the "Protein-Packed" Snack

For many years, the myth has been to avoid carbohydrates, because they "turn to sugar." This is partially true, especially white flour products—however, healthful diets *must* include healthful carbohydrates —particularly when young athletes need their most efficient source of energy to erupt during their practices.

"Energy-Loading" Lentil Soup

This is a quick boost of protein and carbohydrate energy—add some whole grain crackers or a whole grain roll, and the combination will assist in a great game!

INGREDIENTS | SERVES 3–4

Nonstick cooking spray
1 tablespoon olive oil
2 stalks celery
1 small onion, chopped finely
2 to 3 large carrots, chopped finely
1 cup lentils, dry
2 to 3 (16-ounce) cans chicken broth
1 (15-ounce) can diced tomatoes
Pepper and garlic to taste

1. In a medium skillet, spray nonstick cooking spray.

2. Heat olive oil on low heat. Add celery, onions, and carrots, and sauté until tender.

3. In a medium saucepan, cook lentils according to directions.

4. Add broth and the can of diced tomatoes.

5. Add vegetables, and continue to simmer, until hearty stew texture, about 30 to 45 minutes.

Bean Soups Versus Creamed Soups

Generally made without cream, bean soups such as a white bean soup, minestrone, pasta fagioli, lentil, and black bean soup are much healthier than creamed soups such as New England clam chowder or cream of broccoli. Always encourage children to choose the non-creamed versions; cream is highly saturated with fat.

Funny Face Pizza

Just a cute way to get the children involved in making their pizza—including those great vegetables, too!

INGREDIENTS | SERVES 4–6

1 prepared pizza crust (preferably whole wheat)

Nonstick cooking spray

1 (24-ounce) jar spaghetti or pizza sauce

2 cups shredded low-fat mozzarella cheese

Oregano, parsley, pepper, and garlic to taste

1 cup steamed broccoli florets

1 olive

4 large carrots, grated

2 round zucchini slices

1 thin slice red pepper

1. Preheat oven to 350°F.

2. Lay out pizza crust on a large piece of aluminum foil, sprayed with nonstick cooking spray.

3. Cover pizza crust with tomato sauce, mozzarella cheese, and spices.

4. Decorate with vegetables using grated carrots for hair and eyebrows. Use an olive for the nose, and broccoli florets for the eyes. Use red pepper slice for the mouth, and zucchini for the cheeks; or use different vegetable favorites and your imagination.

5. Cook pizza according to package directions.

Spinach Frittata

Do not be shocked, as this pancake may come out looking light green. Feel free to change the cheese selections to fit your family's tastes. Yet another wonderful punch of protein!

INGREDIENTS | SERVES 2–3

3 whole eggs

4 egg whites

⅓ cup low-fat milk

4 ounces part-skim mozzarella cheese, cubed

4 ounces low-fat Cheddar cheese, shredded

2 cups fresh spinach

1 teaspoon garlic powder

½ teaspoon white pepper

Salt to taste

Nonstick cooking spray

1. Place eggs, egg whites, milk, cheeses, spinach, garlic powder, white pepper, and salt in blender. Blend to a liquid consistency.

2. Spray skillet (which has a cover/lid) with nonstick cooking spray. Heat on medium heat for 1 minute.

3. Add egg mixture and reduce heat to low.

4. Cover and cook slowly for 20 minutes, turning once.

When They're Ready to Cook

This is a great way to introduce your teens to some cooking independence. Scrambling eggs and making an "egg pancake" is quite easy. Teach them the safety of the frying pan, cooking mostly on low heat, and how to scramble up those eggs and make their own frittata!

Goal-Scoring Chili

Beans don't get the respect they deserve. An excellent source of protein, and one of the top-notch sources of iron for energy into the cells. Add 6 to 8 whole grain crackers during this quick pre-practice snack, and this has all the makings for many winning goals.

INGREDIENTS | SERVES 6

Nonstick cooking spray
2 pounds ground sirloin
4 medium onions, chopped finely
1 medium green bell pepper, chopped
1 medium red pepper, chopped
1 (15-ounce) can tomato sauce
1 teaspoon garlic powder
¼ teaspoon pepper
2 tablespoons chili powder (amount optional—depending on your tolerance for spice)
1 (15-ounce) can kidney beans, rinsed and drained

1. Spray medium skillet with nonstick cooking spray.

2. Sauté onions and ground beef until beef is brown and cooked through. Drain fat from pan.

3. Add green and red pepper; cook 5 minutes.

4. Add tomato sauce, garlic powder, pepper, and chili powder, and mix well. Simmer 10 minutes on low heat.

5. Add kidney beans and mix. Simmer 10 more minutes and serve.

Mexican Chicken Triangles

You can use fresh turkey, or just cheese triangles as alternatives to the chicken.

INGREDIENTS | SERVES 4–6

Nonstick cooking spray
4 flour or corn tortillas
1½ cups low-fat Cheddar cheese, shredded
1½ cups shredded chicken breast, cooked
½ cup medium salsa
⅓ cup canned corn
½ cup red and yellow pepper, chopped
1 tablespoon chopped cilantro (optional)

1. Preheat oven to 350°F.

2. Spray cooking spray on a baking sheet, and place tortillas on the baking sheet. Bake 5 minutes until lightly browned. Remove from oven, and sprinkle 3 to 4 tablespoons of the cheese on each tortilla.

3. In a small mixing bowl, mix chicken with salsa.

4. Spoon chicken mixture over the cheese. Top with corn, red and yellow pepper, and remaining cheese.

5. Bake 7 to 10 minutes or until cheese is melted.

6. Sprinkle with cilantro (optional). Cut into quarters.

Grand Slam Mozzarella Marinara Sticks

Kids love mozzarella sticks! This is a bit of a healthier version. Serve with some carrot sticks, too—like a little cocktail party.

INGREDIENTS | SERVES 8

Pan-fried cheese:

1½ cups seasoned breadcrumbs

2 tablespoons Parmesan cheese

2 eggs

8 sticks of part-skim mozzarella cheese, about 1 inch in width, and 3 inches in length

2 to 3 tablespoons olive oil (for frying)

Marinara sauce:

Nonstick cooking spray

2 tablespoons olive oil

1 large garlic clove, minced

1 tablespoon parsley, minced

½ teaspoon basil

½ teaspoon oregano

1 (16-ounce) can crushed tomatoes, drained

1 (8-ounce) can tomato sauce

1. On a plate, mix breadcrumbs and Parmesan cheese together.

2. Crack the eggs into a small bowl, and beat well.

3. Dip each stick of cheese into beaten eggs and then into the breadcrumb mixture.

4. Place breaded cheese in a single layer on a plate and cover with plastic wrap. Place in refrigerator at least 30 minutes, so crumbs can adhere to the cheese.

5. In large skillet, on low heat, heat olive oil and fry cheese until brown on one side. Turn the cheese sticks and brown on other side. Remove from pan and drain on a paper towel.

6. Prepare marinara sauce in same large skillet. Spray skillet with nonstick cooking spray, and on low heat, sauté garlic.

7. Add remaining ingredients of sauce to skillet, and mix well.

8. Cook on medium heat for about 15 minutes or until thickened, stirring occasionally.

9. Simmer an additional 45 minutes.

10. Serve cheese sticks with warm sauce.

Amazing Apple Omelet

What a neat and distinctive combination of flavors; perfect for a quick snack, breakfast, weekend lunch, or dinner.

INGREDIENTS | **SERVES 4**

2 eggs, separated

3 tablespoons white sugar, divided

3 tablespoons all-purpose flour

¼ teaspoon baking powder

3 tablespoons low-fat milk

½ teaspoon vanilla

1 tablespoon lemon juice

Nonstick cooking spray

1 large Red Delicious apple, peeled, cored, and very thinly sliced

¼ teaspoon ground cinnamon

1. Preheat oven to 350°F.

2. In a small bowl, whip egg whites with an electric mixer until foamy.

3. As egg whites foam, add 2 tablespoons sugar, while continuing to whip until stiff peaks form.

4. In another medium mixing bowl, combine flour and baking powder.

5. Blend in the milk, egg yolks, vanilla, and lemon juice until well blended.

6. Fold in the egg whites with a spatula until blended and smooth.

7. Spray round baking pan with nonstick cooking spray. Pour batter evenly in the pan.

8. Place the apples on top of the batter. Sprinkle with cinnamon and remaining 1 tablespoon sugar.

9. Bake for 10 to 15 minutes, until the apples are just golden.

Maximum Power Mini Quiche

Your athletes will love this—quick, easy, full of protein and omega-3s. Substitute their favorite low-fat cheeses and even different vegetables for a great game-winning snack.

INGREDIENTS | SERVES 12

Nonstick cooking spray

12 slices whole wheat bread

1 medium onion, grated

½ cup low-fat Swiss or mozzarella cheese, shredded

1 cup low-fat milk

4 eggs

1 teaspoon dry mustard

1 pinch black pepper

1 teaspoon salt

Make It Quick—Practice Starts Soon

On sports days, it is critical to feed kids "correctly" before they go to athletic practice. To allow them to eat a bag of chips and a glass of fruit juice will not serve them well. Their needs are for high energy that will last them an hour or more. A source of protein plus a healthful carb are necessary to provide this.

1. Preheat oven to 375°F. Lightly spray a 12-muffin tin with nonstick cooking spray, or use paper liners.

2. Cut bread into circles that will fit in the muffin tins. Place circles in bottom of muffin tins.

3. Distribute the onion and shredded cheese evenly between the muffin tins.

4. In a medium bowl, combine milk, eggs, mustard, and pepper. Divide the mixture between the 12 compartments.

5. Bake in oven 20 minutes, or until a toothpick inserted into center of a quiche comes out clean.

White Bean Bisque

A thick and robust bean soup, giving great protein and "good carbs" for the afternoon basketball practice—though it can be a great meal anytime, too. Just add a big salad and a whole grain roll, for that "complete protein" meal.

INGREDIENTS | SERVES 6

Nonstick cooking spray

1 medium onion, chopped

1 small garlic clove, minced

2 (15-ounce) cans white cannellini beans, drained

1 cup frozen corn kernels

3 to 4 fresh carrots, grated

½ cup diced celery

1 cup chicken broth

1 to 2 teaspoons chili powder

2 cups low-fat milk

1 tablespoon cornstarch

1 cup low-fat Cheddar cheese, shredded

1. In a large skillet, spray nonstick cooking spray. Add onion and garlic, and heat over medium heat until onion and garlic are softened, about 5 minutes.

2. Add 1 can of beans to the skillet. Mash the beans with a fork.

3. Stir in second can of beans, corn, carrots, celery, chicken broth, and chili powder. Bring mixture to a simmer.

4. In a small bowl, mix cornstarch and milk and stir. Add to skillet. Bring slowly to a boil, stirring frequently.

5. Reduce heat and simmer 10 minutes or until mixture thickens and vegetables are tender.

6. Stir in cheese just until melted, and serve.

Fresh Fruit Pudding Mixer

Have the kids choose their favorite fruits and their favorite pudding flavors, and this can be such a fun healthy milkshake!

INGREDIENTS | SERVES 4

3½ cups low-fat milk

1 package (4 serving size) vanilla sugar-free, fat-free pudding

½ medium mango, cut into chunks

½ cup strawberries

1. Place all ingredients in blender container; cover.

2. Blend 1 to 2 minutes or until smooth.

3. Serve immediately.

Goat Cheese Crostini

Feta or farmer cheese can be good alternatives—a quick and delicious snack.

INGREDIENTS | SERVES 4

1 (8-ounce) package goat cheese

2 teaspoons fresh lemon juice

1 garlic clove, minced

8 small whole grain rolls, cut in half

Nonstick cooking spray

1. Preheat oven to 400°F.

2. Combine goat cheese, lemon juice, and garlic in a medium mixing bowl.

3. Slice rolls in half. Spray baking sheet with nonstick cooking spray. Place rolls in a single layer on the baking sheet.

4. Spoon goat cheese mixture onto each half of roll.

5. Bake for 8 minutes or until toasted. Serve immediately.

Pre-Football Fast Fajitas

Perfect when there are chicken (or steak) leftovers, too. Slice up the chicken and make some fast fajitas. Always remember a healthful higher-fiber carbohydrate plus a protein is the best recipe for an afternoon of football practice.

INGREDIENTS | SERVES 4

¼ cup fresh lime juice

2 teaspoons olive oil

½ teaspoon chili powder

4 skinless, boneless chicken breast halves (4 ounces each)

Nonstick cooking spray

2 medium red bell peppers, cut into thin strips

8 whole wheat flour or corn tortillas

2 medium tomatoes, chopped

½ cup scallions, finely chopped

4 leaves romaine lettuce, cleaned

2 teaspoons cilantro

Salsa as desired

1. In a medium shallow bowl, combine lime juice, oil, and chili powder. Mix well; reserve 2 tablespoons of marinade for later.

2. Add chicken to dish; turn on both sides to coat with marinade. Cover bowl with plastic wrap; refrigerate for 30 minutes.

3. Preheat the broiler.

4. After 30 minutes, drain the chicken from the marinade. Place chicken on a broiler pan sprayed with nonstick cooking spray.

5. Broil the chicken, basting with the reserved marinade and turning once, until cooked through (about 10 minutes). Place chicken on a plate and cover to keep warm.

6. Leave broiler on, and place bell pepper slices on the broiler pan. Broil until lightly grilled, turning once (about 6 to 8 minutes).

7. Cut chicken into strips.

8. In the tortilla, place chicken, broiled pepper, tomatoes, scallions, lettuce, and cilantro.

9. Fold tortillas tightly to enclose filling. Hold closed with several toothpicks, especially if packing in the lunch box. Serve with salsa (or pack it in a plastic container or snack size plastic bag).

Southwestern Nachos

Baked chips are a must—and everything else can be replaced with your children's favorites: different types of cheeses, beans or fat-free refried beans, pulled pork, chicken, spicy salsa.

INGREDIENTS | SERVES 4

Nonstick cooking spray

4 servings (about 8 chips per serving) baked tortilla chips

½ cup low-fat Cheddar cheese, shredded

½ cup low-fat Monterey jack cheese, shredded

2 medium tomatoes, chopped finely (about 2 cups)

½ cup scallions, chopped finely

1 clove garlic, minced

1 tablespoon red wine vinegar

¾ cup salsa (spice level as desired)

1. Preheat the broiler. Spray a baking sheet with nonstick cooking spray.

2. Place chips in a single layer on baking sheet; set aside.

3. In a small bowl, combine the cheeses; set aside.

4. In a medium bowl, combine tomatoes, scallions, garlic, and vinegar. Mix well. Spread this mixture evenly on top of chips.

5. Sprinkle cheeses evenly on top of tomato mixture.

6. Place the baking sheet in the broiler. Broil until the cheese melts (about 2 minutes—watch carefully).

7. Using a spatula, place nachos on a serving platter. Serve immediately with salsa on the side.

French Cinnamon Toast

Eggs and milk are used here as the dipping foundation—great protein sources as the afternoon practice gets underway. Another unique, good carb/protein snack.

INGREDIENTS | SERVES 4

1 whole egg

2 egg whites

½ cup low-fat milk

1 teaspoon vanilla extract

1 teaspoon ground cinnamon

⅛ teaspoon nutmeg

Nonstick cooking spray

8 whole wheat Italian bread slices, 1 inch thick, diagonally cut (or regular slices of whole grain bread)

Cinnamon and sugar or reduced-calorie maple syrup

1. In a shallow bowl, using a fork, beat the egg and egg whites until foamy.

2. Add milk, vanilla, cinnamon, and nutmeg. Beat well.

3. Spray large skillet with nonstick cooking spray. Heat over low heat.

4. Dip the bread slices into the egg mixture, coating on both sides.

5. Pan fry until golden brown, turning once.

6. Sprinkle lightly with cinnamon and sugar, or top with maple syrup. Serve immediately.

Dunkin' Drummettes

Who doesn't love chicken wings? These are a healthier version of chicken wings, with more meat and less fat.

INGREDIENTS | SERVES 4–6

2½ pounds chicken drummettes

1 (10-ounce) jar low-sugar apricot preserves

1 (8-ounce) low-fat French or Catalina dressing

1 envelope onion soup mix

Nonstick cooking spray

1. Remove skin from drummettes.

2. In a small mixing bowl, combine preserves, dressing, and onion soup mix.

3. Spray a shallow baking dish with nonstick cooking spray. Place the drummettes in a single layer in the baking dish.

4. Pour the preserve mixture over the drummettes, and allow to marinate for at least 1 hour.

5. Preheat oven to 300°F. Bake uncovered for approximately 2 hours, basting during cooking time.

CHAPTER 7

Hassle-Free Dinnertimes

Want Pizza?

For variety, add mushrooms, peppers, pineapple—anything that will excite your pizza (and your children)! And that's a sure-fire way to get in some vegetables, too!

INGREDIENTS | SERVES 3–4

1 large prepared pizza crust (whole wheat crust)

1 (26-ounce) jar tomato sauce

8 ounces shredded cooked chicken

12 ounces pineapple tidbits

1 (16-ounce) package shredded part-skim mozzarella cheese

Garlic powder, oregano, and basil to taste

1. Place pizza crust on a cookie sheet or pizza tray.

2. Pour tomato sauce onto crust, add chicken and pineapple and sprinkle cheese on top.

3. Add spices as desired.

4. Bake at 450°F for 8 to 10 minutes.

This Is No Daunting or Overwhelming Task

It does take some planning—just a little. This chapter highlights the many different types of meals that can be put together, taking 10 to 15 minutes, for most school nights—and those that will give your family a little more gourmet (or relaxing) feeling on the weekend. When children become old enough to be more helpful in the kitchen, reel them in to set the table, wash the vegetables, help choose the meal components, and clean up!

Chicken Fingers with Honey Mustard Sauce

*Serve the fingers with a chopped romaine or green leafy salad and a baked potato,
for a tasty, kid-friendly meal. Offer their favorite low-fat salad dressing,
and a trans-fat-free margarine for their baked potato.*

INGREDIENTS | SERVES 4–6

1 cup all-purpose flour or Wondra gravy mix

½ teaspoon salt

¼ teaspoon pepper

¾ cup low-fat milk (or 3 egg whites)

4 chicken breasts, skinless, boneless, cut in strips

¼ cup olive oil

⅓ cup honey

¼ cup Dijon mustard

Those Infamous Chicken Fingers

We equate kids with "chicken fingers." They are usually breaded with trans fat (the dangerous kind), artery-clogging and deep-fried—truly, a very poor choice as our children's staple food, especially in a restaurant or fast-food establishment. Your kids are chicken nugget freaks? Make your own. They can be just as delicious, pan-fried or baked.

1. Mix flour, salt, and pepper in a shallow bowl.

2. Place milk (or egg whites) in a shallow bowl and dip chicken into it.

3. Dip into flour mixture. Coat well. Place chicken on waxed paper.

4. Heat oil in skillet and pan-fry chicken strips until golden brown.

5. Mix together the honey and Dijon mustard to prepare sauce; in fact, try to prepare this sauce the night before for a richer flavor. Dip chicken in sauce and enjoy.

Groovy Grilled Flank Steak

An inexpensive, delicious way to serve a lean protein, along with lots of B vitamins and iron, for that long-term energy source. Place grilled steak on a chopped salad, or serve with a pureed squash and an ear of corn.

INGREDIENTS | SERVES 4

1½ pounds flank steak

3 tablespoons ketchup

3 tablespoons brown sugar

1 garlic clove, finely chopped

1. Marinate flank steak in ketchup, brown sugar, and garlic for a minimum of 2 hours.

2. Place on the grill for 5 to 6 minutes, each side.

Red Meat—Known for Its "Unhealthy" Reputation

Not necessarily anymore. For growing children, lean sources of protein, including meat, fish, and chicken, are critical nutrients for continued growth and development—especially of the brain. For years, it has been suggested that people curtail their intake of red meat, due to high-fat and elevated cholesterol issues. As long as you choose lean sources, and offer it 1 to 2 times per week, your kids should be in good shape, along with their healthy brains.

Broiled Shrimp Parmesan

A unique blend of seafood and cheese. Serve with steamed green pea pods, and a whole wheat pasta for a wonderful meal.

INGREDIENTS | SERVES 3–4

2 teaspoons olive oil

2 cloves garlic, minced

1 pound large shrimp, peeled and deveined

2 fresh medium tomatoes, coarsely chopped

¼ cup dry white wine

½ cup shredded part-skim mozzarella cheese

½ cup parmesan cheese

1. Preheat oven to broil.

2. Heat oil in an ovenproof skillet on low heat. Add garlic and sauté, stirring constantly, until lightly browned. Add the shrimp and tomato. Continue cooking on low heat until shrimp are cooked through, about 8 to 10 minutes.

3. Add wine and continue cooking for 1 to 2 minutes.

4. Sprinkle cheese evenly over the shrimp.

5. Place skillet in oven under broiler for 2 to 4 minutes, until cheese is melted and golden brown.

Sizzling Sirloin Shish Kabobs

For the best flavor, prepare marinade and leave sirloin chunks in the marinade overnight.

INGREDIENTS | SERVES 6–8

2½ pounds lean sirloin, cubed in 2-inch squares

2 medium green bell peppers, cut in 1-inch chunks

1 pound cherry tomatoes

1 pound large mushrooms, sliced in half

3 medium onions, cut in quarters

Skewer sticks

Marinade:

1½ cups olive oil

¾ cup low-sodium soy sauce

¼ cup Worcestershire sauce

2 tablespoons dry mustard

2 teaspoons salt

2 teaspoons parsley flakes

1 tablespoon fresh ground pepper

½ cup red wine vinegar

1 clove garlic, crushed

⅓ cup lemon juice

1. Prepare marinade by blending all ingredients in a blender for 30 seconds.

2. Marinate beef overnight.

3. When ready to prepare, place beef and vegetables on skewers, alternating meat with vegetable.

4. Broil or grill for 15 minutes, turning frequently.

Dinner Is Much Easier When Majority Rules

The bottom line here is that moms and dads should not be short-order cooks. There is no time, nor usually the desire, to create several meals per night that everyone will like. Therefore, from the get-go, begin to serve meals that can either "grow" on your children, or spouse, or prepare popular meals that everyone enjoys—and just vary them a little bit.

Lip-Smacking Lemony Chicken

A light and delightful dish—substitute fish fillet or thin veal tenderloins in place of the chicken.

INGREDIENTS | SERVES 4

4 tablespoons olive oil

4 large chicken breasts, boneless and skinless

1½ cups seasoned bread crumbs

2 whole eggs

2 to 3 egg whites

¼ cup olive oil

½ cup cooking wine

¼ cup lemon juice

1. Preheat oven to 350°F.

2. In a large skillet, heat 4 tablespoons of olive oil on low heat.

3. Place whole eggs and egg whites in a small bowl and beat together.

4. Dip chicken breasts in egg mixture, then bread crumbs.

5. Sauté chicken in skillet over low heat until cooked through.

6. Prepare mixture of ¼ cup olive oil, wine, and lemon juice.

7. Transfer chicken to baking or casserole dish. Pour wine-lemon mixture over chicken.

8. Bake for 20 to 30 minutes.

Baked Ziti with Spinach

This recipe is a quick, low-fat version of baked ziti. It's also a great source of calcium, not only from the cheeses but from the spinach, too.

INGREDIENTS | **SERVES 6–8**

1 pound ziti rigatoni noodles, whole wheat

1 cup part-skim ricotta cheese

1 cup shredded part-skim mozzarella cheese

1 (10-ounce) box chopped frozen spinach, thawed and drained

2 eggs

2 cups marinara or tomato sauce

Garlic, parsley, and oregano to taste

Nonstick cooking spray

½ cup grated Parmesan cheese

1. Preheat oven to 350°F.

2. Partially cook noodles, about 5 minutes and drain.

3. In a large mixing bowl, combine ricotta and mozzarella cheese, spinach, and eggs. Combine with the pasta and sauce. Add spices as desired.

4. Spray a large casserole dish with nonstick cooking spray. Pour pasta mixture into casserole dish. Sprinkle with Parmesan cheese.

5. Bake for 45 to 60 minutes.

Glazed Chicken Drums

A delicious Asian twist on "chicken wings." There is more meat on the drumstick and much less fat.

INGREDIENTS | **SERVES 10**

Nonstick cooking spray

3 scallions, chopped

3 tablespoons sherry

⅓ cup reduced-sodium soy sauce

2 teaspoons sugar

2 pounds chicken drumsticks, skinned

1. Spray cooking spray in a large skillet, over low heat.

2. Place scallions, sherry, soy sauce, and sugar in skillet. Bring to a boil, and then reduce heat.

3. Add chicken drumsticks. Cover skillet and simmer for 20 minutes.

4. Turn chicken several times during cooking.

Grand Chicken Soup

A wonderful, hearty chicken soup—sure to become a family favorite.

INGREDIENTS | SERVES 10–12

5 quarts water

2 whole chickens, cleaned and quartered

1 large onion, quartered

1 to 2 large sweet potatoes, peeled, quartered

4 large carrots, peeled and sliced

1 tablespoon fresh dill

1 tablespoon fresh parsley

1. Bring water to a boil in a large pot.

2. Add chicken parts, onions, sweet potatoes, carrots, dill, and parsley to the boiling water.

3. Cook covered, on simmer only, about 1½ to 2 hours.

4. Skim fat several times from the top of the pot while cooking.

5. Serve hot.

Mom's "Better" Meatloaf

Everyone loves this meatloaf—it just feels like home! For less saturated fat, mix ground beef with ground veal or ground turkey breast.

INGREDIENTS | SERVES 6–8

1 small (6-ounce) can tomato sauce

1 medium onion, chopped finely

¼ cup bread crumbs

Juice of 1 lemon

⅓ cup brown sugar

1 egg

1 tablespoon parsley

Salt and pepper to taste

2 pounds ground round or sirloin

3 tablespoons ketchup

1. Preheat oven to 350°F.

2. In medium bowl, combine tomato sauce, chopped onion, bread crumbs, lemon juice, sugar, egg, and spices.

3. Add meat in small chunks, and mix.

4. Shape into a loaf and place on a broiling pan.

5. Brush with ketchup. Bake 1 hour.

Grilled Vegetable and Lamb Shish Kebobs

It's a colorful dish—vary the vegetables with your kids' "favorites."

INGREDIENTS | SERVES 6

2½ to 3 pounds lamb, cut in 2-inch squares

12 cherry tomatoes

12 medium-sized mushrooms

3 large onions, cut in quarters

2 red peppers, cut in 1-inch squares

2 to 3 yellow squash, cut in small slices

Marinade for lamb:

⅓ cup reduced-sodium soy sauce

¾ cup canola oil

⅛ cup Worcestershire sauce

1 tablespoon dry mustard

1 teaspoon parsley flakes

1½ teaspoons ground pepper

¼ cup wine vinegar

1 teaspoon garlic powder

¼ cup lemon juice

1. Mix all ingredients together for the marinade and blend for 1 to 2 minutes.

2. Marinate lamb chunks for several hours or all day.

3. Assemble lamb on skewers, alternating with vegetables. Brush with extra marinade.

4. Place on the grill turning skewers several times for 15 minutes, or until cooked through.

Introduce Lamb as a Beef Alternative

Once again, variety, variety, variety. When the children are young enough, and aren't quite set in their ways yet, continue to familiarize them with as many new foods as possible. This recipe has crunch, color, and a marinade that is so tasty, the kids will add this to their "sophisticated" repertoire of foods. Beware: lamb is a little higher in fat than some of the leaner beef cuts.

Amazingly Simple Arroz con Pollo

For a truly healthy meal, prepare this dish with brown rice instead of yellow rice.
Add a bouillon cube to the water when preparing the brown rice for additional flavor.

INGREDIENTS | SERVES 6

3 pounds chicken, quartered

¼ cup olive oil

1 medium onion, chopped finely

2 tablespoons parsley flakes

3 cups canned tomatoes

⅛ teaspoon cumin

1 cup yellow rice, uncooked

1 teaspoon salt

¼ teaspoon pepper

2 cloves garlic, chopped

1 bay leaf

1. Preheat oven to 350°F.

2. In large ovenproof skillet, sauté chicken in olive oil until browned. Remove the chicken and place on a plate.

3. Use the remaining olive oil to cook the onions.

4. Place chicken back in the skillet.

5. Add all other ingredients, placing the bay leaf on the top.

6. Cover and place skillet in oven. Bake for 45 to 60 minutes. Remove bay leaf before serving.

Rice Portions Can Add an Extra 300 to 400 Calories

One of the issues with American eating is the size of the portions. No other country in the world "super-sizes" like Americans do, from the size of fast-food burgers and orders of French fries, to portions in a restaurant. To help with portion control prepare "the serving" of rice for each family member; that tends to be ½ cup to 1 cup, cooked, depending on the age of the family members, their activity levels, etc. The more you cook, the more they will eat.

Chicken a l'Orange

For the working parents, prepare the marinade the night before, and this becomes a quick dish to pan-fry when you get home. Smile knowing there are oranges, raisins, and carrots in this dish, which will give your family a vitamin C boost.

INGREDIENTS | SERVES 4–6

1 cup orange juice
1 cup white wine
1 teaspoon salt
½ teaspoon pepper
1 teaspoon paprika
1 large carrot, sliced thinly
1 celery stalk, sliced thinly
1 medium onion, sliced thinly
3 pounds chicken, skinless
Nonstick cooking spray
2 medium oranges, peeled and sectioned
½ cup golden raisins

A Million Marinades

Chicken (or meat or fish) is a lean and popular protein entrée that can be made in an endless number of ways for the family. Commercial marinades, though generally high in salt (sodium) can also be used, and there are many great flavors. Find fun marinades, pour the bottle into a plastic bag, throw the raw chicken in the bag, seal, and leave at the bottom of the refrigerator when you leave for work. It's ready to be cooked as soon as you walk in the door.

1. Preheat oven to 350°F.

2. Combine orange juice, wine, salt, pepper, and paprika with the sliced vegetables.

3. Place the chicken in a shallow pan and marinate with the juice-wine mixture for at least 1 hour. Turn 2 to 3 times during the marinating time.

4. Spray large skillet with cooking spray, and put over medium heat.

5. Place chicken in skillet and brown on both sides. Remove from pan.

6. In a baking dish, arrange the chicken, bone side up. Pour the marinade, orange sections and raisins on top of chicken.

7. Cover and bake 1 hour.

8. After an hour, uncover and continue baking for 30 minutes, or until browned.

9. Strain the pan juices, pour over chicken, and serve.

Salmon Pancakes

A delicious way to serve fish—pancake style! Sometimes ketchup on the side really does the trick! A vegetable and a baked potato completes this easy dinner.

INGREDIENTS | SERVES 6–8

1 (15½-ounce) can red or pink salmon, skinned and boned, juice reserved

2 eggs

⅔ cup onion, finely chopped

½ cup breadcrumbs

Salt and pepper to taste

¼ cup olive oil

Salmon—One of the *Best* Fish Around!

Offer salmon to your youngsters. The notable part about salmon is that you can vary its preparation in different ways, so if they don't love it poached, you can make salmon burgers, throw salmon on the grill basted with a little olive oil, or soaked in a wonderful marinade and then grilled or baked.

1. In a large bowl, combine the salmon with the reserved juice, eggs, onion, and breadcrumbs. Add salt and pepper as desired. Set aside for 15 minutes.

2. With wet hands, mold mixture into thick pancake shapes.

3. In a large skillet, heat oil on low heat.

4. Pan-fry pancakes until golden brown, turning once. Drain on paper towel and serve.

Ground Meat Asian Lettuce Wraps

Substitute sliced chicken or sliced flank steak, and add whatever vegetables, such as sliced peppers or mushrooms—whatever will make the entire family happy!

INGREDIENTS | SERVES 4–6

6 to 10 Boston or Bibb lettuce leaves
Make-It-Simple Meat Sauce (Page 181)
1 pound shredded carrots
½ cup hoisin sauce

1. Wash lettuce leaves.

2. Place ⅓ cup Meat Sauce in each lettuce leaf.

3. Garnish with carrots and 1 to 2 tablespoons hoisin sauce.

4. Roll up and enjoy.

Think Out of the Box

Asian and Japanese dishes are quite popular these days—lettuce wraps, dumplings, sushi. Offering these foods is a very sophisticated way to introduce children to different cultural foods. Caution: young children should not eat raw fish. Stick to the cooked versions.

Grilled Marinated Mahi-Mahi

*This recipe is easy, and delicious with tilapia, baja, or salmon.
The longer it is marinated, the better the flavor.*

INGREDIENTS | SERVES 4–6

2 lemons, juiced
2 medium oranges, juiced
Lemon and orange zest (from above)
2 tablespoons brown sugar
1½ to 2 pounds mahi-mahi

1. Prepare the marinade by blending the lemon and orange juice, lemon and orange zest, and brown sugar in shallow dish.

2. Place the fish into the marinade and refrigerate for a minimum of 2 hours.

3. Grill fish until opaque inside.

First-Rate Baked Steak

Baking or broiling is always an alternative when cooking beef. It can limit time spent grilling—which, when the use of the grill is more than 2 to 3 times per week—may be considered cancer-causing.

INGREDIENTS | SERVES 4–6

3 pounds lean sirloin, approximate 2-inch thickness

Black pepper to taste

½ cup ketchup

2 tablespoons Worcestershire sauce

2 green bell peppers, sliced thinly

1 large white onion, sliced thinly

Feed Your Family Leaner Cuts of Red Meat

It's best to chose the leaner cuts of red meat when cooking with it. Try these, the leaner of the options: tenderloin/filet mignon, sirloin, lean ground beef, flank steak, London broil, eye round, bottom round.

1. Preheat oven to 350°F.

2. Place steak in shallow roasting pan. Sprinkle steak with black pepper.

3. Coat steak completely with ketchup, covering the top and sides.

4. Add Worcestershire sauce. Top with the pepper and onion slices.

5. Bake for 1 hour.

Cheesy Chicken Casserole

For the extra spicy version, include the optional jalapeno pepper.

INGREDIENTS | SERVES 4–6

2 cups brown rice, cooked

2 cups white rice, cooked

2 large tomatoes, chopped

1 medium onion, chopped

3 cups cooked chicken breast, diced in small cubes

Pepper to taste

2 cups low-fat sour cream

12 ounces low-fat Monterey jack or mozzarella cheese, shredded

1 (12-ounce) can black olives, drained and sliced

1 jalapeño, seeded and cut into strips (optional)

1. Preheat oven to 350°F.

2. In a large bowl, combine the cooked brown and white rice, tomatoes, onion, and diced chicken. Season with pepper.

3. Spoon about half of this mixture into a shallow, greased, 2- to 3-quart casserole dish.

4. Cover with 1 cup sour cream, half of the cheese and half of the olives.

5. Repeat the above layers.

6. Bake uncovered for 45 minutes.

Special Sweet and Sour Pork

The tenderloin of the pork is a very lean cut of protein, quite lower in fat and saturated fat than beef.

INGREDIENTS | SERVES 8

2 pounds lean pork tenderloin

1 teaspoon salt

1 teaspoon pepper

2 tablespoons olive oil

1 (15-ounce) can crushed pineapple

¼ cup apple vinegar

¾ cup water

2 tablespoons reduced-sodium teriyaki sauce

¼ cup brown sugar

1 green bell pepper, sliced

1 red pepper, sliced

2 cups brown rice, cooked

Serve High-Vitamin C and Iron "Power-Packed Meals"

Meat, poultry, veal, pork, etc. are iron-rich foods. Iron helps to supply oxygen to your cells, the foundation of your body. The trick to a better absorption of iron in our bloodstream is to combine a food rich in vitamin C at the same meal with the high-iron food. The Sweet and Sour Pork recipe does just that: combines the pork with pineapple and red peppers—great sources of vitamin C.

1. Season pork with salt and pepper.

2. In large frying pan, add olive oil, and heat over low heat.

3. In mixing bowl, combine pineapple, vinegar, water, teriyaki sauce, and sugar. Mix well.

4. Slice pork into thin strips, and place into frying pan. Sauté pork until cooked thoroughly (no pink inside), about 10 to 20 minutes.

5. Add the liquid ingredients to the frying pan, and allow the pork to continue cooking.

6. Add the vegetables and cook until they are al dente, about 5 to 10 minutes.

7. Serve over brown rice.

Shrimp and Vegetable Paella

*A real mix of seafood, vegetables, and healthier brown rice, too—
vegetables and protein source can be alternated, too.*

INGREDIENTS | SERVES 4–6

2 tablespoons olive oil

1 clove garlic, minced

1 pound shrimp, deveined

Nonstick cooking spray

1 medium onion, chopped

1 (4-ounce) jar sliced pimientos, drained

1 large tomato, chopped

2 tablespoons minced garlic

Salt and pepper to taste

1 cup white rice, uncooked

1 cup brown rice, uncooked

3 cups chicken broth

1 cup water

3 to 4 tablespoons dried parsley

1 cup frozen peas

1 cup fresh or frozen carrots, chopped

½ pound fresh green beans, cleaned and cut in 1-inch pieces

1 (19-ounce) can cannellini or great northern beans, drained and rinsed

Brown and White Rice Are Joining Forces

Recently it has been proven that "white" carbohydrates are not very nutritious— white flour, white rice, regular pasta. In the long run, they can harm the way you make energy in your body, and leave you vulnerable to diseases such as diabetes, high cholesterol, and heart problems. What your children see (or eat) early in their lives is what they get accustomed to. When cooking brown rice, add that bouillon cube for more flavor; switch to a whole grain pasta, and when you add a delicious sauce, no one will complain.

1. In large skillet, heat oil over low heat. Add garlic to skillet.

2. Add shrimp and cook until cooked through, about 8 to 10 minutes.

3. Remove shrimp from heat and place in separate dish.

4. Spray nonstick cooking spray into same skillet, and sauté onion until tender.

5. Add pimientos, tomato, and garlic. Cook 2 minutes, stirring occasionally.

6. Add salt, pepper, and both types of uncooked rice. Add broth, water, and parsley. Increase to medium heat and bring to a boil.

7. Stir often, until most of the liquid has been absorbed, about 10 minutes.

8. Stir in vegetables and beans. Reduce heat to low and continue to simmer, covered, for about 10 to 15 minutes.

9. Add shrimp for the final few minutes, until shrimp is hot.

10. Remove from heat and allow to stand for about 10 minutes before serving.

Rockin' Roasted Salmon

Another simple way to prepare salmon—this marinade works well with many varieties of fish.

INGREDIENTS | SERVES 4

1½ pounds fresh salmon fillet, sliced in 4 pieces

1 tablespoon olive oil

Garlic powder to taste

Salt and pepper to taste

2 tablespoons fresh chives, chopped

1 lemon, juiced

1. Preheat oven to 425°F.

2. Rub salmon with olive oil. Season with garlic, salt, pepper and the juice of the lemon.

3. Place in upper third of oven and bake on a foil-lined baking sheet, 15 to 20 minutes.

4. Remove from oven, sprinkle with chives, and serve.

BBQ Roast with Potatoes

Home cooking come true—serve with a Caesar salad (with light dressing) for a perfect meal.

INGREDIENTS | SERVES 8–10

3 to 4 pounds lean roast (chuck or bottom round)

12 to 18 ounces barbecue sauce

½ cup ketchup

2 tablespoons onion soup mix

Pepper to taste

Garlic powder to taste

4 medium potatoes, cubed

1. Preheat oven to 375°F. Line roasting pan with aluminum foil.

2. Mix together the barbecue sauce, ketchup, onion soup mix, pepper, and garlic powder, and rub mixture on the roast.

3. Place in a large pot and cook on top of stove for 30 to 40 minutes, turning constantly.

4. Place in the prepared roasting pan and bake 1 to 1½ hours.

5. Place potatoes in pan. Bake together in oven for 1 hour or until desired doneness.

Brave Bean Burritos

A quick dinner for all—everyone can assemble the burritos themselves—
and in 10 minutes, dinner is ready. Add a big fruit salad and voilà!

INGREDIENTS | SERVES 4

4 corn tortillas

2 cups canned black beans, drained

½ cup prepared salsa (optional spice level)

½ cup romaine lettuce, chopped finely

½ cup tomatoes, chopped finely

2 ounces low-fat cheddar cheese, shredded

1. Warm tortillas and roll up in aluminum foil.

2. When ready to serve, fill each tortilla equally with beans, salsa, lettuce, tomato and cheese and close the burrito.

3. Warm in microwave about 30 seconds until beans are hot and cheese is melted.

Anatomy of a Burrito

As is, this recipe uses black beans—however, kidney beans or white beans or even fat-free refried beans offer great variety. Of course, the "spice-level" of the salsa can be altered, the vegetables that go inside the tortilla can also be different. Lettuce and tomato are the norm, but how about raw mushrooms, sliced colored peppers, jalapenos, shaved carrots, or cucumbers? Cheeses will add some additional protein and calcium—offer the children's favorite low-fat cheeses. This makes the crowd roar!

Mrs. Paco Taco

Prepare taco meat. Shred lettuce and chop tomatoes, and serve with baked tortilla chips, or wrap in a corn tortilla for a unique soft taco.

INGREDIENTS | SERVES 4–6

Nonstick cooking spray
1 pound ground sirloin
¼ teaspoon nutmeg
¼ teaspoon pepper
½ teaspoon salt
½ teaspoon dried oregano
2 cloves garlic, minced
½ small onion, chopped
Water to cover

1. Spray medium skillet with nonstick cooking spray.

2. Combine beef, nutmeg, pepper, salt, oregano, garlic, and onion.

3. Cook on medium heat until beef is cooked and onion begins to soften.

4. Just barely cover with water.

5. Cook 30 to 40 minutes on low heat, until water is absorbed.

6. Serve with corn chips or put into a corn tortilla and serve.

CHAPTER 8

How to Get Them to Try Something New

Baked Cheese Crepes

There are different varieties of frozen blintzes—blueberry or potato blintzes could be substituted for cheese blintzes. It's generally something children like.

INGREDIENTS | SERVES 6

2 (13-ounce) packages frozen cheese "blintzes"

Nonstick cooking spray

4 whole eggs

4 egg whites

½ cup sugar

¼ cup orange juice

¾ cup canola oil

2 teaspoons vanilla

¼ teaspoon salt

Cinnamon and sugar to taste

1. Preheat oven to 350°F.

2. Thaw the blintzes for a few minutes, just long enough to separate them easily. Spray 9" × 13" pan with nonstick cooking spray. Layer the blintzes in the pan.

3. In a large bowl, beat the eggs and egg whites until light and fluffy.

4. Add the sugar, orange juice, oil, vanilla, and salt. Pour the mixture evenly over the blintzes.

5. Sprinkle with cinnamon and sugar.

6. Bake for 1 hour.

Kids Wouldn't Be Kids If They Weren't Picky

Not every kid, or adult, likes every food. Kids go through food phases; one day, they adore corn, and the next week, they hate it. This is where the patience of a parent needs to be saint like. Studies reveal that the continuous exposure of a child to a food will increase the likelihood that he will eat it. The magic number seems to be *ten*. Key tip: try and attempt this task at the dinner table. If the rest of the family is enjoying that "new food" you want your child to try, that is the perfect setup for success.

Brown Rice and Noodle Casserole

Take baby steps to change from a white pasta noodle to a whole wheat one—and from white rice to brown rice. This dish can be one of those steps. It is an unusual side dish, and quite a bit healthier with the higher fiber versions.

INGREDIENTS | SERVES 8–10

1 (16-ounce) box angel hair spaghetti, whole wheat

¼ cup trans-fat-free margarine

2 cups brown minute rice, uncooked

1 cup water

1 tablespoon low-sodium soy sauce

2 (15-ounce) cans chicken broth

2 (15-ounce) cans low-sodium onion soup

1 (15-ounce) can sliced water chestnuts (optional)

1. Preheat oven to 350°F.

2. Break the spaghetti noodles in half before boiling. Partially cook noodles (approximately 3 to 4 minutes).

3. Heat margarine in skillet on low heat. Place cooked noodles in skillet and brown them for about 5 to 7 minutes.

4. In large casserole dish, mix the noodles with the remaining ingredients.

5. Bake uncovered for 45 minutes.

Baked Broccoli

This is a terrific way to introduce children to broccoli—with a cheesy twist! Give fresh green beans a try, too, as an alternative to the broccoli.

INGREDIENTS | SERVES 4

1 large head of broccoli, chopped

2 tablespoons olive oil

1 cup grated Parmesan cheese, plus extra for garnish

3 to 4 tablespoons minced garlic

Nonstick cooking spray

1. Preheat oven to 350°F.

2. Place all ingredients, except the cooking spray, in a plastic bag. Shake well.

3. Spray nonstick cooking spray on a cookie sheet. Spread broccoli on cookie sheet.

4. Sprinkle with a little extra Parmesan cheese.

5. Bake for 20 to 30 minutes or until slightly browned.

Hawaiian Fruit Salad

A sweet and colorful way to serve fruit. It's a kids' favorite. Feel free to double and triple the recipe and alternate the fruits, too.

INGREDIENTS | SERVES 6–8

1 cup canned mandarin oranges, drained

1 cup canned pineapple chunks (in own juice), drained

1 cup shredded coconut

1 cup mini-marshmallows

1 cup low-fat sour cream

1. Mix all ingredients in a large bowl, carefully.

2. Refrigerate for 1 hour and then serve.

Tropical Fruits—Kid-Friendly and Healthful

Any way you can continue to promote fruits of all kinds, even if it means a little extra sweetness added, just do it. Although coconut is not a good oil to use when cooking due to its high saturation content, the fruit itself is an excellent source of fiber and potassium. Potassium is a needed mineral in children's growing bodies; it assists in healthy muscles and a healthy heartbeat.

Grand Ol' Guacamole Dip

Let kids dip baked tortilla chips into this wonderfully healthy dip— very high in monounsaturated fat and quite heart-healthy.

INGREDIENTS | SERVES 8–10

½ package onion soup mix

1 cup low-fat sour cream

1 medium avocado, mashed

1 large tomato, chopped

1 teaspoon lemon juice

Dash of Worcestershire sauce

Salt to taste

1. Blend onion soup mix and sour cream together.

2. Add the mashed avocado, chopped tomato, lemon juice, Worcestershire sauce, and salt.

3. Mix well and refrigerate for at least 2 hours before serving.

This Is a Versatile and Fun Dip

For that Super Bowl party, holiday, or just a weekend hang-out with the kids, serve either with baked chips, or cut-up carrots, peppers, and celery, for plenty of crunch and great color! This is really a bold victory for them if they are willing to taste avocado, a vegetable known for its monounsaturated fats—those "good" fats!

Pumpkin Cake

*Packed with vitamin A and beta-carotene—pumpkins are great
for eyesight and prevention of cancer in later years.*

INGREDIENTS | SERVES 16

1½ cups sugar

½ cup canola oil

3 eggs

1 teaspoon vanilla extract

1 (15-ounce) can pumpkin

3 cups cake flour, sifted

1 teaspoon baking powder

1 teaspoon baking soda

1 teaspoon ground cinnamon

¼ teaspoon ground nutmeg

½ teaspoon salt

Nonstick cooking spray

Glaze:

½ cup powdered sugar

½ cup whipped cream cheese

½ teaspoon vanilla extract

3 tablespoons fresh orange juice

1. Preheat oven to 350°F.

2. In a large bowl, mix sugar and oil. Beat at medium speed until well blended, 3 to 5 minutes.

3. Add eggs, vanilla, and pumpkin.

4. In a separate bowl, mix flour, baking powder, baking soda, cinnamon, nutmeg, and salt. Stir carefully with a wire whisk.

5. Fold flour mixture into pumpkin mixture.

6. Spray a tube pan with nonstick cooking spray. Pour batter into pan.

7. Bake for 50 to 60 minutes, until toothpick comes out clean and dry.

8. To prepare glaze, place powdered sugar and whipped cream cheese in a bowl. Beat at medium speed until well blended.

9. Add vanilla and orange juice, and beat well.

10. After cake is removed from oven, and cooled for 15 minutes, drizzle cake with glaze.

Tantalizing Tuna Nuggets

Another neat way to get fish into the children's regular diet. Looks like a meatball, but a much greater benefit from the healthful fat, in an attempt to avoid heart disease in later years.

INGREDIENTS | SERVES 8

2 (7-ounce) cans tuna packed in water
6 ounces whipped cream cheese
1 tablespoon lemon juice
2 tablespoons horseradish
1 cup chopped parsley
2 teaspoons garlic powder

1. Drain tuna and place in a mixing bowl. Flake the tuna with a fork.

2. Whip together cream cheese, lemon juice, horseradish, parsley, and garlic powder until smooth and fluffy.

3. Add tuna and mix well.

4. Shape into small balls.

5. Refrigerate for 30 minutes and serve.

Give "Dark/Chunk Tuna" a Try

It has been noted over the years that fish with high levels of mercury are quite toxic to the body. Several kinds of fish have pretty high mercury levels: shark, tuna, swordfish, and king mackerel. Solid white tuna has higher levels than dark. The recommendation is to choose the solid white only once per week, and to avoid it completely during pregnancy and lactation. As you prepare your dark/chunk tuna, add celery and/or relish, garlic and/or onion, a little pepper—and it is delicious. This type can be eaten several times a week and no worries about mercury poisoning.

Sweet Cheese Crepes

This is a time-consuming recipe, but a delicious one—worth the work.

INGREDIENTS | SERVES 6

Batter:
2 eggs
2 tablespoons canola oil
1 teaspoon vanilla
1 cup low-fat milk
¾ cup flour, sifted
½ teaspoon salt
Nonstick cooking spray

Filling:
2 egg yolks
6 tablespoons sugar
¼ pound whipped cream cheese, room temperature
¼ pound 2% low-fat cottage cheese, small curd

A Much Lower-Fat, Lower-Sugar Version

Shh! No one will know the difference! A recipe around for years—using high-fat products such as regular cottage cheese, sour cream, whole milk, and cream cheese. Everything used here is a low-fat adaptation, with a little less sugar than the original, too. It remains a delicious, high-calcium crepe!

1. To make the crepes, beat eggs, oil, vanilla, and milk.

2. Add flour and salt, and beat until smooth.

3. Chill for 30 minutes.

4. Spray nonstick cooking spray into small frying pan, over low heat.

5. Using about ¼ cup batter, pour into frying pan and cook for 2 to 3 minutes. It is not necessary to flip the crepe since it is thin enough to cook through without flipping.

6. To prepare filling, beat egg yolks and sugar in a medium bowl.

7. Add cream cheese and cottage cheese. Mix well.

8. Now ready to fill the crepe, put about ¼ cup cheese mixture into the crepe, using the "less cooked" side of the crepe to fill.

9. Fold so that the filling is safely inside. Remove from pan. Place on large piece of wax paper.

10. Prepare the remaining crepes with filling. Place them all on the wax paper.

11. Wrap all the crepes in large piece of foil and freeze for 1 hour.

12. When ready to fry the crepes, place 2 to 3 tablespoons canola oil in a frying pan over low heat, cooking for 2 to 3 minutes.

13. Serve with fresh fruit or hot blueberry sauce or applesauce.

Crunchy Chinese Salad

What a colorful and crunchy salad! Full of great vegetables, fruits, and nuts.
Hint: look for the rice noodles in the ethnic section of the grocery store.

INGREDIENTS | SERVES 8–10

1 cup slivered almonds

1 bag (16–20 ounces) shredded cabbage

1 medium bag fresh snow peas, blanched

1 (10-ounce) can mandarin oranges in own juice, drained

1 package rice noodles

Salad dressing:

⅓ cup canola oil

1 tablespoon reduced-sodium soy sauce

1 tablespoon sesame oil

½ cup sugar

¼ cup wine vinegar

1. Toast almonds in oven (or toaster oven), for about 5 to 10 minutes.

2. Toss all salad ingredients, except for almonds and rice noodles.

3. Prepare salad dressing by combining all ingredients in a small bowl and mixing well.

4. Add salad dressing to salad, and sprinkle almonds and rice noodles on top.

The Salads Will "Grow" on Them

Studies reveal that many children are just not good salad eaters. Is this because you, as a parent, do not enjoy or prepare them? Do you just take it for granted that they will not eat something so healthy? Encourage and influence your children early to become salad eaters. Though dressings tend to hold much of the calories and fat in salads, you can offer low-fat dressings. Throw in the fruits and vegetables you know they'll eat!

Israeli Salad

Vary the vegetables to include the ones the children like best, and/or add chopped Romaine lettuce for a more traditional salad.

INGREDIENTS | SERVES 8–10

3 carrots, diced
5 radishes, diced
2 green bell peppers, diced
2 red peppers, diced
2 cucumbers, peeled and diced
6 plum tomatoes, diced
3 stalks celery, diced
2 tablespoons parsley, chopped finely

Salad Dressing:
¼ cup olive oil
¼ cup lemon juice
Salt and pepper to taste

1. Combine all the vegetables in a large bowl.

2. Create the dressing by combining oil, lemon juice, salt, and pepper in a small bowl and mixing well.

3. Add salad dressing to the salad; toss well.

Veggies Are Key for Kids' Health

Vegetables are a crucial part of kids' diets—providing fiber and keeping everything moving throughout the "system." Vegetables keep you feeling "full and satisfied" long after you've finished eating them. Additionally, the vitamin C, potassium, iron, vitamin A, and beta-carotene are perfect for prevention of colds and illnesses and provide good fuel for the muscles and antioxidants for long-term cancer and heart disease prevention.

Marvelous Mahi-Mahi Marinara

Try this with mahi-mahi first. This is a mild fish. Feel free to experiment with other fish fillets as the kids begin to like this dish.

INGREDIENTS | SERVES 4–6

1½ to 2 pounds mahi-mahi fillets
1 large tomato, sliced thinly
1 large onion, sliced thinly
1 cup marinara sauce (jarred)
¾ cup Parmesan cheese

1. Preheat oven to 475°F. Place large piece of aluminum foil on a baking sheet.

2. Rinse the fish and place on the aluminum foil.

3. Place tomatoes and onion slices on top of each piece of fish.

4. Cover each piece of fish with marinara sauce and sprinkle with Parmesan cheese.

5. Close up tin foil to form a tent. Bake for 1 hour.

Delicious Dilled Potato Salad

Let's try another way for the kids to eat potatoes—other than the fried version! This will fit in great with your next barbecue.

INGREDIENTS | SERVES 8

1 cup low-fat mayonnaise

1 tablespoon Dijon mustard

1½ teaspoons dried dill

½ teaspoon salt

¼ teaspoon pepper

2 pounds small red potatoes, cooked and quartered

⅓ cup scallions, chopped

1. Combine mayonnaise, mustard, dill, salt, and pepper.

2. Add potatoes and scallions.

3. Cover and chill in refrigerator for about 1 hour before serving.

Encourage Potato Skins

No, no—not the fried potato skins in restaurants! One of the healthiest parts of the potato is, by far, the skin. Recent research suggests that the white potato, though a great source of vitamin C and potassium, can raise blood sugar levels quickly. However, when eaten with a meal, and with the skin (fantastic fiber), the blood sugars don't rise as quickly.

Kid-Friendly Honey Mustard Salad Dressing

The children will probably love this dressing—try it with chopped romaine lettuce, or chopped cucumber and tomato.

INGREDIENTS | SERVES 4–6

½ cup low-fat mayonnaise

1½ tablespoons Dijon mustard

1 tablespoon honey

1. Combine ingredients. Stir well until completely blended.

2. Chill 20 to 30 minutes and serve on their favorite salad.

Salad Dressings—a Huge Source of Fat Calories

When ordering salad in a restaurant ask if they have "light" dressings, and see if your children will choose any of the flavors. You should also ask for salad dressing on the side, and suggest how much should be used. Consider more vinaigrette-based dressings, rather than heavy bleu cheese. And at home purchase low-fat dressings *only*. There are so many wonderful varieties today: Caesar, Ranch, even light bleu cheese. Look for those that are about 80 calories per serving and olive oil based.

Rotini with Perfect Peanut Sauce

Of course, any shape noodle can be used for this recipe. An important tip is to use healthier peanut butter, without trans fat (or partially hydrogenated vegetable oil), and a whole wheat noodle.

INGREDIENTS | SERVES 4–6

½ to ¾ pounds whole wheat rotini pasta noodles

Peanut Sauce:

4 to 5 tablespoons trans-fat-free peanut butter

2 teaspoons brown sugar

2 garlic cloves, peeled and minced

2 tablespoons canola oil

2 tablespoons reduced-sodium soy sauce

1 tablespoon cider vinegar

1 tablespoon sesame oil

4 to 5 tablespoons hot water

1. Bring to a boil a large pot of water. Cook the pasta until just soft. Drain and set aside.

2. Combine the peanut butter, brown sugar, garlic, canola oil, soy sauce, cider vinegar, and sesame oil. Blend well.

3. Add the hot water and mix until a creamy consistency.

4. Add the sauce to the pasta. Serve immediately for best flavor.

A Really Neat Twist on Pasta

Peanut butter with pasta? Now that Japanese/Asian food is so popular, why not prepare this pasta dish with a peanut sauce? To increase the protein level for this dish, add sliced chicken or cooked shrimp—more protein will always keep the children satiated. Yet another way to have them eat whole wheat pasta, too, without complaints!

Tofu Triangles and Pita

A pleasant way to introduce the vegetarian product tofu, made from soybeans and quite healthy. Experiment with the children when they are young—they will be great eaters!

INGREDIENTS | SERVES 4

1 (14-ounce) package firm tofu, drained

¼ cup all-purpose flour or Wondra coating

1 tablespoon canola oil

1 medium onion, thinly sliced

½ teaspoon salt

¼ teaspoon ground cumin

¼ teaspoon black pepper

3 to 4 plum tomatoes, diced

2 tablespoons fresh cilantro, chopped

1 tablespoon brown sugar

½ cup water

3 tablespoons red wine vinegar

2 to 3 whole wheat pitas, cut in triangle shapes

Tofu, a Great Protein Alternative

Children, whose bodies are still developing, require so many nutrients through their adolescent period. Tofu, a product of soybeans, if prepared pleasingly, can be another protein choice for the kids. Protein sources that do not come from animals are what we call "incomplete proteins." Therefore, incomplete proteins such as beans, nuts, and corn have to be combined with a source of rice or wheat in order to be considered a "complete protein"—better for the children, and their parents. For a protein to be considered a complete protein it must contain about 20 amino acids (the building blocks of protein).

1. Cut tofu into 6 to 7 slices, about ¾ inch thick. Place the tofu on 2 layers of paper towels. Cover with paper towel. Let stand for 10 minutes, pressing down on tofu once or twice, to remove excess water.

2. Place flour in a shallow dish. Dredge the tofu in flour on both sides.

3. Heat canola oil in a large skillet, over low heat. Sauté tofu 3 to 5 minutes on each side. Remove from the oil, and place on a large plate.

4. In the skillet, place the onions, salt, cumin, and pepper, and continue sautéing for about 5 minutes, until onions are tender.

5. Add tomato, cilantro, and sugar, and continue cooking for an additional 2 to 3 minutes.

6. Add the water and vinegar and bring to a slight boil. Cook 2 minutes.

7. Place pita triangles on a serving dish. Place cooked tofu on top of each piece of pita.

8. Spoon the onion sauce over the tofu and serve.

Spaghetti Pie

When this dish is prepared, no one even notices the cheeses are lower-fat versions. That is the greatest—when no one knows the difference, and can still enjoy it immensely!

INGREDIENTS | SERVES 4

½ pound whole wheat spaghetti
2 tablespoons olive oil
2 eggs, beaten
1 cup Parmesan cheese, grated
Nonstick cooking spray
1 cup low-fat ricotta cheese
1 cup marinara sauce, jarred
½ to 1 cup part-skim mozzarella cheese, shredded

1. Preheat oven to 350°F.

2. Cook spaghetti as per directions on the box.

3. Place cooked spaghetti in a large bowl and toss with the olive oil.

4. In a small bowl, combine eggs and ½ cup Parmesan cheese.

5. Add to pasta and mix.

6. Spray nonstick cooking spray into a pie pan.

7. Pour spaghetti into the pie pan, creating a "pie crust."

8. Spread the ricotta cheese inside the "crust."

9. Pour marinara sauce on top.

10. Bake for 25 minutes.

11. Add mozzarella and remainder of Parmesan cheese.

12. Continue to bake for an additional 5 to 10 minutes, until cheese is melted.

Citrus-Braised Duck

Recent information suggests that ducks are being raised a bit healthier—
and are therefore less "fatty" than they used to be.

INGREDIENTS | SERVES 6–8

2 large ducks, quartered

4 cups orange juice

1 teaspoon salt

¼ teaspoon white pepper

2 cups chicken broth

1 cup low-sugar apricot preserves

2 to 3 tablespoons potato or cornstarch

¼ cup cold water

Breeding Ducks with a Little Less Fat

Over the last several years, duck has become a lower-fat poultry, thanks to the healthier feeding and raising of ducks. One of the keys to keeping poultry servings lower in fat is to leave the skin behind on your plate. That may be a tough one, but poultry skin is loaded with saturated fat, the ultimate artery-clogger.

1. In a large mixing bowl, marinate the duck in 2 cups of the orange juice. Refrigerate for 1 day, if possible. Dispose of the orange juice marinade.

2. Preheat oven to 400°F. Place the duck in a roasting pan, on a rack, for fat to drip off.

3. Roast the duck for 30 to 40 minutes, then reduce heat to 325°F.

4. Pull the duck out, and quickly season the duck with salt and pepper.

5. In a mixing bowl, combine the remaining 2 cups of orange juice and chicken broth. Pour over the duck and cover with aluminum foil.

6. Continuing baking for 1 hour or so, until fully cooked and tender.

7. Using a spoon, skim the fat from the juices at the bottom of the pan, and keep the remaining liquid.

8. Add the apricot preserves to the liquid or drippings and stir.

9. Pour the mixture into a saucepan, and add potato starch and cold water.

10. Cook over low heat, until gravy has thickened, stirring constantly for about 5 to 7 minutes.

11. Pour the gravy over the duck and serve immediately.

Gazpacho Soup for the Daring

A refreshing cold soup for a great summer day—as mild or as spicy as you like.

INGREDIENTS | SERVES 4

1½ quarts low-sodium V-8 juice
1 cucumber, peeled, seeded, and chopped
2 plum tomatoes, chopped
1 medium white onion, chopped
1 small red onion, chopped
1 green bell pepper, chopped
Black pepper and Tabasco sauce to taste

1. Mix all ingredients together.

2. Refrigerate overnight; serve.

Role Modeling—a Parent's Ultimate Responsibility

Gazpacho is a refreshing twist on a cold tomato soup. One of the greatest lessons you can teach as a parent, is to "do as I do," not just "do as I say." There is much greater power in being a role model for your children, by *doing* what you expect them to do. So, even though you might not love a food, please try it, or eat it, in front of your child—with a smile on your face.

Grandma's Rice Pudding

What a wonderful way to get in some bone-enhancing calcium! Always a memorable favorite, and you can even give brown rice pudding a try.

INGREDIENTS | SERVES 12

1 cup whole milk
4 cups 2% milk
¾ cup sugar
½ cup uncooked rice
Cinnamon to taste
Orange zest for garnish (optional)

1. Preheat oven to 325°F.

2. In a casserole dish, combine milks, sugar, and rice (shallow dish preferable to deep dish).

3. Bake 2 hours in the oven, uncovered, without stirring.

4. Remove from the oven and let sit for half an hour to set.

5. Serve pudding warm or cold, garnished with cinnamon and orange zest, if desired.

Super Spinach Crustless Quiche

Another easy way to disguise other vegetables—this is delicious with mushrooms and colored peppers, too. This quiche is also crustless and is therefore all the more healthier than standard quiche.

INGREDIENTS | SERVES 8–10

2 (10-ounce) packages frozen chopped spinach

1 medium onion, sliced

Nonstick cooking spray

1 pint low-fat sour cream

4 tablespoons low-fat Cheddar cheese

4 tablespoons low-fat American cheese

Salt and pepper to taste

2 teaspoons dried parsley

4 whole eggs

2 egg whites

2 (6-ounce) cans mushroom pieces or 1 cup fresh mushrooms, finely chopped (optional)

1. Preheat oven to 350°F.

2. Cook spinach in the microwave, following package directions. Drain spinach for 30 minutes in strainer, getting out all the water.

3. In small frying pan, spray nonstick cooking spray. Sauté onions until tender.

4. Combine all ingredients in a large bowl.

5. Spray nonstick cooking spray into a quiche pan. Pour egg mixture into pan.

6. Bake for 45 to 50 minutes, or until quiche is firm to the touch.

Phenomenal Fish with Sesame Vegetables

Tilapia is a very mild fish. Mixed with the vegetables, it is very pleasing to the eye and to the palate.

INGREDIENTS | SERVES 4-6

6 Tilapia fillets
2 medium lemons (juice only)
2 teaspoons garlic powder
1 teaspoon pepper
2 teaspoons oregano
3 tablespoons olive oil
1 small onion, sliced
½ cup flour
1 (14-ounce) bag frozen mixed vegetables
¼ cup light soy sauce (preferably citrus soy sauce)
4 tablespoons sesame oil
1 tablespoon rice vinegar
Sesame seeds to garnish

1. Cut fish in medium size pieces.

2. Prepare marinade with lemon juice, garlic powder, pepper, and oregano. Place fish in marinade and refrigerate for 1 hour.

3. In a small skillet, heat olive oil on low heat, and sauté onions until golden, about 4 to 5 minutes.

4. Dip fish pieces in flour and sauté on both sides until golden, about 4 minutes on each side.

5. Remove the fish from the pan and set aside.

6. Add vegetables, soy sauce, sesame oil and vinegar to the frying pan. Sauté the vegetables for a few minutes, and then place fish carefully on top. Place lid on pan and cook for 10 minutes.

7. Add a little more sauce if needed, sprinkle with sesame seeds, and serve.

Sweet 'n Sour Shrimp

Shrimp is always a great way to get children to eat some sort of seafood. This is a very tasty dish, with the brown rice (or even a baked potato) and a salad, a beautiful meal.

INGREDIENTS | SERVES 4

2 tablespoons cornstarch

1 cup pineapple juice, unsweetened

½ cup chicken broth

⅓ cup red wine vinegar

¼ cup dry sherry

1 medium red pepper, diced

20 raw fresh shrimp, shelled and deveined

2 cups brown rice, cooked

Shrimp—a Wonderful Seafood Source

In the past it was believed that shrimp were high in cholesterol and should be limited or avoided. However, recent research shows that the high percentage of "good fats" in shrimp reduces the impact of the cholesterol. Shrimp tend to be a seafood that kids will eat. Avoid the fried version! Certainly sauté in olive oil, serve as a shrimp cocktail, or barbecue on skewers. So, enjoy shrimp without guilt—and serve it to the kids, often.

1. In a saucepan, combine cornstarch, pineapple juice, and broth.

2. Bring to a boil over medium heat, stirring occasionally, until thickened. Turn down the heat, and simmer for 1 to 2 minutes.

3. Stir in vinegar and sherry.

4. Add red pepper and shrimp, and cook for 4 to 6 minutes, until tender.

5. Spoon over brown rice.

"You're All Heart" Salad

Take steps toward turning out good vegetable eaters. Allow your children to munch on this creative little salad—and then venture off into different vegetables; just keep the heart shape!

INGREDIENTS | SERVES 2

1 small green bell pepper, cored, seeded, and cut into quarters

1 small red bell pepper, cored, seeded, and cut into quarters

½ cucumber, cut into ½-inch-thick slices

1 slice low-fat American cheese (or other favorite low-fat cheese choice)

2 tablespoons favorite low-fat salad dressing

1. Using a small heart-shaped cookie cutter, shape peppers, cucumber, and cheese into heart shapes.

2. On a plate, assemble the veggies and the cheese.

3. Drizzle with low-fat dressing.

CHAPTER 9

More Dairy:
A Must for Optimum Growth

Cream of Carrot Soup

Carrots, in any form, along with all fruits and vegetables that are orange in color, are an incredible source of antioxidants and phytochemicals—cancer fighting, heart-healthy nutrients. Incorporate them daily into your family's diets.

INGREDIENTS | SERVES 4–6

8 large carrots, scraped and thinly sliced

2 celery stalks, chopped fine

3 cups chicken or vegetable stock

Salt and pepper to taste

1 small bay leaf

1 egg yolk, beaten

¼ cup heavy whipping cream

½ cup 2% reduced fat milk

Phytochemicals

Over the past ten years or so, phytochemicals have been found to have an impact similar to antioxidants. Protecting our cells from damage, reducing the risk of developing certain types of cancer, and helping to reduce osteoporosis. Sneak these foods in whenever you can. Phytochemicals can be found in foods such as tomatoes, carrots, broccoli, soy products, beans, and fruits such as blueberries, cranberries, and cherries.

1. In a large saucepan, combine carrots, celery, stock, salt and pepper, and bay leaf.

2. Bring to a boil and then simmer until carrots are tender, about 10 to 20 minutes.

3. Discard bay leaf. Pour soup mixture into a blender or food processor and purée until smooth.

5. Return to saucepan and bring to a boil.

6. In a medium bowl combine beaten egg, cream, and milk. Mix a little of the soup with the egg/milk mixture, and then add that mixture to the soup.

7. Stir and bring to a boil for 1 minute.

8. Serve hot or cold.

Mango Bisque

What a sweet way to get in the calcium, and pleasing to the eye, too! Mango is one of the primary fruits for vitamin C and surely beta-carotene, the cancer-fighting nutrient. Everyone will love this easy, refreshing treat.

INGREDIENTS | SERVES 4–6

3 ripe mangos, peeled, seeded, and cubed

Juice of 1 to 2 limes

1 cup plain or vanilla low-fat yogurt

1 cup low-fat milk

Dash of cinnamon and/or nutmeg

1. Place all ingredients in a blender or food processor.

2. Blend until smooth.

3. Chill and serve.

Kids Have One Chance to Grow to Their Max

Dairy is a must for healthy bones and teeth. It is not always easy to keep children eating and drinking calcium sources consistently throughout their childhood. They get one chance to fill their bones with strength; in adulthood, calcium begins to be pulled from the bones. Milk and dairy products are the best absorbed choices—however, there are others, e.g., spinach, sardines, molasses.

Cheesy Egg Delight

Protein and plenty of calcium. Eggs are a wonderful source of protein (and a "new" source of omega-3 fatty acids). Cheese is one of the best sources of calcium, which is great for a healthy heart, decreasing inflammation throughout the body, and strengthening those bones.

INGREDIENTS | SERVES 1

Nonstick cooking spray

2 eggs

3 to 4 tablespoons low-fat milk

2 ounces shredded part-skim mozzarella cheese

1. Spray nonstick cooking spray into pan.

2. Whip eggs and milk together in a small bowl.

3. Pour into pan, and scramble or form into omelet. Add cheese as the eggs begin to cook, until the cheese melts and the eggs are cooked to your desired consistency.

Eggs Are a Marvelously Adaptable Food

There are so many ways to prepare eggs. Scramble them, poach them, hard boil them, turn them into egg salad. Eat them for breakfast and snacks, pack them in any form for lunch, and make them into a frittata or omelet for dinner. Recent research allows you to have a few more yolks weekly—3 or 4—due to the high amount of omega-3 fatty acids, that healthy fat.

Yummy Yogurt Pie

Sneaking in the calcium in a sweet and sinful way! Suggest to your children they pick the pie flavor—using different flavored pudding mixes.

INGREDIENTS | SERVES 12

1 (1.5-ounce) package fat-free sugar-free pudding mix (vanilla, chocolate, pistachio)

16-ounce low-fat vanilla or plain yogurt

1 (16-ounce) container low-fat whipped topping

1 teaspoon vanilla extract

1 prepared graham cracker crust

1. In a large bowl, combine pudding mix and yogurt together. Stir until well blended.

2. Add whipped topping and vanilla. Continue mixing until smooth.

3. Pour pie mixture into pie crust. Refrigerate for 2 to 3 hours before serving.

Yogurt—One of the Highest Calcium Foods

Yogurt is a wonderful choice as one of your child's first foods, due its different flavors and colors. Encourage them to have yogurt, certainly through their puberty. Their bones and teeth will thank them. Remember how versatile yogurt can be, too—in a cold soup, in a milkshake or smoothie, even in a pie.

Luscious and Light Fruit Dip

Serve this as dessert after dinner with your child's favorite fruits. It's a luscious treat.

INGREDIENTS | SERVES 12–16

4 ounces whipped cream cheese

1 cup whole berry cranberry sauce

8 ounces low-fat plain yogurt

1 cup low-fat whipped topping

Fresh fruit chunks—pineapple, cantaloupe, kiwi, strawberries

1. With electric mixer, beat cream cheese, cranberry sauce, and yogurt. Blend well.

2. Gently fold in whipped topping.

3. Cover and refrigerate at least 1 hour before serving. Serve with favorite fresh fruits.

Cheesy Corn Soufflé

This is a terrific dish, which provides fiber from the corn and a lot of calcium!

INGREDIENTS | SERVES 10–12

4 ounces whipped cream cheese

¾ cup low-fat milk

3 eggs

1 (15-ounce) can whole kernel corn, drained

1 can (15-ounce) creamed corn

1 package corn muffin mix

8 ounces low-fat Cheddar cheese

Nonstick cooking spray

1. Preheat oven to 375°F.

2. Blend cream cheese and milk until smooth.

3. Add in remainder of ingredients and beat until well blended.

4. Spray 9" × 13" baking dish with nonstick cooking spray.

5. Pour mixture into baking dish. Bake 35 to 40 minutes, or until golden brown.

Cottage Cheese Pancakes

These pancakes are delicious and conceal the high protein and calcium. Remember to purchase the cottage cheese with "twice the calcium" to get more bang for your buck.

INGREDIENTS | SERVES 3–4

1 cup "twice the calcium" low-fat cottage cheese

3 eggs

2 tablespoons trans-fat-free margarine

¼ cup flour

1 teaspoon vanilla extract

¼ teaspoon salt

Nonstick cooking spray

Sugar-free pancake syrup

1. Drain liquid from cottage cheese by placing it in a strainer for 1 hour.

2. Place drained cottage cheese, eggs, margarine, flour, vanilla, and salt in a mixing bowl. Beat until well blended. Cover and let stand for 30 minutes.

3. Spray nonstick cooking spray into skillet.

4. Cook pancakes on low heat, turning once until golden brown.

5. Serve with sugar-free pancake syrup.

Grilled Eggplant Bundles

Eggplant, filled with wonderful fiber and antioxidants, is included in this lasagna-type dish, filled with cheese for a nice source of protein.

INGREDIENTS | SERVES 8

2 large eggplants
1 (8-ounce) block of low-fat mozzarella cheese
2 large plum tomatoes
10 fresh basil leaves
2 teaspoons olive oil
Salt and pepper to taste

Dressing:

4 tablespoons olive oil
1 teaspoon balsamic vinegar
1 tablespoon sundried tomato paste
1 tablespoon lemon juice
2 tablespoons toasted pine nuts, for garnish
Fresh basil leaves, chopped, for garnish

1. Wash eggplants well and remove the stalks. Slice them lengthways into thin slices using a long-bladed knife, about ¼-inch-thick slices (try to get 6 slices from each, discarding the first and last slices).

2. Bring a large pot of water to a boil and cook the eggplant slices for about 2 minutes. Drain slices and pat dry on a paper towel.

3. Slice the mozzarella cheese into eight slices.

4. Slice each tomato into 8 slices.

5. Take 2 slices of eggplant and arrange in a "T" formation.

6. Place a slice of tomato in the center, add ½ of a basil leaf, followed by a slice of mozzarella, another basil leaf, and another slice of tomato.

7. Fold both ends of the eggplant slices around the filling to make a neat bundle. Repeat with the rest of assembled ingredients to make eight bundles. Chill in the refrigerator for about 20 minutes.

8. To make the dressing, whisk together the olive oil, vinegar, sundried tomato paste and lemon juice. Season to taste.

9. Remove the bundles from the refrigerator, brush them with olive oil, and either cook on a hot grill for about 5 minutes on each side or under the oven broiler, just until golden.

10. Serve hot, with the dressing on the side. Sprinkle with pine nuts and basil (optional).

The Famous Caprese Salad

When the children are ready to take a reprieve from the lettuce salads, this is a great way to get lots of necessary vitamins, calcium, and healthy fats.

INGREDIENTS | SERVES 4–6

3 to 4 large ripe tomatoes
1 pound fresh part-skim mozzarella
¼ cup olive oil
8 to 10 fresh basil leaves, chopped
Salt and pepper to taste

Get the Calcium in Any Way You Can!

Encouraging your child to consume dairy products—in any way, shape, or form—is non-negotiable. The consumption of calcium is the supreme nutrient for your child to achieve their optimum growth, especially their height. The best-absorbed calcium does come from dairy products. The less absorbed calcium comes from certain vegetables, such as spinach, broccoli, kale, and asparagus. Stick with the dairy sources of low-fat milk, low-fat chocolate milk (low sugar, when possible), low-fat yogurts, low-fat cheeses, and cottage cheese, fortified with calcium whenever possible.

1. Slice the tomatoes ½-inch thick.

2. Slice the mozzarella cheese into ¼-inch slices.

3. Arrange 2 to 3 slices of tomato and 2 to 3 slices of cheese on a small plate, alternating slices.

4. Drizzle olive oil on top.

5. Sprinkle the chopped basil leaves. Season with salt and pepper as desired.

6. For best flavor, refrigerate for 30 minutes prior to serving.

Mighty Baked Macaroni and Cheese

Have you ever met a child who doesn't love mac and cheese? Try this healthier, high calcium version—once again, they won't know the difference between this and the higher fat, artery-clogging one.

INGREDIENTS | SERVES 8

1 pound macaroni noodles
3 tablespoons trans-fat-free margarine
3 tablespoons flour
Salt and pepper to taste
3 cups low-fat milk
3 cups low-fat Cheddar cheese, shredded
Nonstick cooking spray
½ cup corn flake crumbs

A Word about Those Whole Grains

If your children do not grow up with "that brown bread," it is much harder to introduce whole grains into their world as they get older. Be sure that the whole wheat bread that is purchased reads "whole wheat flour" as the very first ingredient on the label. This goes for whole wheat pasta as well. Always remember, what they "grow up" on is what they get comfortable with. Hint: there are companies now making whole wheat bread, with nice amounts of fiber, that are "white" in color—if you really come up against resistance. It is certainly better than eating pure white bread.

1. Preheat oven to 350°F.

2. Cook macaroni as per package directions, and set aside.

3. Melt margarine in a small pot over low heat. Add flour, salt, and pepper to make a paste.

4. Slowly add milk, whisking until thickened.

5. Add cheese to mixture, and continue to mix until smooth and cheese is melted.

6. Pour the sauce over the noodles, and mix well.

7. Spray cooking spray into a casserole dish. Pour noodles into casserole dish.

8. Sprinkle with corn flake crumbs.

9. Bake for 1 hour.

Bull's Eye Soy Burger

A vegetarian dish, fun to prepare, and loaded with calcium—reports show high intakes of calcium may also keep blood pressure lower.

INGREDIENTS | SERVES 6

Nonstick cooking spray

6 frozen prepared soy burgers

6 slices low-fat white American cheese

6 slices low-fat Cheddar cheese

6 tablespoons ketchup

24 sticks of celery, washed and tops cut off

Sneak in a Little Vegetarianism—You Can't Go Wrong!

Most children tend to shy away from vegetarian food items (many adults, too). Begin to introduce some soy products to the kids, as studies show us that soybeans as a source of protein, iron, fiber, and a non-animal source of fat are quite healthy for them.

1. In medium skillet, spray nonstick cooking spray.

2. Pan-fry soy burgers on low heat until cooked through.

3. With white American cheese slices, cut off edges, making round slices.

4. With Cheddar cheese slices, cut off edges, creating smaller, round slices.

5. To assemble bull's eye burger, place burger on a serving plate.

6. Top with white American cheese, then Cheddar cheese on top.

7. Place 1 tablespoon ketchup on top of the Cheddar cheese.

8. To create the bull's eye stand, place 2 celery stalks at base of the burger, about 2 inches apart.

9. Cut celery stick in half, and place them on top of the burger, with their tips touching.

10. Cut another celery stick in half, and cut lengthwise, too.

11. Place one half between the bottom celery stick, horizontally, close to the burger.

12. Place the final half smack in the middle of the ketchup dollop.

Penne with Tomatoes and Mozzarella

Pasta is a classic in the lives of children. A healthier twist: use a whole wheat noodle, and the chunks of mozzarella cheese will add the equivalent of a glass of milk for the day.

INGREDIENTS | SERVES 6–8

1 tablespoon olive oil

¼ cup fresh basil, chopped

6 to 8 fresh tomatoes, chopped

6 to 8 ounces mozzarella cheese, cut in small cubes

Salt and pepper to taste

1 pound penne noodles, whole wheat

⅓ cup Parmesan cheese

1. In a medium bowl, place olive oil, basil, tomatoes, and mozzarella cheese. Mix well. Season with salt and pepper. Set aside and let stand.

2. Cook penne noodles according to package directions.

3. Toss pasta and tomato mixture.

4. Sprinkle with Parmesan cheese and serve.

Rotini Ricotta and Spinach Pasta

Another child-friendly pasta dish—ricotta, mozzarella, and spinach are all good sources of calcium. If your kids have a different favorite vegetable, feel free to substitute it.

INGREDIENTS | SERVES 6

1 pound whole wheat Rotini noodles

1 (12-ounce) package frozen chopped spinach

16 ounces low-fat ricotta cheese (part-skim)

8 ounces shredded low-fat mozzarella cheese

3 tablespoons trans-fat-free margarine, melted

Salt, pepper, and garlic to taste

1. In a large saucepan, cook pasta according to package directions.

2. Cook spinach according to package directions, and drain.

3. In a mixing bowl, blend ricotta cheese, cooked spinach, mozzarella cheese, melted margarine and seasonings.

4. Place noodles back in the saucepan, and combine cheese mixture with the noodles.

5. Reheat on a low heat, and serve.

The Champ's Cheddar Ziti

A neat, low-fat twist on baked ziti—always a favorite. Add a low-fat coleslaw and a large cup of fresh berries, and dinner is done.

INGREDIENTS | SERVES 6–8

1 (16-ounce) package whole wheat ziti noodles

1 (10-ounce) package frozen peas

1 (14-ounce) jar spaghetti sauce

2 cups low-fat milk

8 ounces low-fat shredded Cheddar cheese

1 teaspoon Italian seasoning

½ cup grated Parmesan cheese

1. Preheat oven to 350°F.

2. Prepare ziti noodles according to package directions. Drain noodles. Set aside.

3. Rinse frozen peas with running cold water to separate. Drain and set aside.

4. In a large casserole dish, combine spaghetti sauce, milk, cheese, and Italian seasoning. Add noodles and peas to the casserole dish, and mix well.

5. Sprinkle with Parmesan cheese. Bake about 45 minutes or until heated through and bubbly.

Fluffy Fruit Dip

What a fluffy and tasty calcium booster—mix with any fruits your kids love!

INGREDIENTS | SERVES 12

2 (3-ounce) packages instant vanilla sugar-free, fat-free pudding mix

1 cup low-fat milk

1 teaspoon vanilla extract

1 (16-ounce) container frozen lite whipped topping, thawed

1. In a medium bowl, mix together the vanilla pudding mix, milk, and vanilla.

2. Blend in the whipped topping.

3. Chill 1 hour in refrigerator before serving.

Make It Fun!

While feeding the children healthfully, try to keep it fun. Either allow them to help prepare something cool, or present appropriate foods in a neat way. This is one of them. Cut up their favorite fruits, and offer this unique dip to make the fruit more interesting. Food is a very significant part of our world—try to keep the children happy with their healthy food repertoire.

Blueberry Pie and Frozen Yogurt Smoothie

There are so many ways to adapt smoothies to your children's liking. Keep the dairy coming, even through the age of seventeen or eighteen. Substitute favorite flavors of frozen yogurt and different fruits, too.

INGREDIENTS | SERVES 2

½ cup blueberries, cleaned

1 cup low-fat or nonfat vanilla frozen yogurt

½ cup low-fat milk

1 teaspoon vanilla extract

¼ teaspoon ground cinnamon

2 tablespoons vanilla wafer crumbs

1. Place the blueberries in a microwave-safe bowl. Microwave on high power for 1 minute.

2. Remove from microwave and put in the refrigerator for 10 to 15 minutes.

3. In a blender, add the frozen yogurt, milk, vanilla, cinnamon, and blueberries. Purée until smooth.

4. Pour into 2 separate glasses. Sprinkle each smoothie with the vanilla wafer crumbs.

Choose Smart Smoothies

Make smoothies at home, and order very few out of the house. Though smoothies have become the "new milkshake," and certainly a healthier choice, most smoothies are loaded with sugar, and therefore, calories. Yes, fresh fruit is great in the smoothie, but the sugar and the additional fruit juice tend to really make the calories similar to that milkshake. Preparing smoothies at home is a sensational idea, and generally much healthier.

Mouth-Watering Pina Colada Chiller

This is a very refreshing high-calcium, high-protein drink, for a speedy after-school snack or a power boost prior to any sports workout.

INGREDIENTS | SERVES 4

2 cups low-fat milk

2 cups pineapple juice, unsweetened

1 tablespoon vanilla extract

1 tablespoon coconut extract

2 tablespoons Splenda (or sugar if children are less than ten years old)

6 to 8 ice cubes

1. In a blender, combine all ingredients.

2. Blend until smooth.

3. Pour into 4 glasses and serve.

Are Artificial Sweeteners Safe for Children?

Until your children reach the age of ten and older, avoid the artificial sweeteners—including Splenda, Sweet 'n Low, Equal, and any others. Though sugar is not a healthy nutrient when overly consumed, it only has about 16 calories per teaspoon. It's not a terrible item in *small* amounts. There are insufficient studies on children as to what side effects these artificial sweeteners can have on their growing bodies.

Creamy Cucumber Salad

Cucumbers tend to be well received by many children. Sometimes they need the seeds removed. This is a creamy salad, and when served with dinner is usually a big hit.

INGREDIENTS | SERVES 4–6

2 large cucumbers, peeled and sliced

2 teaspoons salt

2 cups low-fat plain yogurt

1 clove garlic, minced

1 teaspoon fresh dill

2 tablespoons lemon juice

2 tablespoons olive oil

Salt and pepper to taste

1. Place sliced cucumbers in a medium bowl. Sprinkle with salt and let stand 15 to 20 minutes.

2. In a small mixing bowl, combine yogurt, garlic, dill, and lemon juice. Blend well.

3. Add olive oil, and salt and pepper to taste.

4. If there is any liquid surrounding the cucumbers, pour the liquid off. Add yogurt mixture to the cucumbers.

5. Chill for at least 1 hour before serving.

MVP Power Pudding

Packed with calcium, protein, and a little sweetness, this recipe tastes just like those old-fashioned milk and cookies! Substitute favorite fruits or pudding flavors.

INGREDIENTS | SERVES 6

4 cups low-fat milk

2 packages (4 serving size) sugar-free, fat-free vanilla pudding mix

4 to 6 (100-calorie) packages of Oreo low-fat cookies

2 cups sliced bananas

1 cup blueberries

1. In a medium mixing bowl, prepare pudding mix according to directions on box using low-fat milk. Refrigerate until pudding is thickened.

2. In a medium glass bowl, layer half of the vanilla pudding, 1 cup of the sliced bananas and a ½ cup of blueberries.

3. Crumble ½ the cookies on top of the fruit.

4. Repeat layers with remainder of ingredients.

5. Cover and refrigerate for 1 hour.

The Powerful Purple Cow

The purple cow can become any color, any flavor—let your children be creative!

INGREDIENTS | SERVES 1–2

¾ cup low-fat milk

1½ tablespoons frozen, concentrated grape juice

¼ cup low-fat vanilla yogurt

1. Pour the milk, frozen grape juice, and yogurt into a blender.

2. Blend well for 1 to 2 minutes.

3. Serve immediately.

CHAPTER 10

How to Get Them to
Eat Those "Yucky" Vegetables

Mandarin Orange Salad

*A sweet salad that kids seem to love. Dress this up with nuts,
canola, and sesame oil, for a little heart-healthy boost.*

INGREDIENTS | SERVES 6

½ head romaine lettuce, chopped
1 cup celery, chopped
12 ounces peanut brittle

Dressing:
1 teaspoon mustard
3 tablespoons sugar
½ cup canola oil
2 tablespoons sesame oil
6 tablespoons rice wine vinegar
1 (15-ounce) can mandarin oranges

1. Prepare salad using chopped lettuce and celery.

2. Prepare dressing by blending mustard, sugar, canola oil, sesame oil, and vinegar in a small bowl and mixing well.

3. When ready to serve, add small chunks of peanut brittle and mandarin oranges, and top with dressing.

There Are 55 Nutrients Needed per Day

Between the major nutrient groups and the vitamins and minerals, our incredible machines can work for many years. It is a "high-maintenance" job to take care of your body. From making healthful choices to structuring some long-term physical activity, it continues to be your responsibility to teach our children how to do this. Start with their learning to eat vegetables and salads.

Broccolini (Baby Broccoli)

Just another creative way to get kids to eat their vegetables—tasty, colorful, and "kid-friendly"! Broccolini is generally easy to find in your local grocery store.

INGREDIENTS | SERVES 6–8

2 tablespoons olive oil

2 large garlic cloves, minced

4 medium bunches of broccolini, ends trimmed

½ teaspoon salt

3 tablespoons water

1. Heat oil and garlic in skillet, using low heat.

2. Add broccolini to skillet. Cook about 4 to 5 minutes, tossing often.

3. Add the water and salt and continue tossing for 2 more minutes until tender.

4. Serve immediately.

Offer It Ten Times, They Will Eat It!

Learn how to mask vegetables for those youngsters who wrinkle their nose at the green beans and zucchini. The rule of thumb for making sure your toddler becomes a good veggie eater is to introduce the same vegetable ten times—with a little break in between, if they are not crazy about that vegetable. It is the repetition that reminds them, at some point, to take a bite, even if it is just one! Believe it or not, most will end up enjoying the vegetables, sooner or later.

Oven-Roasted Veggies

Cut and mold these vegetables into creative shapes for more fun—and one more thing, leave the skin on the potatoes for some additional fiber.

INGREDIENTS | SERVES 6

4 large carrots, sliced into thick sticks

4 small red potatoes, scrubbed clean and cut into quarters

2 medium squash or zucchini, sliced into thick chunks

2 onions, sliced in quarters

¼ cup olive oil

1 teaspoon dried rosemary

1 teaspoon dried thyme

½ teaspoon salt

¼ teaspoon black pepper

1. Preheat oven to 425°F.

2. In a pan, combine all the vegetables except for the squash (or zucchini) and toss in olive oil.

3. Then, transfer to a casserole dish. Sprinkle with herbs and seasonings.

4. Bake covered for 25 minutes. Add squash (or zucchini) and continue cooking for 20 minutes or until vegetables are tender.

Easy Peasy Snap Peas

This is such an easy recipe to make—older kids can even make it themselves. The olive oil gives it a nice flavor, along with the heart-healthy benefits of the snap peas and the healthy fat.

INGREDIENTS | SERVES 6–8

1 pound fresh snap peas

3 to 4 tablespoons olive oil

2 teaspoons minced garlic

3 to 4 tablespoons Parmesan cheese

1. Clean snap peas, and cut off the ends.

2. Pour olive oil into a large skillet.

3. On low heat, sauté garlic for 2 minutes.

4. Add snap peas, stirring constantly.

5. Sauté until snap peas are cooked, about 8 to 10 minutes.

6. When ready to serve, sprinkle with Parmesan cheese.

Cauliflower-Broccoli Casserole

Colorful and tasty, broccoli and cauliflower add lots of vitamins, minerals, and fiber to this dish.

INGREDIENTS | SERVES 12–16

3 tablespoons low-fat mayonnaise

1 package onion soup mix

2 egg whites

Nonstick cooking spray

3 to 4 cups fresh broccoli florets or 1 (14-ounce) bag frozen broccoli florets

3 to 4 cups fresh cauliflower florets 1 (14-ounce) bag frozen cauliflower florets

½ cup corn flake crumbs

1. Preheat oven to 350°F.

2. Mix together mayonnaise, onion soup mix, and egg whites.

3. Spray casserole dish with nonstick cooking spray. Place broccoli and cauliflower in the casserole dish.

4. Add mayonnaise mixture to vegetables and stir. Sprinkle with corn flake crumbs.

5. Bake for 1 hour.

Special Salsa

Serve with baked tortilla chips or fresh cut-up vegetables for a tasty snack. They love the zesty salsa!

INGREDIENTS | SERVES 10

1 (28-ounce) can diced tomatoes

1 bunch fresh cilantro, finely chopped

1 medium onion, chopped

4 cloves fresh garlic, minced

1 teaspoon salt

1 teaspoon black pepper

½ teaspoon cumin

2 tablespoons olive oil

2 tablespoons red wine vinegar

1. Drain juice from the tomatoes, preserving 1 cup of the juice. Place tomatoes in a medium mixing bowl.

2. Add cilantro, onions, and garlic to the tomatoes.

3. Add reserved juice, salt, pepper, cumin, oil, and vinegar.

4. Mix well and serve.

The Ultimate Vegetable Soup

A warm and wonderful way to enjoy vegetables—full of needed nutrients—as a great snack or a meal! Slice in a chicken breast for another good source of protein.

INGREDIENTS | SERVES 16

2 cups vegetable stock/broth

1 (15-ounce) can whole tomatoes

1 stalk celery, chopped

½ cup frozen corn kernels

2 medium potatoes, cubed

2 medium carrots, peeled and chopped

1 medium onion, finely chopped

1 cup snap peas

1 (15-ounce) can kidney beans, drained

1 clove garlic, minced

1 teaspoon black pepper

To Complete This as a Meatless Meal . . .

Since this hearty soup contains beans, add a whole grain roll or pita. This is a fine vegetarian pair; the combination of beans and a grain make a "complete" protein, just as if you were eating an animal protein such as beef or chicken. Don't forget a salad of some kind—maybe chopped cucumbers and tomato, or a wedge of Boston lettuce, for a change.

1. In a large soup pot, combine all ingredients. Breaking up tomatoes with a spoon.

2. Bring to a boil, and cook for 20 minutes.

3. Reduce heat and simmer for another 20 minutes, or until vegetables are soft.

Carrots and Honey Glaze

Kids seem to like carrots. This sweet version will have them asking for more. Good thing—the cancer fighting properties are endless.

INGREDIENTS | SERVES 6

8 large carrots, cleaned and peeled
1½ to 2 cups orange juice
4 tablespoons honey
Salt to taste
3 tablespoons canola oil
Rind of 1 lemon

1. Slice carrots or cut into desired shape.

2. Place in large pot, and cover with orange juice. Boil for 10 minutes.

3. Add the honey, salt, and oil.

4. Simmer for 1 hour, until the liquid is almost absorbed.

5. Sprinkle with lemon rind bits, and simmer another 10 to 15 minutes.

Any Veggie Will Do!

There are endless easy ways to help kids eat their vegetables—unique ways of preparing them—soups, quiches, soufflés, on pizza. Cooked vegetables are one way to complete a meal, but raw veggies count, too. At every lunch and dinner meal, some type of vegetable should be presented to your children—raw baby carrots, cut-up colored peppers, cucumbers, grape tomatoes, black olives, or celery. If they do not seem terribly interested, include a low-fat dip, salsa, or even a homemade bean dip. Serve salads when kids are old enough to eat them—use romaine or leafy lettuce, not iceberg (no nutritional value there).

Corn and Potato Chowder

A conglomeration of terrific vegetables in a very tasty soup—there's something in here for everyone!

INGREDIENTS | SERVES 6-8

1 cup fresh carrots, chopped finely
1 medium onion, diced
1 tablespoon minced garlic
3 medium potatoes, cut in small pieces
1 cup celery, chopped finely
4 cups chicken broth
½ teaspoon chili powder
¼ teaspoon white pepper
2 teaspoons low-sodium soy sauce
2 tablespoons rice vinegar
3 cups frozen corn

1. Steam carrots in microwave in ¼ cup water for 3 to 4 minutes. Set aside.

2. In a large frying pan, simmer onions, garlic, potatoes, and celery in 1½ cups chicken broth for about 10 minutes.

3. Add remaining chicken broth, spices, soy sauce, and vinegar. Bring to a boil and simmer for 30 to 45 minutes.

4. Pour soup mixture into a blender and purée until smooth.

5. Return mixture to pan. Add corn and carrots, and simmer for additional 15 to 20 minutes before serving.

Cauliflower Bake

This is an interesting way to introduce cauliflower. You can substitute broccoli, too.

Cauliflower to the Rescue

Cauliflower is one of those cruciferous vegetables that needs to get some extra credit. Extremely high in fiber, folic acid, vitamins C and K, cauliflower can be prepared in several different tasty ways—sauté in olive oil, cook and purée in a blender with a little olive oil, or of course, roast with other vegetables. Available in grocery stores year round, the best cauliflower season is truly from December to March. Recent data suggest cauliflower, too, has cancer-fighting compounds, in studies focusing especially on breast, colon, lung, and prostate cancer.

1. Preheat oven to 375°F.

2. Remove and discard the core of the cauliflower.

3. Place in microwaveable dish with ¼ cup water. Microwave for 5 to 6 minutes, or until tender.

4. In a small pan, melt margarine. Stir in shallots and bread crumbs.

5. In a baking dish, place cauliflower, and top with bread crumb mixture.

6. Bake for 15 to 20 minutes.

Un-Fried Fried Potatoes and Onions

Pan-fried, and then broiled for that crunchy, "French-fried" feeling. This doesn't mean never eat regular French fries; however, this is an awesome substitute for that weekly craving.

INGREDIENTS | SERVES 6

2 tablespoons olive oil

2 medium onions, thinly sliced

4 large potatoes, Yukon Gold

Salt and pepper to taste

2½ to 3 cups chicken broth

¼ cup seasoned bread crumbs

¼ cup grated Parmesan cheese

Everything in Moderation

As of now, French fries continue to be the number one vegetable choice for children. Though, as the saying goes, "everything in moderation." French fries should *really* be offered in moderation—especially the fast food versions; as the oil soaks into French fries, this becomes a very high fat "vegetable." It is quite simple to make them at home, slicing potatoes (unpeeled), spraying with nonstick cooking spray on top and bottom, sprinkling favorite seasoning, and baking until tender.

1. Heat olive oil in large, oven-safe skillet, on low heat. Sauté onions until golden brown.

2. Clean potatoes, and slice into ¼-inch round slices.

3. Combine potatoes with the onions and season with salt and pepper.

4. Add broth, enough to cover the potatoes. Bring to a boil, and boil for 2 to 3 minutes.

5. Lower heat and simmer for 15 minutes, or until potatoes are soft.

6. Sprinkle with bread crumbs and Parmesan cheese.

7. Turn oven to broil. Place potatoes and onions under the broiler for 1 to 2 minutes.

Carrots, Potatoes, and Fruits—Oh My!

The most colorful "fruit stew" you will ever see! Feel free to combine other fruits and/or vegetables, for instance, acorn squash, raisins, different varieties of apples, and nuts. You may easily substitute canned yams for fresh sweet potatoes if you are pressed for time.

INGREDIENTS | SERVES 8–10

4 large carrots, sliced

2 cups sliced sweet potatoes, peeled

10 to 12 pitted prunes

3 Red Delicious apples, peeled and sliced

½ cup chopped pecans

1 (10-ounce) can crushed pineapple, in its own juice

¾ cup brown sugar

¾ cup orange juice

1½ teaspoons cinnamon

Nonstick cooking spray

1. Preheat oven to 300°F.

2. In a large mixing bowl, combine all ingredients.

3. Spray casserole dish with nonstick cooking spray. Pour mixture into casserole dish, and cover.

4. Bake for 3 to 4 hours.

These Vegetables and Fruits—Gems to the Body

In recent years, it has been proven that fruits and vegetables bright in color, e.g., carrots, sweet potatoes, cantaloupe, red and yellow peppers, etc. are long-term cancer-preventers. They are high in a vitamin A derivative called beta-carotene. Historically, it was acceptable to take a beta-carotene vitamin supplement and get the same benefit. However, the use of supplementation is discouraged today— and it is strongly advisable to get this critical vitamin from foods only. This recipe will take care of it, for both children and adults.

Spectacular Spinach Lasagna

Sneak in the vegetables and 2 or 3 servings of high-calcium cheese right in one meal. Add a tossed salad, and the meal is really all-inclusive.

INGREDIENTS | SERVES 8–10

2 (10-ounce) packages frozen chopped spinach

32 ounces low-fat cottage cheese

2 eggs

Garlic powder and pepper to taste

Nonstick cooking spray

8 ounces oven-ready lasagna noodles

2 cups reduced-fat Monterey jack cheese

1 cup grated Parmesan cheese

1. Preheat oven to 350°F.

2. Cook spinach according to the package directions. Drain.

3. In a medium mixing bowl, blend cottage cheese, eggs, garlic powder and pepper.

4. Spray 13" × 9" Pyrex with cooking spray.

5. Place a layer of noodles on the bottom of the pan. Layer the cottage cheese mixture. Top with Monterey jack cheese, cooked spinach, and Parmesan cheese.

6. Repeat layers, ending with the cheese on top.

7. Bake for 30 to 45 minutes.

Black Bean and Corn Mexican Salsa

*Serve with whole grain crackers or baked chips—perfect for
a sports party or even the kids' birthday parties.*

INGREDIENTS | SERVES 10

1 (15-ounce) can black beans, drained and rinsed

1 (14-ounce) can salsa-style chunky tomatoes

1 (7-ounce) can whole-kernel corn, drained

1 teaspoon chili powder

1. In a food processor, place beans and tomatoes, blend until finely chopped.

2. Stir in corn and chili powder.

3. Chill and serve.

Vegetable Salsa Full of Finesse!

Again, start children with diverse tastes, and who knows what they will surprise you with! Salsas such as these can add powerful nutrients—beans, tomatoes, corn, and any other vegetables the kids can come up with! This is an outstanding source of protein, iron, vitamin C, all mixed together—a fun food! And spice it up as their hearts desire.

Cheesy Greeny Zucchini

Eggplant, Brussels sprouts, or yellow squash could be used as an experimental alternative.

INGREDIENTS | SERVES 6

Nonstick cooking spray

6 zucchini, sliced thinly

12 to 16 ounces part-skim mozzarella cheese, shredded

¾ to 1 cup seasoned bread crumbs

2 tablespoons trans-fat-free margarine, melted

1. Preheat oven to 350°F.

2. Spray 13" × 9" glass dish with nonstick cooking spray.

3. Layer the slices of zucchini, then mozzarella.

4. Repeat these layers.

5. Sprinkle the top with bread crumbs and melted margarine.

6. Bake for 30 to 45 minutes.

Grande Vegetable Casserole

This is a beautifully presented dish of wonderful vegetables, generally the ones children like—the sweet ones included. It is worth the little bit of work it entails.

INGREDIENTS | SERVES 12–15

1 pound white potatoes, cut into 1-inch chunks

1 pound sweet potatoes, peeled, cut into 1-inch chunks

1½ pounds parsnips, peeled, cut into 1-inch chunks

3 pounds butternut squash

1 medium onion, chopped

8 ounces low-fat sour cream

¼ cup low-fat milk

Salt to taste

½ teaspoon ground nutmeg

Nonstick cooking spray

1. Preheat oven to 350°F.

2. In a large saucepan, pour several cups of water, and place potatoes and parsnips into saucepan. Boil, and then reduce heat to low. Simmer for 15 to 20 minutes, until vegetables are tender.

3. In the meantime, cut squash in quarters, take out seeds, and peel.

4. Drain potatoes and parsnips. Add squash and onions and boil the squash until tender, about 10 to 15 minutes.

5. Place white potatoes and parsnips in a large mixing bowl, and with potato masher, mash potatoes with sour cream, milk, and salt.

6. Mash sweet potatoes separately and add ¼ teaspoon nutmeg.

7. Drain squash. Mash squash with ¼ teaspoon nutmeg.

8. In a large casserole dish, spray nonstick cooking spray. Spoon rows of mixtures in this order: squash, mashed potatoes, and sweet potatoes.

9. Cover with aluminum foil and bake for 40 minutes, or until hot.

Pretty Peas with Shallots and Spinach

The kids probably did not enjoy the baby puréed peas, but let's give it another shot, a little dressed up.

INGREDIENTS | SERVES 4–5

1 tablespoon canola oil

2 medium shallots, finely chopped

1 clove garlic, minced

1 (10-ounce) package frozen peas

¼ cup water

5 ounces fresh baby spinach, washed

¾ teaspoon salt

¼ teaspoon black pepper

1. Pour canola oil into medium skillet, and heat over low heat. Cook shallots and garlic in oil, stirring until shallots are soft, about 5 minutes.

2. Stir in peas and water, and cover. Stir occasionally, until peas are tender, about 5 minutes.

3. Toss in spinach, add salt and pepper, and continue cooking about 1 minute, stirring occasionally.

The Many Benefits of Fiber

Fiber has been studied for many years. It is most recently responsible in the nutrition science world for regulating blood sugar levels—keeping blood glucose calm and normal. We also know it helps to regulate the bowels; reduce risks of cancer, especially colon and rectal cancer; lower cholesterol levels; and reduce the risk of heart disease and diabetes.

Baked Vegetable Omelet

A nice way to mix different vegetables and cheese—replace with any of the kids' favorite vegetables anytime.

INGREDIENTS | SERVES 6

Nonstick cooking spray

2 cups shredded low-fat mozzarella cheese

1½ cups chopped frozen broccoli, defrosted and drained (or fresh broccoli)

2 medium tomatoes, diced

1 cup asparagus spears, chopped (discard hard ends)

1 cup shredded low-fat Cheddar cheese

1 cup low-fat milk

¼ cup all-purpose flour

¼ teaspoon salt

3 whole eggs

1. Preheat oven to 350°F. Spray nonstick cooking spray into a square 8" × 8" pan.

2. Layer mozzarella cheese on the bottom of the pan, followed by broccoli, tomatoes, and asparagus.

3. Layer Cheddar cheese on top of the vegetables.

4. Beat milk, flour, salt, and eggs until smooth. Pour over casserole.

5. Bake uncovered for 40 to 45 minutes, or until egg mixture is set.

6. Let stand 10 minutes before serving.

Veggie and Cheese Pockets

Substitute any vegetables—as long as they have the roasted flavor, this is a quick and delicious party appetizer or an easy meal.

INGREDIENTS | SERVES 4

Nonstick cooking spray

2 large zucchini, sliced

2 yellow squash, sliced

2 large carrots, sliced thinly

2 tablespoons canola or olive oil

4 large whole wheat pita bread rounds

8 ounces low-fat mozzarella cheese, shredded

1. Preheat oven to broil.

2. On a baking sheet sprayed with cooking spray, spread zucchini, squash, and carrots. Brush 1 tablespoon oil onto vegetables. Place in oven for 5 to 10 minutes, until vegetables are soft.

3. Cut each pita in half.

4. Place remaining tablespoon of oil in small skillet.

5. Heat each pita for 1 minute on each side.

6. Stuff pitas equally with cheese and vegetables.

Nutty Green Beans

Snow peas or string beans can be substituted for green beans, and certainly any type of nut may be included here, too.

INGREDIENTS | SERVES 15–20

Nonstick cooking spray

2 medium onions, diced

4 cloves garlic, thinly sliced

Pepper to taste

2 large (1-pound) bags fresh green beans, cleaned and sliced in half

¼ cup light soy sauce

¼ cup olive oil

2 to 3 cups almonds and pecans, chopped and toasted

Aww—Nuts!

Years ago, health professionals suggested avoiding large handfuls of nuts—they were very high in fat, and quite high in calories. Though a good source of fiber and protein, nuts do have a lot of calories. That being said, nuts are back on the "eat them" list—just eat them about 12 cashews at a time. Nuts are rich in marvelous monounsaturated fats, wonderful for heart disease prevention.

1. Preheat oven to 300°F.

2. In a medium skillet, spray cooking spray, and sauté onions on medium heat, until translucent.

3. Add garlic slices and continue to cook. Cook for 5 minutes; add pepper.

4. Using the microwave, place green beans in microwaveable-safe dish, and cook approximately 8 to 10 minutes, until beans are al dente.

5. Add green beans to frying pan with olive oil, onions and garlic. Add soy sauce and mix well. Place in a casserole dish.

6. Separately toast nuts for 5 to 6 minutes in a toaster oven.

7. Sprinkle nuts on top of casserole.

8. Bake for 15 minutes, uncovered.

CHAPTER 11

How to Get Them to Eat More Protein

Pan-Fried Tantalizing Tilapia

Breaded and pan-fried fish is a wonderful way to get your children to try fish. Always attempt mild fish such as tilapia, mahi-mahi, or swordfish.

INGREDIENTS | SERVES 4

3 tablespoons olive or canola oil

1 cup flour or quick-mixing flour (Wondra)

Garlic powder

Salt and pepper to taste

2 eggs, beaten

4 tilapia fillets

1. Heat oil in skillet over low heat.

2. Mix flour with garlic powder, salt and pepper.

3. Dip fish fillet in egg, then flour mixture.

4. Pan-fry until golden brown, 5 to 6 minutes on each side, turning once.

The Benefits of Fish

Studies have proven that fish is one of the most important foods to incorporate into your diet. Include shellfish, such as shrimp, scallops, mussels, clams, in pasta for a delicious fish dish. Even if fish is not one of your favorites, try to get your family to enjoy it in some fashion!

Marinated Flank Steak

Filled with B vitamins and iron, this is a great lean protein dish. Marinate overnight for best flavor. This is a delicious marinade for chicken and fish, too.

INGREDIENTS | SERVES 8–10

¼ cup low-sodium soy sauce

3 tablespoons white vinegar

¼ cup onion, chopped

¼ cup honey

½ cup olive oil

1 clove garlic, minced

4 pounds flank steak

1. In a blender, mix all ingredients (except steak).

2. Place marinade and steak in a zip-top plastic bag. Seal and place the bag on the bottom shelf of refrigerator, on a plate. Marinate several hours or overnight, if possible.

3. Broil or grill 7 to 8 minutes on each side.

Children Should Avoid Rare Meat at All Costs

Research has shown that rare meat products can carry bacteria, and children should be eating meat products that are cooked through—at the very least, cooked to pink, or medium (teens and older). Medium well is even better.

Make-It-Simple Meat Sauce

Always a family favorite—loaded with protein, iron, healthy carbohydrates, fiber, and vitamin C—all in one meal. Add a crunchy Bibb lettuce salad, with a low-fat dressing, and it's perfect!

INGREDIENTS | SERVES 4–6

Nonstick cooking spray
1 medium onion, chopped
2 tablespoons minced garlic
1½ pounds ground sirloin, chopped
1 (12-ounce) can crushed tomatoes
2 (6-ounce) cans tomato paste
1 can water (use can from tomato paste)
4 tablespoons parsley
½ teaspoon salt
1 tablespoon oregano
1 tablespoon sugar

1. In a large pot, spray nonstick cooking spray, and sauté garlic and onion.

2. Add ground sirloin and cook through, about 10 to 15 minutes.

3. Mix remainder of all ingredients together in the large pot.

4. Simmer for at least 1 hour. Serve over whole wheat pasta of your choice.

Lean Forms of Protein

In young children, as brain development continues, and muscles and organ systems continue to develop, protein is a crucial nutrient. The protein source for an infant is found in formula or breast milk. When solid foods are introduced into the diet, then it is imperative to offer a source of protein at each meal and each snack. For those children who do not love the animal sources of protein, then dairy is adequate, as are eggs. Beans and nuts are a good source of protein; however, there is a "formula" to this. Beans and nuts are called *incomplete* sources of protein (since they do not contain all the building blocks, amino acids, of protein), so they need to be combined with other foods (i.e., beans *and* rice, or peas *and* wheat), in order for the body to consider them a "complete protein" and contribute these benefits.

Grilled Chicken Citrus

With orange juice, squeeze in some potassium and vitamin C—all nutrients to assist in terrific growth and development of your young ones.

INGREDIENTS | SERVES 4

6 medium oranges
1 cup barbecue sauce
4 small chicken breast halves, boneless and skinless

Safety Precaution

The safest way to prevent food poisoning is to keep raw meat, fish, and poultry refrigerated at all times. Always place the container with the raw food on the bottom shelf of the refrigerator, preventing raw juices from dripping into other foods. Even if you are defrosting these items, keep them refrigerated, on a plate, using the same process.

1. Squeeze juice from 3 oranges and mix with the barbecue sauce. Pour half of the mixture into a large resealable plastic bag. Refrigerate the extra sauce.

2. Add the chicken, seal the bag, and marinate for at least 1 hour.

3. Remove the chicken from the marinade, and discard the used marinade.

4. Heat the grill. Place the chicken on the grill.

5. Place the 3 remaining oranges, peeled and sliced, on the grill, along with the chicken.

6. Cook through, brushing reserved sauce on the chicken.

7. Place chicken on a serving dish, layering the grilled oranges on top.

Lemon Garlic Shrimp

With omega-3s, and low levels of total fat and calories, this is a great choice for the heart, and a superb way to get your kids to eat seafood. Shrimp is a family favorite—easy to get everyone to eat it!

INGREDIENTS | SERVES 3–4

¼ cup olive oil

5 to 6 medium cloves garlic, crushed

2 pounds large shrimp, peeled and deveined

3 tablespoons lemon juice

¼ cup fresh parsley, chopped

1. In a large skillet, heat olive oil on low heat.

2. Add the garlic, and sauté for 2 minutes.

3. Add the shrimp, turning often, until the shrimp are pink (about 5 minutes).

4. Add parsley and lemon juice. Mix well.

5. Remove from heat and then serve.

The Current Cholesterol Situation

Foods that increase cholesterol are those that come from animal products. The more fat in the food—e.g., whole milk and whole milk dairy products, ice cream, fatty meats—the higher the blood cholesterol levels will be. Though paying attention and curbing your intake of cholesterol-rich foods is critical, it is more important to concentrate on your total fat consumption. Shrimp, though a higher cholesterol food, is very low in total fat. Obviously you should not consume it 4 or 5 times per week, but a couple of times a week certainly gives those healthy fats, too!

Simply Grilled Lamb Chops

*Season lamb chops and leave in the refrigerator for several
hours. When grilled, they are perfectly delicious.*

INGREDIENTS | SERVES 4

8 to 10 lamb rib chops, about 1-inch
thick

2 teaspoons coarse salt

2 to 3 tablespoons minced garlic

2 teaspoons ground black pepper

1. Season lamb chops with salt, garlic, and pepper. Place
   in refrigerator and allow to sit for 1 to 2 hours.

2. Place lamb chops on a grill pan.

3. Grill (or broil) chops 5 to 7 minutes on each side.

Cannellini Bean Dip

*A quick and easy recipe—serve with whole grain crackers, pita chips,
baked tortilla chips, or cut-up carrots and colored peppers.*

INGREDIENTS | SERVES 6–8

1 (19-ounce) can white kidney beans
(cannellini beans), drained and rinsed

3 tablespoons lemon juice

3 tablespoons olive oil

2 teaspoons minced garlic

½ teaspoon dried oregano (or 1
teaspoon fresh chopped)

Salt to taste

1. Combine the beans, lemon juice, oil, garlic, half of the
   oregano, and salt in a food processor. Process until
   smooth.

2. Pour into a small, shallow bowl. Sprinkle with
   oregano, and serve.

Island Chicken Satay

This is a fun family project. Let the kids help with this one.

INGREDIENTS | SERVES 6–8

1 pound chicken breasts, skinned and boned

18 wooden skewers

2 tablespoons lemon juice

3 tablespoons reduced-sodium soy sauce

2 tablespoons honey

2 tablespoons trans-fat-free peanut butter

½ cup water

1. Cut chicken into 1-inch chunks. Place chucks on the skewers.

2. Put remaining ingredients into a large skillet. Bring to a boil, stirring constantly.

3. Reduce to simmer, and place skewers in the skillet. Leave space between the skewers. Cook for about 10 minutes.

4. Remove skewers and place them on a serving dish.

5. Reduce sauce (continue simmering) to 1 cup. Pour over the chicken and serve. (This can also be served cold.)

Honey Garlic Chicken Wings and Drums

Chicken drums have more meat, and less fat, than chicken wings. Have the children remove the skin off all poultry, always.

INGREDIENTS | SERVES 5–6

4 tablespoons canola oil

10 chicken wings

10 chicken drummettes, skinless

4 tablespoons reduced-sodium soy sauce

4 tablespoons honey

1 tablespoon sugar

4 tablespoons red wine

6 garlic cloves, chopped

Black pepper to taste

1. Preheat oven to 350°F.

2. In a large skillet, heat oil over low heat.

3. Place wings and drums in oil, and fry for 3 to 5 minutes.

4. Mix soy sauce, honey, sugar, wine, garlic, and pepper in a large casserole dish.

5. Add the chicken to the sauce.

6. Bake for 10 to 20 minutes, or until golden brown.

Sweet and Sour Chinese Veal Meatballs

Cooking with veal means less fat than regular beef. The key to great-tasting veal products is to season the veal well. It is a more bland meat.

INGREDIENTS | SERVES 4

1 pound ground veal

1 teaspoon salt

1 teaspoon pepper

1 teaspoon garlic powder

2 tablespoons canola oil

1 green bell pepper, cut into ¼-inch cubes

1 medium onion, chopped

2 large carrots, grated

2 tablespoons vinegar

3 tablespoons brown sugar

2 teaspoons reduced-sodium soy sauce

2 teaspoons dry sherry

2 tablespoons cornstarch

½ cup chilled chicken broth

1. Mix together veal, salt, pepper, and garlic powder in a medium bowl.

2. Roll veal mixture into 1-inch meatballs.

3. Heat oil in a large skillet, over low heat.

4. Brown the meatballs on all sides, approximately 3 to 5 minutes.

5. Add bell pepper, onion, carrots, vinegar, brown sugar, soy sauce, and sherry. Cover and simmer, stirring constantly.

6. Mix cornstarch and chicken broth in a small bowl. Add to skillet.

7. Wait for mixture to thicken, and cook 5 to 10 more minutes.

8. Serve immediately, perhaps over brown rice.

Black Bean Tortilla Casserole

This is a terrific recipe, filled with healthy ingredients, from beans to vegetables.

INGREDIENTS | **SERVES 6–8**

Nonstick cooking spray

2 cups chopped onion

2 cloves minced garlic

1 medium green bell pepper, chopped

1 medium red pepper, chopped

¾ cup picante sauce

2 (15-ounce) cans black beans, drained

1 (15-ounce) can stewed tomatoes

12 medium corn tortillas

6 to 8 ounces part-skim mozzarella or Monterey jack cheese, divided

1 cup shredded romaine lettuce

1 cup chopped tomatoes

4 tablespoons low-fat sour cream (optional)

1. Preheat oven to 350°F.

2. Spray a large skillet with cooking spray. Add onion and garlic and sauté 4 to 5 minutes.

3. Add green and red peppers, and sauté 3 to 4 additional minutes.

4. Add picante sauce, beans, and tomatoes. Cook 5 to 7 minutes, stirring constantly. Turn heat off; set aside.

5. Spray cooking spray into a 13" × 9" baking dish. Spoon 1 cup of the black bean mixture into the bottom of the baking dish. Arrange 6 tortillas in a single layer over the bean mixture.

6. Sprinkle tortillas with ¾ cup cheese. Add 2½ cups of the bean mixture over the cheese.

7. Arrange the remaining 6 tortillas over the cheese. Top with the remaining bean mixture.

8. Cover and bake for 30 minutes.

9. Uncover and top with remaining cheese. Bake uncovered 10 minutes, or until cheese melts.

10. Let stand 5 minutes before serving. Top with lettuce and tomato. Cut into 4-inch to 5-inch squares. Top with sour cream, if desired.

Easy Roasted Lemon Chicken

A lemon-y twist on chicken—easy for when there isn't much time for cooking.

INGREDIENTS | SERVES 6

7- to 8-pound roasting chicken
2 fresh lemons
2 teaspoons lemon pepper

Chicken—Low-Fat, High-Protein, and a Million Ways to Cook It!

This seems to be an easy protein source for children to comfortably include in their diets. Whether it is breaded and pan-fried, baked strips, a fruity marinade, or chicken and rice, chicken (and poultry) is pretty versatile. Remember to pull off the skin, or even better, cook the chicken skinless.

1. Preheat oven to 350°F.

2. Clean chicken and remove contents from its cavity.

3. Puncture the lemons in several places and place both lemons inside the cavity.

4. Coat the chicken on the outside with lemon pepper.

5. Bake 15 to 20 minutes per pound, basting every 30 minutes.

Puddin' and Pie Milkshake

Just like a thick milkshake—with much less calories and fat!
The kids can make it, and then use a spoon to eat it! '

INGREDIENTS | SERVES 4

3 to 4 cups low-fat milk
1 (4-ounce) package favorite flavor sugar-free, fat-free pudding mix
1 teaspoon vanilla extract
1 medium ripe banana, sliced
1 cup strawberries, sliced

1. Place all ingredients in blender.

2. Blend until smooth.

3. Pour into 4 chilled glasses.

Splendid Stuffed Cabbage

For the daring—those willing to taste something new and delicious. This sweet, ethnic delicacy is a wonderful dish and a great source of many nutrients—fiber, protein, iron, to name a few.

INGREDIENTS | SERVES 6

2 tablespoons olive oil

3 large onions, chopped

2 (16-ounce) cans tomato sauce

2 slices wheat bread, soaked in water

2 large heads green cabbage

¾ cup sugar

2 teaspoons salt

2 pounds ground sirloin or lean ground beef

3 eggs

½ cup raisins

Garlic powder to taste

Cabbage? Not Too Many Children Will Eat It!

What a great way to mask one of the unfavorable vegetables in a child's world. This stuffed cabbage recipe is so delicious, and has so many flavors intertwined, that the cabbage itself is a very mild flavor. Cabbage is filled with fiber, vitamin K and vitamin C, and has been touted in lowering the risk of certain cancers. Make this dish a few times, and see if you get a smile!

1. Preheat oven to 350°F.

2. In a large pot, sauté onions in olive oil, until transparent. Add the tomato sauce and mix well and simmer. Add sugar and 1 teaspoon salt and mix well

3. Place the bread in a small bowl of water and leave for several minutes.

4. Boil cabbages in a large uncovered pot. Boil for a few minutes, and cool. Peel the leaves, trying to keep them whole, and set aside. If the leaves inside appear hard, place back in the boiling water to soften. When you have about 10 to 12 cabbage leaves in good condition, lay them out flat.

5. Drain water from the bread and place in a food processor, until crumb-like.

6. In a large mixing bowl, mix the bread, ground beef, 1 teaspoon salt, eggs, and raisins.

7. Transfer the tomato sauce mixture into a large casserole dish.

8. Spoon a large spoonful of ground beef into the cabbage leaf, toward the bottom of the leaf. To fold the leaf, bring up the bottom of the leaf about 1 to 2 inches, and fold in each side. Tuck the top part of the leaf inside.

9. Transfer the stuffed cabbage into the tomato sauce mixture. Repeat until all the cabbage are stuffed with ground beef. Cover and bake in the oven for 2 hours.

Turkey Scallopini with Cranberry Relish

This is a delightful, easy, and child-friendly dish—chicken or veal cutlets can be substituted, too.

INGREDIENTS | SERVES 4

1 pound turkey cutlets, about ½-inch thick

3 tablespoons Wondra gravy mix or flour

½ teaspoon salt

½ teaspoon pepper

½ teaspoon garlic powder

2 eggs

2 tablespoons olive oil

¾ cup whole cranberry sauce

1 tablespoon lemon juice

1 teaspoon cornstarch

1 bouillon cube, chicken-flavored

1 cup water

1. Cut turkey cutlets into 3" × 3" pieces.

2. On a plate or a large piece of waxed paper, combine the gravy mix, salt, pepper, and garlic.

3. In a small bowl, beat the eggs.

4. Dip turkey cutlets in egg mixture, and then in Wondra or flour to form coating.

5. In a large nonstick skillet, heat olive oil on low heat.

6. Pan-fry turkey cutlets, 2 to 3 minutes on each side, until lightly browned. Place on a dish.

7. In the same skillet, add cranberry sauce, lemon juice, cornstarch, bouillon, and 1 cup water.

8. Cook until boiling, stirring constantly. Allow to boil for 1 to 2 minutes.

9. Return turkey cutlets to the skillet to reheat.

10. Place turkey on a serving dish, and cover with cranberry mixture.

Chicken Finger Stir-Fry

Feel like you are in a Chinese restaurant with a delicious combination of chicken and vegetables. Substitute any of the kids' favorite vegetables.

INGREDIENTS | SERVES 4

¾ cup orange juice

3 tablespoons low-sodium soy sauce

1 tablespoon honey

1 tablespoon cornstarch

1½ pounds chicken breast, boneless, skinless

Salt and pepper to taste

3 tablespoons olive or canola oil

4 medium carrots, sliced thinly

1½ cups snow peas

1 large clove garlic, crushed

2 scallions, chopped

2 cups quick cooking brown rice, uncooked

1¾ cups water

1 bouillon cube, vegetable or chicken

1. In a small bowl, mix orange juice, soy sauce, honey, and cornstarch.

2. Clean chicken and slice in strips.

3. Season with salt and pepper.

4. In a medium skillet, heat canola or olive oil on low heat.

5. Cook the chicken strips 5 to 7 minutes, until thoroughly cooked. Remove from pan.

6. Add 1 tablespoon oil to the skillet, and place carrots, snow peas, scallions, and garlic in the pan.

7. Cook 4 to 5 minutes, until desired doneness.

8. Add chicken back into the skillet.

9. Stir orange juice mixture, and add to the skillet, covering the chicken and the vegetables.

10. Cook 2 to 3 minutes, until hot.

11. Add a few tablespoons of water if sauce becomes too thick.

12. Prepare brown rice, using package directions.

13. Add the bouillon cube to the cooking water.

14. Serve chicken and vegetables over rice.

Japanese Brown Rice and Beef Teriyaki

This meal can be prepared with chicken or shrimp, and is a terrific transformation of a "healthier stir-fry."

INGREDIENTS | SERVES 4

3 tablespoons low-sodium soy sauce

1 tablespoon dry sherry

1 tablespoon brown sugar

1 teaspoon minced garlic

1 pound flank steak, cut into thin strips

1 tablespoon olive oil

3 cups mixed vegetables: broccoli, snap peas, carrots (chopped)

1 cup beef broth

4 teaspoons cornstarch

2 cups brown rice, cooked

1. In a medium mixing bowl, combine soy sauce, sherry, brown sugar, and garlic.

2. Add steak strips to bowl, and allow to marinate for 10 to 30 minutes.

3. In a large frying pan, heat oil over low heat. Stir-fry the beef until browned. Add vegetables and continue cooking, until vegetables are tender.

4. Mix cornstarch with broth, and add to skillet. Boil for 1 minute.

5. Serve beef and vegetables over the cooked brown rice.

Salmon with Lemon Sauce

Another easy fish preparation that can be made with so many different types of fish.

INGREDIENTS | SERVES 2–3

1 pound salmon fillets

½ to 1 cup water

2 lemons, juiced

1 teaspoon dried parsley

Salt and pepper to taste

2 eggs

1. Wash fish and cut into serving-size pieces. Place in heavy skillet. Add water half way up the side of fish pieces.

2. Squeeze in juice of 1 lemon. Add parsley and ground pepper. Cover and place on medium heat for 10 to 15 minutes.

3. In a small mixing bowl, beat eggs with juice of second lemon.

4. Remove fish from heat and uncover. Quickly pour egg/lemon mixture over fish, shaking pan so that the mix creates a sauce. Cover pan and let sit a few minutes until sauce thickens.

Balsamic BBQ Tuna

This oil and vinegar–based marinade can be used for so many other entrees—chicken, turkey, fish, etc.

INGREDIENTS | SERVES 2

2 tuna steaks, about 5 ounces each
2 tablespoons olive oil
2 tablespoons balsamic vinegar
1 clove garlic, crushed
Salt and black pepper to taste
¼ cup barbecue sauce
Nonstick cooking spray

1. Rinse the tuna steaks. Poke several holes on both sides of the steaks, so the marinade can infuse in.

2. Create marinade by mixing olive oil, balsamic vinegar, garlic, salt, and black pepper together.

3. Place the tuna in a small bowl and pour the marinade over the fish. Let marinate in refrigerator for 30 minutes to 1 hour. Drain marinade from tuna.

4. Light grill, making sure your grill grates are clean. Spray with nonstick cooking spray. Place the tuna on the grill for 3 to 4 minutes, turn over and repeat the process.

5. With about 3 minutes left in cooking, brush with barbecue sauce.

Fruity Cornish Hen with Stuffing

This is a beautiful and creative dish for a family dinner, a holiday, or a party. This recipe is not just for Cornish hens, but can be used with chicken or turkey, too.

INGREDIENTS | **SERVES 6–8**

3 Cornish hens

1 to 2 tablespoons garlic powder

1 tablespoon paprika

Salt to taste

1 (15-ounce) can sliced pineapple

1 small jar maraschino cherries

3 scallions, chopped

½ pound sliced mushrooms

1 to 2 cups baby carrots

Nonstick cooking spray

2 medium onions, chopped

1 box seasoned stuffing mix

1. Preheat oven to 350°F.

2. Clean the hens, inside and out. Line a large roasting pan with aluminum foil and place hens in the pan.

3. Sprinkle garlic powder, paprika, and salt on hens, covering entire surface.

4. Place 1 pineapple slice on top of each hen with 3 cherries in the center of pineapple slice. Top with chopped scallions.

5. Place the mushrooms and carrots around the hens, covering the bottom of the roasting pan.

6. Cook hens for 1 hour.

7. In a small skillet, spray nonstick cooking spray. Sauté onions until soft.

8. Prepare the stuffing as directed. Add the sautéed onions to the stuffing and mix.

9. After 1 hour, check hens for doneness. Serve with stuffing.

Cashew Chicken Lettuce Cups

This is a great little dish that can be served as an appetizer or snack, at a party, or for a holiday—one of the most versatile recipes. Switch up the nuts, the vegetables, leave the chicken in or take it out. A delicious treat.

INGREDIENTS | SERVES 4

3 tablespoons low-sodium soy sauce

3 tablespoons honey

1½ pounds boneless, skinless chicken breasts

2 tablespoons canola or olive oil

2 cloves garlic, finely chopped

1 tablespoon grated ginger

1 (8-ounce) can sliced water chestnuts, drained and chopped

½ pound fresh green beans, cleaned and chopped

1 small head Boston or Bibb lettuce leaves, washed and separated

1 cup roasted unsalted cashews

1. In a small bowl, combine the soy sauce and honey. Set aside.

2. Cut chicken into bite-size pieces. Heat the oil in a large skillet over low heat. Sauté the chicken about 3 minutes.

3. Add garlic and ginger, and continue mixing.

4. Stir in water chestnuts and green beans, and half the soy sauce mixture. Continue to cook until the chicken is cooked through, about 5 more minutes.

5. Place lettuce leaves on a serving dish. Spoon the chicken mixture into the lettuce leaves. Sprinkle with cashews. Drizzle the remaining soy sauce and serve.

Broiled Salmon and Wasabi Sandwich

Dress up the salmon, and hopefully the children will learn to be good fish eaters.
It is so critical to their health, and reducing inflammation.

INGREDIENTS | SERVES 4

1 (1-pound) salmon fillet, skinned
½ teaspoon salt
¼ teaspoon black pepper
Nonstick cooking spray
½ teaspoon wasabi powder
1 teaspoon water
⅓ cup low-fat mayonnaise
¼ cup scallions, chopped
1 teaspoon low-sodium soy sauce
¼ teaspoon sesame oil
4 romaine or Boston lettuce leaves
4 whole grain rolls

1. Preheat the broiler.

2. Sprinkle salmon with salt and pepper.

3. Spray nonstick cooking spray on a broiler pan. Broil salmon 8 to 10 minutes, or until fish flakes easily with a fork. Allow fish to cool. Cut into 2-inch pieces.

4. In a small mixing bowl, combine wasabi powder and water. Add mayonnaise, scallions, soy sauce, and oil, and blend well.

5. Add fish to sauce and toss gently.

6. Place one lettuce leaf on each of the rolls. Divide fish evenly over lettuce.

Aging Is a "Disease"

It has been suggested that the aging process is a disease. As people age, body parts tend to fall apart, some sooner than others. Fish has been named *the number one* food with anti-inflammatory properties (salmon especially)—that means little or less inflammation throughout the body as you get older. Be sure to encourage your children to eat fish for their health now and in the future.

Pad Thai with Shrimp

This is usually a sweet, delicious, and popular Asian favorite. Shrimp would be a first choice—fish, fish, fish—however, this dish can be made with pork, chicken, steak, or just vegetables for a side dish.

INGREDIENTS | SERVES 6–8

8 ounces wide rice noodles

¼ cup ketchup

2 tablespoons sugar

2 tablespoons canola oil, divided

2 pounds medium shrimp, peeled and deveined

2 large eggs, lightly beaten

¾ cup scallions, finely chopped

2 teaspoons minced garlic

2 tablespoons chopped unsalted peanuts

1. Place noodles in a large mixing bowl filled with hot water. Let stand about 15 minutes or until softened. Drain noodles in a colander.

2. Combine ketchup and sugar in a small bowl.

3. Heat 1 tablespoon oil in a large skillet over low heat. Add shrimp; sauté 2 to 3 minutes, or until shrimp are done. Remove shrimp from the skillet, but keep it covered and warm.

4. Heat 1 tablespoon oil in same skillet over low heat.

5. Add eggs; cook 30 seconds, or until soft-scrambled, stirring constantly.

6. Add scallions and garlic; cook 2 to 3 minutes.

7. Add noodles, ketchup mixture, and shrimp. Cook 5 minutes until heated.

8. Sprinkle with peanuts and serve.

Grilled Mahi-Mahi and Pineapple Skewers

No leftovers here! A sweet sauce along with the Mahi-Mahi makes for a popular dish.
Select other mild, thick fish varieties such as swordfish for an alternative.

INGREDIENTS | SERVES 4

½ cup chopped onion

⅓ cup honey

½ cup dry red wine

2 tablespoons balsamic vinegar

2 tablespoons pineapple juice

1 tablespoon low-sodium soy sauce

2 cups diced fresh or canned pineapple

1½ pounds mahi-mahi steaks, cut into 24 (1-inch) pieces

24 (1-inch) cubes fresh pineapple

24 (1-inch) pieces red and/or yellow bell pepper

¼ teaspoon salt

¼ teaspoon black pepper

Nonstick cooking spray

8 skewers for grilling

1. Heat a medium nonstick skillet over low heat. Combine chopped onions and honey in the skillet. Cook 10 to 12 minutes or until tender and browned, stirring occasionally.

2. Add red wine, vinegar, pineapple juice, and soy sauce. Mix well. Cook about 10 minutes, stirring occasionally.

3. Stir in diced pineapple; cook for 5 minutes; keep sauce warm.

4. Prepare the grill.

5. In preparing the skewers, place 3 mahi-mahi pieces, 3 pineapple cubes and 3 bell pepper pieces, alternately, onto each of the 8 (12-inch) skewers. Sprinkle with salt and pepper.

6. Place kebobs on a grill rack coated with nonstick cooking spray. Grill kebobs 8 to 10 minutes or until fish is done, turning once.

7. Serve with pineapple sauce.

Picture-Perfect Picadillo

This traditional Latin dish can be made with lean ground beef or ground veal. Ground turkey breast is certainly the lowest in saturated and total fat, however, season it up good, as ground turkey needs it!

INGREDIENTS | SERVES 4

1 teaspoon olive oil

1 cup finely chopped onion

1 pound ground turkey breast

3 garlic cloves, minced

1 cup beef broth

1/3 cup coarsely chopped pimiento-stuffed olives

1 tablespoon tomato paste

1/4 teaspoon freshly ground pepper

3 cups hot cooked brown rice

1. In a large skillet over low heat, heat olive oil. Add chopped onions and sauté for 5 minutes, until tender.

2. Add turkey and garlic to the skillet. Cook 5 to 7 minutes, stirring to break up turkey chunks.

3. Add broth, olives, tomato paste and ground pepper. Mix well. Increase heat and bring to a boil.

4. After bringing to a boil, cover and reduce heat. Simmer 25 to 35 minutes. Serve with brown rice.

CHAPTER 12

I Want Dessert!

Let's Meringue!

For a lower sugar content, use ½ cup sugar and ¼ cup Splenda (for your older children). This cuts some of the sugar and calories from this splendid dessert.

INGREDIENTS | SERVES 8–10

4 egg whites
1 teaspoon vanilla
¼ teaspoon cream of tartar
¾ cup sugar
¼ cup semi-sweet mini-morsels

Doesn't Everyone Love Dessert!

And dessert is *never* off limits. It is not a forbidden food. In fact, if you do ban it, the children generally will get it from somewhere, and will overindulge whenever they get the chance. So, in this chapter, dessert recipes have been compiled for that occasional, really yummy, not-so-healthy treat. Then, there are those that could be included on a once-or-twice-a-week basis, along with the rest of our moderate healthy lifestyle.

1. Leave egg whites at room temperature for 1 hour.

2. Preheat oven to 225°F.

3. Beat egg whites until stiff. As the egg whites are being whipped, add vanilla and cream of tartar.

4. When egg whites become fluffy and peaked, slowly add sugar. Continue beating until very stiff.

5. Fold in chocolate chips.

6. Place by teaspoonful onto ungreased cookie sheet (lined with wax paper).

7. Bake for 1 hour 30 minutes.

8. Turn oven off, and let meringues cool in the oven for another hour or so.

Most Wonderful White Trifle

Though a delicious dessert, here is a way to infuse some fresh fruit into the children without a ton of fat and sugar.

INGREDIENTS | SERVES 8–10

2 medium bananas (not too ripe), sliced

1 tablespoon lemon juice

1 (4-ounce) package fat-free, sugar-free vanilla instant pudding

1 cup fat-free condensed milk

1 cup water

1 large container low-fat whipped topping

1 fat free (or low-fat) pound cake, sliced, and halved

½ pint fresh strawberries, sliced

1. Soak sliced bananas in lemon juice for several minutes.

2. In a mixing bowl, mix pudding, condensed milk, and water. Refrigerate the mixture until it is the texture of pudding.

3. When pudding mixture is stiff, fold in whipped topping and blend carefully.

4. Cut pound cake slices in half.

5. In a trifle bowl, layer the following: pound cake, pudding mixture, sliced strawberries and banana. Repeat. Decorate the top of the trifle with strawberry and banana slices.

The Scoop on "Fat-Free" Products

Many years ago, fat free was the way to go, and the way you were told to eat. Why? It was determined that any food that contained fat had twice as many calories as that which contained carbohydrate or protein. While this is true, it has been found since that our calorie intake really didn't drop—all of the fat-free products no longer contained unhealthy fat, but were substituted with large amounts of sugar. Many people seemed to feel that if the food were "fat free," they could eat even more of it!

Apple Crisp

Use any variety of apples—try Granny Smith for a more tart taste.
Even the topping has a little "here's to health" thrown in!

INGREDIENTS | SERVES 8–10

Nonstick cooking spray
½ cup flour
¾ cup brown sugar
3 tablespoons trans-fat-free margarine
1 cup rolled oats
6 to 8 Golden Delicious apples, peeled, cored, and sliced
¼ cup sugar
¼ teaspoon cinnamon
1 tablespoon lemon juice

No Need to Give Up Dessert

The goal for keeping your family healthy is the concept of moderation. It is important that you teach this to your children, and allow them, even prepare for them, healthier desserts. Incorporate them into your mealtime on occasion. Let them learn that there are no foods that are "off limits"—self-control is the ultimate lesson here, which will hopefully last them a lifetime!

1. Preheat oven to 350°F.

2. Use a shallow round pie pan, and spray with nonstick cooking spray.

3. Prepare streusel by placing flour, sugar, and margarine in food processor, pulsing until a coarse texture. Add oatmeal, and continue pulsing to break it up.

4. Place half the streusel mixture on the bottom of pan.

5. Mix the apples, sugar, cinnamon, and lemon juice. Place mixture on top of the streusel. Top with remaining streusel.

6. Bake for 1 hour; cover for the first 20 minutes. Uncover for the remainder of the baking time.

Fluorescent Green Delight

This one couldn't be easier—and the kids find the color really cool. It also looks beautiful on a holiday table.

INGREDIENTS | SERVES 6–8

1 (12-ounce) container low-fat whipped topping

2 (4-ounce) packages fat-free sugar-free pistachio pudding

1 (16-ounce) can crushed pineapple (in its own juice), drained

1. Mix pudding powder and whipped topping together.

2. Add pineapple.

3. Place in a decorative bowl and refrigerate for about 1 hour. Serve chilled.

Banana Ice Cream Pie

Taking your favorite recipes, and modifying them with lower-fat, lower-sugar items, can make a big difference in your child's health, while they probably don't notice that much of a difference in taste—it's all a matter of what they can get used to.

INGREDIENTS | SERVES 8–10

Prepared graham cracker crust

3 to 4 ripe bananas, sliced

1½ cups low-fat vanilla ice cream

½ cup low-fat milk

1 (4-ounce) package sugar-free instant vanilla pudding mix

1 cup low-fat whipped topping

1. Layer bottom of graham cracker crust with sliced bananas.

2. Mix together ice cream, milk, and pudding mix. Spread over bananas.

3. Cover the top with additional sliced bananas, and whipped topping.

4. Freeze for 1 to 2 hours, then serve.

Raspberry Meringue Cake

*This becomes a beautiful dessert, even for a holiday or party. Everyone enjoys it—
and the fruits can be varied to include blueberries, kiwi, or blackberries.*

INGREDIENTS | SERVES 12

4 egg whites, room temperature

¼ teaspoon cream of tartar

1 cup sugar

1½ cups low-fat milk, cold

1 (4-ounce) package fat-free, sugar-free vanilla pudding mix

1 cup low-fat whipped topping

2 cups raspberries

2 tablespoons powdered sugar

Meringue: A Dessert Everyone Seems to Enjoy

Being whipped through and through when prepared, and therefore light and airy, meringue is one of the lower calorie options around. Though made with sugar, it is a delicate dessert that can be made in "cookie" form, cake form, or as a topping. Hint: it has to be beaten just until the stiff peaks form—if it is overbeaten, you may end up with meringue soup!

1. Preheat oven to 225°F.

2. Beat egg whites with electric mixer on high speed until soft peaks form.

3. Add cream of tartar.

4. Slowly, add sugar, and continue beating until stiff peaks form.

5. Place parchment paper on a large baking sheet. Spoon meringue onto baking sheet, creating a 10-inch to 12-inch circle.

6. Form a large "hole" in the middle, so that the outer portion creates a "crust," and there is space to add the whipped topping and fruit.

7. Bake for 1 to 1½ hours, until hard and crusty. Cool for 30 minutes.

8. To make the pudding mixture, pour milk into a large mixing bowl. Add pudding mix. Beat with a wire whisk until well blended. Fold in whipped topping.

9. Refrigerate for 30 minutes or until pudding thickens.

10. To assemble "cake," place the meringue on a serving dish. Spoon pudding mixture into the center, leaving the crust, or border of meringue, to show. Top with raspberries and sprinkle with powdered sugar.

Chocolate Tower Trifle

Even better on Day 2, a vanilla cake can be substituted for the chocolate; any flavor pudding can be substituted for a fun variety of this delicious dessert!

INGREDIENTS | SERVES 12–16

1 box Devil's food prepared cake mix (low sugar, if available)

2 (16-ounce) containers low-fat whipped topping

2 (4-ounce) sugar-free, fat-free chocolate pudding mix

1 large bag individually wrapped Heath bars

1 teaspoon vanilla extract

Practice Good Old Portion Control

So, when you decide to "splurge" on this divine cake, remember moderation. Desserts are part of life—the children's too—it is the serving you allow them or teach them, that will entitle them to eat dessert on a regular basis. There are no more super-size or monster-size slices of cake served at home, and all desserts at home or even in a restaurant should probably just be cut in half.

1. Prepare Devil's food cake according to package directions. Bake in 2 separate baking pans.

2. Mix pudding mix and whipped topping together until well blended. Place in refrigerator for 1 hour, until pudding thickens.

3. Finely chop Heath bars in food processor.

4. Layer the trifle in the following order in a decorative bowl: cake at the bottom, pudding/whipped topping mixture, Heath bars. Repeat same layers.

5. Heath bars should decorate the very top of the trifle.

Nutty Apple Muffins

Delicious muffins—top with low-fat ice cream for a light, sweet dessert.

INGREDIENTS | SERVES 12

Nonstick cooking spray
1 egg
½ cup orange juice
¼ cup canola oil
1½ cups apples, peeled and diced
1½ cups flour
½ cup sugar
2 teaspoons baking powder

Topping:

1 teaspoon cinnamon
¼ cup brown sugar
¼ cup walnuts (optional)

1. Preheat oven to 400°F.

2. Spray 12-cup muffin tray with nonstick cooking spray; or insert paper baking cups into tray.

3. Combine egg, orange juice, canola oil, apples, flour, sugar, and baking powder in a large mixing bowl. Mix thoroughly, until well blended.

4. Pour batter into prepared muffin tray.

5. Prepare topping in a small bowl by combining cinnamon, brown sugar, and walnuts if using. Sprinkle topping over each muffin.

6. Bake for 20 to 25 minutes, until toothpick comes out dry.

Simply Sweet Chocolate Chip Macaroons

This is the easiest recipe—and so much fun to eat!

INGREDIENTS | SERVES 8

1 egg
¼ cup sugar
7 ounces shredded coconut
3 tablespoons trans-fat-free margarine
1 teaspoon vanilla extract
4 ounces mini chocolate morsels
Nonstick cooking spray

1. Preheat oven to 325°F.

2. Mix egg, sugar, and coconut in a medium bowl.

3. Melt margarine, and add margarine and vanilla to the bowl.

4. Fold in chocolate chips.

5. Spray cooking spray onto baking sheet. Drop by heaping tablespoon onto baking sheet.

6. Bake for 15 to 20 minutes.

The Trans Fat Story—the Unhealthiest Fat Ever Created

Trans fats, or partially hydrogenated vegetable oil, as it is usually listed on the label, is the most dangerous type of fat you can eat. Why are the trans fats so harmful? Hydrogenation, or the addition of hydrogen to a somewhat healthy fat, is very dangerous to arteries. Learn to read not only the Nutrition Facts label on all food products, but even more importantly, the actual ingredient list. If the words "partially hydrogenated vegetable oil," or "partially hydrogenated vegetable shortening" appear *anywhere* within the ingredient list, choose another product.

Crispy Oatmeal Crisps

Use "quick-cooking" oatmeal, not an instant oatmeal. In fact, instant oatmeal does not contain as much of the cholesterol-lowering properties as the regular.

INGREDIENTS | SERVES 16–18

Nonstick cooking spray
3 eggs
1 teaspoon cinnamon
1 teaspoon vanilla
½ teaspoon salt
1½ cups granulated sugar
2 tablespoons trans-fat-free margarine, melted and cooled
4 teaspoons baking powder
3½ cups quick-cooking oatmeal

A Healthful Twist on a Cookie?

This is a light oatmeal cookie, thin and crispy. Though a fairly basic cookie recipe, it has enough oatmeal to be able to get cholesterol-lowering benefits—certainly better than a brownie! Indulge the kids once in a while. Teach that it is acceptable to have a sweet treat; however, offer two cookies and a glass of cold low-fat milk, not six cookies!

1. Preheat oven to 350°F.

2. Place aluminum foil on several cookie sheets. Spray with cooking spray.

3. Using an electric mixer, beat eggs until foamy.

4. Add cinnamon, vanilla, salt, and sugar. Beat 2 to 3 minutes until thick and well blended.

5. Add melted margarine and mix. Stir in baking powder and oats.

6. Using a rounded teaspoon, drop batter onto cookie sheet, about 2 inches apart. Continue to stir remaining batter occasionally, as the liquid will start to settle.

7. Bake for 10 minutes, until cookies appear thin and lightly colored, darker on the rim, and lighter in the center. When cookies are done, immediately slide the cookies off the cookie sheet, and cool.

Cheesecake Flan au Chocolat

This is a beautiful dessert and one everyone will love. Save it for that special occasion.

INGREDIENTS | SERVES 12

1½ cups sugar, divided

4 squares semi-sweet baking chocolate

1 (12-ounce) can evaporated skim milk

1 (8-ounce) package low-fat cream cheese, cut in cubes

1 teaspoon vanilla extract

4 eggs

1. Preheat oven to 350°F.

2. In a small saucepan, place 1 cup sugar and cook on medium heat, until sugar is golden brown, stirring constantly. Pour sugar into a 9-inch round pan.

3. Place the chocolate squares in a microwaveable bowl. Microwave on high 2 minutes, until chocolate is almost melted.

4. Put milk and cream cheese in a blender, and blend until smooth.

5. Add remaining sugar, vanilla extract, eggs, and melted chocolate. Blend until smooth. Pour mixture on top of melted sugar in the pan.

6. Create a water bath by setting the pan into a larger pan, filled approximately half way with water.

7. Place in the oven and bake for 1 hour. Remove from oven, and place flan on a wire rack; cool. Refrigerate for several hours, or overnight.

8. Serve chilled.

Chocolate Chip Banana Bread

One for the record books—one of the most delicious desserts in the whole world. Either bake as a banana bread, or use a muffin tin, and fill muffin cups ⅔ of the way full.

INGREDIENTS | SERVES 8–10

1 teaspoon baking soda

¾ cup low-fat sour cream

½ cup trans-fat-free margarine

1½ cups sugar

2 eggs

1 teaspoon vanilla extract

2 large ripe bananas, cut into chunks

1 teaspoon baking powder

2 cups flour

8 to 10 ounces mini chocolate morsels

1. Preheat oven to 350°F.

2. Mix baking soda and sour cream and allow to stand for several minutes.

3. In a food processor, combine margarine, sugar, eggs, and vanilla. Mix for 2 minutes. After 2 minutes, add chunks of banana.

4. Add the baking soda-sour cream mixture, and mix for 10 seconds.

5. Add flour and baking powder slowly.

6. Mix in chocolate chips.

7. Place batter in a loaf pan and bake for 1 hour (or muffins for 20 to 30 minutes).

Very Berry Confection

You can vary the berries, depending on the season. This is a relatively healthful dessert, and beautiful on the table.

INGREDIENTS | SERVES 12

⅓ cup whipped cream cheese
1 teaspoon vanilla extract
¾ cup sugar, divided
2 egg whites
2 teaspoons grated lemon peel
1 cup plus 2 tablespoons flour, divided
½ teaspoon baking soda
⅓ cup low-fat sour cream
1 cup fresh raspberries
1 cup fresh blueberries
1 cup fresh blackberries
2 cups low-fat whipped topping
¼ cup powdered confectioners' sugar
Nonstick cooking spray

Low-Fat Whipped Toppings

Whipped toppings came on the market as a substitute for whipped cream, creating a lower-fat, lighter version of highly saturated whipped cream. However, now with the trans fat issue, learn to read the ingredient label. Therefore, look for a low-fat whipped topping that does not contain partially hydrogenated vegetable oil.

1. Preheat oven to 350°F.

2. With electric mixer, beat cream cheese, vanilla, and ½ cup sugar in a large bowl on medium speed until well blended.

3. Add egg whites and lemon peel and continue to mix.

4. Add 1 cup of the flour and the baking soda.

5. Add sour cream; mix until well blended.

6. Spray 9-inch springform pan with cooking spray. Spread cream cheese batter into pan.

7. Toss 2 cups of the berries with the remaining ¼ cup sugar and 2 tablespoons flour. Pour over the cream cheese mixture, covering the entire batter.

8. Bake 45 minutes. Cool 20 minutes; remove the rim of the pan.

9. Top with layer of whipped topping and remaining berries. Sprinkle with powdered sugar.

Peach Frosty

A fresh summer treat—loaded with vitamin C and potassium—and nice and sweet!

INGREDIENTS | SERVES 2–3

1 cup sliced peaches, in own juice

2 tablespoons powdered sugar

½ cup low-fat milk

1 teaspoon vanilla extract

1 cup low-fat ice cream

The Peach

Whether in a pie, a cobbler, or just sliced as a summer fruit, a peach is a low-calorie, high-fiber, fruit. Keep them at room temperature and they will ripen over the next several days. Do not remove the skin, as that is where most of the fiber lives.

1. Purée the peach slices, powdered sugar, and milk in a blender, until smooth.

2. Add vanilla extract and ice cream and blend again until smooth.

3. Serve immediately.

Luscious Lady Finger Dessert

Enhance the flavor of this dessert by adding one cup strong coffee, cooled, to give it a rich mocha flavor.

INGREDIENTS | SERVES 12

1 (6-ounce) package Lady Fingers, split and separated

1 (8-ounce) package low-fat cream cheese, cut in cubes

1 teaspoon vanilla extract

2 cups cold low-fat milk

2 (4-ounce) packages fat-free, sugar-free pudding mix

8 ounces low-fat whipped topping

1. In a serving bowl or trifle bowl, place Lady Fingers on the bottom and up the sides of the bowl.

2. Beat cream cheese and vanilla with wire whisk until smooth.

3. Gradually add the milk, and beat until smooth. Add pudding mix and half of the whipped topping. Beat softly with wire whisk.

4. Spoon into the trifle bowl. Cover and refrigerate for several hours.

5. Top with a large dollop of whipped topping and a few fresh berries.

Apple Dumpling à la Mode

Served warm, à la mode, these are light and tender dumplings, attractive enough to serve as a holiday or party dessert. Feel free to substitute different types of dried fruits for the center of the apple, and different flavors of low-fat ice cream! Yum!

INGREDIENTS | SERVES 6

2½ cups all-purpose flour

1 teaspoon salt

½ cup light brown sugar

1 cup trans-fat-free margarine, plus 2 tablespoons

1 teaspoon vanilla extract

6 tablespoons cold water

¼ cup chopped apricots

¼ cup raisins

2 teaspoons ground cinnamon

6 small apples, peeled and cored

Nonstick cooking spray

1 egg, beaten

6 or 8 toothpicks

3 cups low-fat ice cream

The Apple Doesn't Fall Far

Apples tend to be a fruit kids will eat. The best part is there are so many varieties, that if you are looking for sweet, tart, or crisp, you can always find it in an apple. Chock full of vitamin C and fiber (in the skin), eating or adding apples to your diet is a good thing. As your children enter their school-age years, urge them to eat the skin. Try not to peel apples if you can help it. And apple juice is not the same. There is no beneficial fiber in fruit juice.

1. Preheat oven to 400°F.

2. In a large bowl, mix flour, salt, and 2 tablespoons brown sugar. Using 2 knives, one in each hand, cut in 1 cup margarine until mixture appears like crumbs.

3. Mix in cold water and vanilla, until dough is stiff. Set dough aside.

4. In a small bowl, mix the apricots and raisins, 2 tablespoons margarine, ¼ cup brown sugar, and half the cinnamon.

5. Prepare apples, and add dried fruit mixture into each apple cavity.

6. Mix remaining 2 tablespoons brown sugar and cinnamon in a small dish. Roll each apple in brown sugar/cinnamon mixture.

7. On a piece of wax paper, pour small amount of flour, and roll a rolling pin in some of the flour. Roll out dough on wax paper, forming large rectangular shape. Cut dough into 7-inch squares.

8. Spray nonstick cooking spray into a large jelly roll pan.

9. Center an apple on a square of dough. Repeat for all apples. Brush each edge of dough with beaten egg. Wrap dough over the top of each apple. Brush with remaining egg. Stick a toothpick or two on the top of the apple, holding the dough in place.

10. Bake for 40 minutes, until the pastry is golden brown in color. Serve with favorite flavor low-fat ice cream.

Crazy Carrot Cake

*An All-American favorite, this carrot cake is a little more healthful—and chock
full of carrots; not quite considered a vegetable serving, however.*

INGREDIENTS | SERVES 10–12

½ cup trans-fat-free margarine, melted

1½ cups sugar

2 cups flour

4 eggs

1 teaspoon vanilla extract

1 teaspoon ginger

2 teaspoons cinnamon

4 cups grated carrots

¼ cup low-fat sour cream

¼ cup powdered sugar

1. Preheat oven to 350°F.

2. In a large mixing bowl, blend margarine and sugar.

3. Add flour, eggs, vanilla, ginger, cinnamon, carrots, and sour cream. Mix well. Pour into round baking dish.

4. Bake 45 minutes to 1 hour.

5. Allow to cool, then sprinkle with powdered sugar.

Delectable Strawberry Mousse

*This is a light and fluffy low-fat version and a delicious treat. At anytime, feel free to change the flavors—
chocolate, pistachio, or even banana sounds great. The kids can be in total charge of this one.*

INGREDIENTS | SERVES 8–10

2 cups water

3 (4-ounce) packages sugar-free, fat-free strawberry Jell-O

1 pint low-fat sour cream

1 pint strawberry low-fat ice cream

1. Boil water in a medium-sized saucepan.

2. Empty Jell-O bag into the boiling water. Stir, and let it sit for 2 minutes.

3. Mix in low-fat sour cream and low-fat ice cream.

4. Refrigerate 4 hours. Serve.

Slumber Party Cake

Certainly a unique and fabulous cake, the children will have a "ball" making this birthday cake.

INGREDIENTS | SERVES 15–20

1 box white cake mix, prepared as per directions

6 cups frosting (choose 2 favorite colors)

6 low-fat Twinkies

6 large marshmallows

6 vanilla wafers

6 to 8 strips licorice

25 to 30 candy dots

3 to 4 strips of fruit leather

Moderation Again

Parties are oodles of fun for kids. The goal is to make the activities more appealing than the food. However, what would a birthday party (or any party, for that matter) be without cake? Do not deprive your children of cake—however, learn to slice small, and make a plan for the leftovers. Freeze it, give it away, or get rid of it. As you may well know, cake lying around calls your name!

1. In a 9½" × 11" baking dish prepare white cake per package directions. Cool; remove from pan and place on a serving dish.

2. Spread a thin layer of icing on the cake.

3. Place Twinkies evenly on the cake, vertically, as if they were "beds." Place a marshmallow at the top of the Twinkie. Place a vanilla wafer on top of the marshmallow. Now there is a pillow and a "head."

4. Use licorice (any color) to create hair, and candy dots for eyes. Use remainder of the icing to make a blanket over the "kids." Use candy dots to create "polka dots" on the blanket.

5. Complete the cake by "framing" blanket and cake with fruit leather.

Perfectly Plaid Cake

This is a magnificent-looking cake, and magnificently tasty, too! You can replace a chocolate butter cream frosting for the cream cheese frosting, too.

INGREDIENTS | SERVES 16

Nonstick cooking spray

1 cup trans-fat-free margarine

2½ cups sugar, divided

3½ cups cake flour

1¼ cups low-fat milk

1 tablespoon baking powder

1 tablespoon vanilla extract

½ teaspoon salt

8 egg whites

8 ounces semi-sweet chocolate squares, melted

2 large decorating bags

Cream Cheese Frosting:

1 cup of trans-fat-free margarine

16 ounces low-fat cream cheese

2 teaspoons vanilla extract

3½ cups powdered sugar

1. Preheat oven to 350°F.

2. Spray three 8-inch round cake pans with nonstick cooking spray.

3. Dust bottoms of pans with flour.

4. In a large bowl, mix with electric mixer margarine and 1½ cups sugar until well blended. Beat at high for 4 to 5 minutes, until light and fluffy.

5. Add flour, milk, baking powder, vanilla, and salt. Beat until just blended, and then increase speed to medium for 2 minutes.

6. In a separate large mixing bowl, beat egg whites and ½ cup sugar until stiff.

7. Gently fold beaten egg white and sugar mixture into flour mixture until well blended.

8. Spoon ½ of batter into another medium bowl.

9. In original bowl, fold melted chocolate until blended, creating a chocolate batter.

10. Pour vanilla batter into the large decorating bag with ½-inch opening (you can also use a large plastic bag, closed at the top, with opening at a bottom corner).

11. Pour chocolate batter into another decorating bag.

12. Pipe a 1½-inch band of chocolate batter around the inside edge of two of the cake pans. Pipe same amount of vanilla batter next to each chocolate band. Fill the rest of the inside of the pan with chocolate batter.

Perfectly Plaid Cake (continued)

13. For the third cake pan, repeat the same process, only begin with the outer band being vanilla batter; follow with chocolate and then vanilla again.

14. Place the three cake pans in the oven for 25 to 30 minutes. Remove from the wax paper and cool.

15. Prepare frosting. With an electric mixer, beat the margarine and cream cheese together on medium speed until smooth.

16. Add vanilla extract and powdered sugar, slowly, and beat well.

17. To assemble the cake, place one of the identical cakes on a cake plate. Spread with ½ cup frosting. Place the nonidentical cake on top of the first layer and spread ½ cup frosting. Top with the final cake layer, and frost the entire cake.

The Kids Will Still Have a Great Time

How do you make your child's birthday party special, where the kids can still have a great time—and not leave with clogged arteries and a million calories eaten? Here are some main meal ideas: 6-foot turkey or roast beef sub sandwiches, BBQ chicken platters, cold cut platters, finger sandwiches: PBJ, turkey, tuna, hamburgers and low-fat hot dogs, pizza, and salad. And to accompany those meals try: Low-fat popcorn, baked chips, nuts and raisins (not for toddler parties—these can be choking foods), dark chocolate, pretzels, 100-calorie packs, S'mores, and fresh fruit salad.

The Chorus Line Cake

A healthy twist on an ice cream cake—that looks like a beautiful top hat!

INGREDIENTS | **SERVES 30–36**

3 pints low-fat ice cream, assorted flavors, softened
Nonstick cooking spray
2 packages white cake mix
2 to 3 cups low-fat whipped topping
Foil paper for decorating

1. The day before assembling the cake, line three 8-inch round cake pans with wax paper. Place one pint of softened ice cream in each pan, and spread evenly. Cover each pan with aluminum foil and place back in the freezer.

2. On the day of assembly, remove ice cream from the pans, and wrap in plastic wrap. Place back in the freezer for the time being.

3. Spray four 8-inch pans with nonstick cooking spray. Also spray a 12-inch round cake pan with nonstick cooking spray.

4. Preheat oven to 350°F.

5. Prepare 2 cake mix packages as directed, and separate them into the four round cake pans, a little less in the 12-inch pan. Bake as directed, though the 12-inch cake should be ready in less time, as it should have less batter.

6. When ready to assemble, take a freezer-safe platter, and place the 12-inch cake on the platter. Then, alternate ice cream layers with cake layers, starting with an ice cream layer, ending with a cake layer. Smooth all edges, and place top hat cake back in the freezer.

7. When ready to serve, take cake out of freezer. Spread whipped topping all around cake, including the brim, until smooth. Decorate as desired.

8. Place back in freezer for 30 minutes.

9. Take it out about 15 minutes prior to serving, so that cutting it can be easier.

"Hats Off to Mother" Cake

Treat Mom on her holiday to a beautiful hat cake—the best part, she didn't have to bake it herself! What a fun recipe for the kids to take control of.

INGREDIENTS | SERVES 15–20

Nonstick cooking spray
1 package white cake mix
3 whole eggs
2 egg whites
¾ cup canola oil
¾ cup low-sugar apricot nectar
3 teaspoons almond extract

Lemon Icing:

½ cup trans-fat-free margarine
4 cups confectioners' sugar
2 teaspoons lemon extract
Pinch of salt
4 tablespoons heavy cream
Assorted candy to decorate

1. Preheat oven to 325°F.

2. Spray nonstick cooking spray and lightly flour a rimmed 12-inch round pizza or cake pan, and a medium metal or oven-proof baking bowl.

3. In a large mixing bowl, combine cake mix, eggs, egg whites, oil, nectar, and almond extract. Beat at medium speed for 4 to 5 minutes.

4. Divide the batter between the pan and the bowl.

5. Bake the large pan for 20 to 25 minutes, and bake the bowl for 45 to 50 minutes (both are ready when a toothpick inserted in the center comes out dry).

6. Let the cakes sit for 5 to 10 minutes before removing them from pans. Cool completely.

7. Prepare icing: In a mixing bowl, beat margarine and add 1 cup of confectioners' sugar slowly.

8. Add lemon extract and salt.

9. Add remainder of confectioners' sugar.

10. Add the heavy cream, and blend until icing texture forms.

11. To assemble the cake, place large round cake on platter. Place the bowl cake in the center of the larger one. Spread icing until cake is completely covered. Decorate cake with candy.

Perfectly Peach Tart

This fruity tart can be made any time of the year for a refreshing treat. Substitute other fruits for peaches, like pears or apricots. Fresh fruit would work, too.

INGREDIENTS | SERVES 15

Nonstick cooking spray
½ cup trans-fat-free margarine
¼ cup sugar
1 teaspoon vanilla extract
1 egg
1 cup all-purpose flour
1 teaspoon baking powder
½ teaspoon salt
1 (29-ounce) can peaches in own juice, drained
3 tablespoons sugar
1 teaspoon cinnamon

1. Preheat oven to 350°F.

2. Spray cooking spray in 9-inch springform pan.

3. In a large bowl, beat margarine and sugar until light and fluffy.

4. Add the egg and vanilla extract. Beat well.

5. Add flour, baking powder, and salt to margarine mixture. Blend well.

6. Spread the dough over the bottom and 1 inch up the sides of the pan. Arrange peach slices in "spoke" fashion over the dough. Sprinkle with cinnamon and sugar.

7. Bake at 350°F for 30 to 35 minutes, or until edges are golden brown. Cool 10 minutes and remove sides of the pan.

Pumpkin Cake in a Cone

Pumpkin cake made in an ice cream cone is one of the most creative favorites—and hiding in the cone is a vast amount of beta-carotene-cancer-fighters—the pumpkin!

INGREDIENTS | SERVES 18

1 package prepared carrot-cake mix
1 cup canned solid pumpkin
3 eggs
⅓ cup canola oil
¼ cup water
1 teaspoon vanilla extract
2 tablespoons brown sugar
1 teaspoon ground cinnamon
18 cake cones

Frosting:

⅔ cup confectioners' sugar
¼ cup canned solid pumpkin
¾ teaspoon vanilla extract
1 (8-ounce) package low-fat cream cheese

1. Preheat oven to 350°F.

2. In a large mixing bowl, combine the carrot cake mix, pumpkin, eggs, oil, water, vanilla extract, brown sugar, and cinnamon. Beat with an electric mixer for 2 to 3 minutes, until well blended.

3. Line up cake cones, and spoon batter among the 18 cones, filling about ⅔ to ¾ full.

4. Bake in the oven for 25 to 30 minutes, until toothpick comes out dry. Cool on a wire rack.

5. To prepare icing, mix together confectioners' sugar, ¼ cup pumpkin, vanilla extract, and cream cheese. Beat with electric mixer, until frosting is smooth. Spread each cone with frosting.

A Versatile Vegetable

Pumpkin might not be the first vegetable you would think to introduce to your children. Maybe it should be! In a soup, a pie, a hot casserole, or even a shake, pumpkin is one of the healthiest vegetables around. An incredible source of antioxidants, potassium (remember the muscle builders), and much-needed vitamins, being that bright orange color makes it a very special vegetable. The red, yellow, and orange vegetables are packed with nutrition power.

Goldilocks and the Strawberry Bear

This is the sweetest of desserts. Bear-shaped molds can be found in kitchenware stores or party supply houses. The dessert can also be prepared in individual dessert bowls.

INGREDIENTS | SERVES 6

1 (6-ounce) package sugar-free, fat-free strawberry-flavored Jell-O

2 cups boiling water

1½ cups cold water

Bear-shaped molds

1 cup low-fat whipped topping

1 teaspoon vanilla extract

1 medium banana

½ cup strawberries, hulled and sliced

Strawberries for garnish (optional)

1 In a medium bowl, dissolve gelatin in boiling water. Stir in cold water.

2. Spoon gelatin into the bear faces, to fill them. Remove 2 cups of the prepared gelatin to another mixing bowl, and refrigerate. Chill the bear molds, and the larger bowl of gelatin, until gelatin is set.

3. When the larger bowl of gelatin is set, fold in whipped topping and vanilla.

4. Spoon whipped topping mixture into molds (on top of the bear gelatin) and refrigerate until set but not firm, about 15 minutes.

5. Slice banana, then add strawberry and banana slices to the top of the mold. Cover bears and chill until set completely, about 4 hours.

6. Unmold onto dessert plates. Garnish plates with strawberries, if desired.

Stars and Stripes Sundae

*Substitute blueberries for blackberries, raspberries for strawberries—
and the ice cream can alternate with a strawberry sorbet!*

INGREDIENTS | **SERVES 4**

1 pound low-fat pound cake
Star cookie cutter
1 pint low-fat vanilla ice cream or frozen yogurt
1 pint fresh strawberries
1 pint fresh blueberries
Red, white, and blue sprinkles

1. Slice pound cake, and using the cookie cutters, cut out 4 to 8 star shapes.

2. On a dessert plate, place ½ cup low-fat ice cream/ frozen yogurt on the center of the plate.

3. Surrounding the ice cream, add fruit and star-shaped cake to decorate. Cover with sprinkles.

CHAPTER 13

Planning That Healthful Holiday

Apple-Honey-Glazed Turkey Breast

This is a great recipe, not only used for holiday time, but for a nice family meal. Turkey seems to be a poultry choice many children enjoy!

INGREDIENTS | SERVES 10

1 tablespoon canola oil

⅓ cup honey

1 tablespoon dry mustard

1 (6-ounce) can frozen apple juice concentrate

2 teaspoons salt

1 teaspoon pepper

1 clove garlic, sliced

4- to 5-pound turkey breast

Always a Holiday Favorite

As soon as the skin is removed, turkey, especially the breast, is a lean source of protein, low in fat, tasty, and certainly versatile. Cook the carcass up in a soup, make a turkey salad with low-fat mayonnaise, or slice up leftovers into a whole wheat baguette.

1. Preheat oven to 325°F.

2. Combine oil, honey, mustard, and apple juice concentrate in a small bowl. Stir well and set aside.

3. Rub salt, pepper, and garlic onto turkey. Place turkey on a rack in a roasting pan. Cover with foil and bake for 1 hour.

4. Uncover, add the honey-mustard glaze and bake for an additional 1 hour.

5. Let cool for 10 minutes.

Guiltless Gravy

A wonderful low-fat gravy courtesy of the National Turkey Federation.

INGREDIENTS | SERVES 16–20

4 cups turkey stock and defatted pan juices

¼ cup cornstarch

¼ cup water

Salt and pepper to taste

The Anatomy of Gravy

Gravy—a high-fat cooking juice, generally very tasty, especially when using high-fat meats. Most gravies are deadly to the arteries, full of saturated fats. An increased intake of saturated fats means very clogged arteries and very high blood cholesterol levels. Commercial gravies can contain up to 200–400 calories per serving. Try this lighter, healthier gravy. Remember, this is all a matter of what your family gets used to.

1. In a large saucepan, over medium heat, bring stock and pan juices to a boil.

2. Meanwhile, blend the cornstarch and water until smooth.

3. Whisking constantly, slowly add the cornstarch mixture to the boiling pan juices. Continue to stir until gravy has thickened.

4. Season to taste with salt and pepper.

Baked Plantains

A baked version of a typically fried Latin delight! They won't know the difference!

INGREDIENTS | SERVES 8

4 ripe plantains
Nonstick cooking spray
½ cup orange juice
Cinnamon to taste
3 tablespoons sugar (or Splenda for children over 10)

A Sweet Latin Favorite

The difference between a plantain and a banana: though they are both in the banana family, a plantain is often known as a starchy potato in Caribbean and Western African countries. A plantain tastes different at each stage of development. Before it ripens, it tastes more starchy and "tuber-like." While it ripens, it becomes much sweeter. Though known for being fried, plantains are quite delicious baked, as the recipe notes.

1. Preheat oven to 350°F.

2. Slice each plantain into 4 pieces.

3. Spray baking sheet with nonstick cooking spray. Place plantains flat in a shallow baking dish.

4. Pour orange juice over plantains.

5. Sprinkle with sugar and cinnamon.

6. Spray the top of the plantains again with cooking spray.

7. Bake for 20 minutes or until tender.

Holiday Tiramisu

A healthier version of a wonderful and popular dessert. It is light and fluffy—and even better the next day!

INGREDIENTS | SERVES 8–10

1½ cups cold low-fat milk

1 (8-ounce) package low-fat cream cheese, softened

2 to 3 tablespoons instant decaffeinated coffee, prepared

1 (4-ounce) package fat-free, sugar-free vanilla pudding

2 cups low-fat whipped topping

24 Lady Fingers, split

½ cup hot water

4 teaspoons instant coffee

½ teaspoon unsweetened cocoa

1. Place ½ cup of the milk and cream cheese in a blender or food processor with a steel blade. Process until well blended.

2. Gradually add remaining 1 cup of milk and the prepared decaf coffee.

3. Blend in pudding mix and fold in the whipped topping.

4. Line the bottom and sides of a 9-inch pie plate with 24 to 36 Lady Finger halves.

5. Mix water and instant coffee. Brush coffee mixture on Lady Fingers.

6. Spoon half the pudding mixture over the Lady Fingers. Top with remaining Lady Fingers; brush with remaining coffee mixture. Again, top with remaining pudding mixture and cover.

7. Refrigerate for a minimum of 4 hours, or overnight. Dust the top with cocoa before serving.

Savory Stuffing Balls

What a hit at the holiday table—kid-friendly and a real twist on a holiday favorite.

INGREDIENTS | SERVES 8

Nonstick cooking spray

1 pound ground veal

Salt and pepper to taste

1 (6-ounce) package stuffing mix

1 cup cranberry sauce

1 egg

1 cup water

¼ cup trans-fat-free margarine

A Really Neat Party Stuffing!

A traditional high-fat, high-carbohydrate legend, regular stuffing helps to take the calorie level of Thanksgiving upwards of 1,000 for the entire meal. Think smaller—start with these little stuffing balls. They also incorporate cranberries, full of cancer-fighting phytochemicals. You can even consider using ground veal, a lower-fat meat.

1. Preheat oven to 350°F.

2. Spray nonstick cooking spray in a frying pan. Cook ground veal until cooked through. Add salt and pepper to veal. Drain excess liquid.

3. Combine veal with dry stuffing mix in a large mixing bowl.

4. Add cranberry sauce, egg, and water.

5. Form mixture into small balls (approximately 16).

6. Spray nonstick cooking spray onto baking sheet. Place stuffing balls on baking sheet. Brush margarine onto the top of the balls.

7. Bake for 20 minutes.

Medallions of Glazed Pork

Use this simple, tasty recipe with chicken, turkey, or beef medallions, too. As an alternative to high-calorie, high-sugar maple syrup, use lower-sugar pancake syrup.

INGREDIENTS | SERVES 4

1½ pounds pork tenderloin, sliced
4 tablespoons maple syrup
4 tablespoons balsamic vinegar
4 teaspoons Dijon mustard
4 tablespoons olive oil

Pork Tenderloin Makes the Grade

Not all pork cuts are created equal. The loin of the pork, or pork tenderloin, is the leanest of the pork products—as lean as skinless chicken. Pork chops, bacon, and ham do not fall into this category. Choose pork wisely, and cook it through.

1. Remove fat from pork tenderloin. Slice into medallions with a 1-inch thickness. Place between parchment or wax paper, and pound to ½-inch thickness.

2. Whisk maple syrup, balsamic vinegar, and Dijon mustard together.

3. Heat olive oil in a frying pan over high heat. Brown the pork medallions for 2 to 3 minutes on each side. Reduce heat to low. Pour maple syrup mixture on top of medallions. Cover and allow to cook for 3 to 4 additional minutes, until cooked thoroughly.

Holiday Potato Wedges

Simple dishes can be quite popular, too. You can always choose different varieties of potatoes—there are many out there.

INGREDIENTS | SERVES 8

4 large white baking potatoes
½ cup low-fat Italian salad dressing
Nonstick cooking spray
2 tablespoons minced garlic
½ cup grated Parmesan cheese
2 tablespoons fresh parsley, chopped

Never Peel Potatoes Again

The most nutrient-rich part of a white potato—the skin. When preparing potatoes for your family, whether baked, pan-fried wedges, even mashed, leave the skin on the potato. It is full of fiber. The potato itself is a real winner—enriched with potassium and vitamin C; a great tuber!

1. Preheat oven to 375°F.

2. Cut potatoes in wedges. Toss potatoes in salad dressing.

3. Spray large baking sheet with nonstick cooking spray. Place wedges on baking sheet. Sprinkle garlic on potatoes.

4. Bake 45 to 60 minutes, turning potatoes after 20 to 30 minutes.

5. With 5 minutes remaining in baking time, sprinkle with Parmesan cheese and parsley.

Hot Spinach-Artichoke Dip

What a delicious hot dip for either fresh vegetables, whole grain crackers, or baked tortilla chips.

INGREDIENTS | SERVES 12

1½ cups low-fat mayonnaise

1½ cups grated Parmesan cheese

1 (10-ounce) package chopped spinach, thawed and drained

1 medium onion, chopped finely

1 teaspoon garlic powder

1 (14-ounce) can artichoke hearts, drained and chopped

1 teaspoon paprika

1. Preheat oven to 350°F.

2. In a small mixing bowl, combine the mayonnaise and Parmesan cheese.

3. Mix in the spinach, onion, garlic, and artichoke hearts.

4. Pour into a casserole dish or glass pie dish. Sprinkle top with paprika for color.

5. Bake for 50 minutes.

Tangy Taco Dip

A unique dip for the holidays—test your spice tolerance with the level of taco sauce you decide to use.

INGREDIENTS | SERVES 8–10

1 (1-ounce) package taco mix (powdered)

1 teaspoon garlic powder

1 (16-ounce) can fat-free refried beans

½ (12 to 16-ounce) jar mild, medium, or hot taco sauce

1 cup low-fat sour cream

1 cup low-fat Cheddar cheese, shredded

1. Preheat oven to 350°F.

2. In a casserole dish, mix dry taco mix and garlic powder with fat-free refried beans. Add layer of taco sauce. Then a layer of sour cream.

3. Top with Cheddar cheese. Bake for 30 to 40 minutes.

There Are Many Varieties of *Baked* Chips

It is no longer necessary to buy regular chips—most of them come baked, and taste just as good. When making dishes like nachos or tacos, use the baked chips for the nachos, and use a soft taco, rather than a hard, fried one. Save lots of calories, and lots of fat.

Festive Vegetable Cheesecake

Prepare this appetizer ahead of time; its very easy to reheat when ready to serve.

INGREDIENTS | SERVES 18

Nonstick cooking spray
1 tablespoon plain bread crumbs
1 tablespoon canola oil
1 cup zucchini, shredded
1 cup carrots, shredded
¼ cup red peppers, chopped
2 (8-ounce) packages whipped cream cheese
2 eggs
½ cup low-fat sour cream
½ cup grated Parmesan cheese
½ cup fresh parsley, chopped
4 tablespoons minced garlic
½ teaspoon dried thyme

1. Preheat oven to 350°F.

2. Spray a springform pan with nonstick cooking spray. Dust with 1 to 2 tablespoons bread crumbs.

3. In a large skillet, heat oil on low heat. Sauté the zucchini, carrots, and peppers. Cook until softened. Allow to cool.

4. In a large mixing bowl, beat the cream cheese until fluffy.

5. Add eggs, sour cream, Parmesan cheese, parsley, garlic, thyme, and vegetable mixture. Pour into the springform pan.

6. Place this pan into a larger pan filled about half way with water.

7. Bake in the water bath for 50 minutes. Cool before serving.

Those 2,000-Calorie Holiday Dinners—a Thing of the Past!

It is not a difficult task to create the habit of "tweaking" some of those favorite family recipes, and see if anyone really tastes a difference. In this recipe, using regular sour cream, cream cheese and eggs (and olive oil, though the healthiest of those fats) brings the total fat content of the recipe to approximately 115 grams of fat. By making the changes, the fat is cut down by about half. Give it a try!

Scrumptious Yeehaw Cornbread Muffins

These are light and moist, and can be prepared in muffin cups or as loaves of cornbread.

INGREDIENTS | SERVES 24

Nonstick cooking spray

3 cups cornmeal

1 cup all-purpose flour

6 tablespoons sugar

2 tablespoons baking powder

1 teaspoon salt

1 cup low-fat milk

1 cup low-fat sour cream

¼ cup trans-fat-free margarine, melted

¼ cup canola oil

3 whole eggs

1 egg white

2 cups canned creamed corn

1. Preheat oven to 400°F.

2. Spray two muffin trays with nonstick cooking spray.

3. Mix the cornmeal, flour, sugar, baking powder, and salt in a large mixing bowl.

4. Combine the milk, sour cream, melted margarine, canola oil, eggs, and egg white in a medium mixing bowl. Mix well.

5. Add milk mixture to the cornmeal mixture and stir.

6. Add in the creamed corn.

7. Bake for 30 to 40 minutes, or until toothpick comes out dry.

A Lighter Cornbread

For many, cornbread is part of a traditional holiday meal or a fabulous BBQ favorite. Cornbread can be quite high in fat, though generally can have a little more fiber, due to the corn, a higher-fiber vegetable. This recipe is a lighter, lower-fat version—and is wonderful. See if your family can tell the difference.

Holiday Blueberry Coffee Cake

A wonderful and light dessert after that heavy holiday meal! Can substitute dried cranberries for an even more festive cake.

INGREDIENTS | SERVES 10–12

Nonstick cooking spray
¾ cup sugar
½ cup canola oil
2 eggs
¾ cup plain low-fat yogurt
½ cup low-fat milk
1 teaspoon vanilla
2 cups flour
¾ teaspoon salt
2 teaspoons baking powder
2 cups fresh blueberries

Topping:
½ cup sugar
⅓ cup flour
1 teaspoon cinnamon
¼ cup trans-fat-free margarine, cut in chunks

1. Preheat oven to 375°F.

2. Spray a 9-inch square baking pan with nonstick cooking spray.

3. Mix sugar, oil, eggs, yogurt, vanilla, and milk in a large bowl.

4. Mix flour, salt, and baking powder together in a medium bowl.

5. Add flour mixture to yogurt mixture.

6. Mix in blueberries carefully.

7. Prepare topping by mixing sugar, flour, cinnamon, and chunks of margarine together, until it resembles a crumb topping.

8. Pour batter into baking pan. Sprinkle crumb topping.

9. Bake 35 to 40 minutes.

Are Those Blueberries Magical?

Research has found that blueberries have properties that make them one of the healthiest fruits around. Certainly a versatile fruit, fresh or frozen, they can be used in cakes, muffins, milkshakes, toppings for low-fat yogurt, jams, and pies. Their incredible nutrients include vitamin K, vitamin C, antioxidants, manganese, and fiber. Studies continue on the intake of blueberries possibly playing a role in less risk of Alzheimer's Disease, macular degeneration of the eye, stroke, cancer, and high blood pressure.

Honey-Glazed Veal Roast

The veal is tender and wonderful—cook a turkey breast, a pork tenderloin, or duck or Cornish hen for a unique twist.

INGREDIENTS | **SERVES 6–8**

1 medium onion, chopped
3 tablespoons brown sugar
1 tablespoon dried basil
1 tablespoon dried thyme
2 teaspoons salt
2 teaspoons pepper
½ cup reduced-sodium soy sauce
½ cup reduced-sodium teriyaki sauce
1 cup honey
½ cup Dijon mustard
3 pounds lean veal roast
Nonstick cooking spray

1. Preheat oven to 400°F.

2. In a large mixing bowl, combine onions, brown sugar, basil, thyme, salt, pepper, soy sauce, teriyaki sauce, honey, and Dijon mustard. Rub mixture on the roast.

3. Spray nonstick cooking spray in a large roasting pan (or cover bottom with aluminum foil).

4. Place veal roast in roasting pan and bake for 50 minutes to 1¼ hours, depending on doneness.

Perfect Holiday Prima Pasta

Why not serve pasta as a starch for a change? This is a light and healthy pasta—substitute any of the children's favorite vegetables.

INGREDIENTS | **SERVES 6–8**

1 (12-ounce) box whole wheat tortellini or rotini noodles
1 pound broccoli rabe, chopped
2 tablespoons olive oil
1 medium onion, chopped finely
2 to 3 cloves garlic, chopped finely
2 cups jarred marinara sauce
¼ to ½ cup Romano cheese, grated
¼ to ½ cup Parmesan cheese, grated

1. In a large saucepan, boil water and cook pasta according to package directions.

2. In the final 3 minutes of cooking the pasta, put the broccoli rabe in the boiling water.

3. In a large skillet, heat olive oil on low heat. Sauté onion and garlic until softened.

4. Add pasta and broccoli rabe to the skillet, tossing constantly.

5. Add in marinara sauce, and cook an additional 2 to 3 minutes, until sauce is hot. Prior to serving, sprinkle with cheeses.

"French" Country Stuffing

Holidays would not be the same without stuffing. Prepare stuffing outside the turkey, for a healthier stuffing (without fat drippings from the turkey). You can substitute cornbread, whole wheat bread, or a combination thereof in lieu of the French bread suggested.

INGREDIENTS | SERVES 10

4 cups 1-day-old French bread, cut in 1-inch cubes.

4 tablespoons olive oil, divided

1 tablespoon dried thyme

Salt and pepper to taste

2 tablespoons minced garlic

1 medium onion, chopped finely

1 cup chopped celery

1 cup dried cranberries

1 cup chopped pecans

1 to 1½ cups chicken broth

1. Preheat oven to 350°F.

2. In a large mixing bowl, place the bread and 2 tablespoons of olive oil, thyme, salt, pepper, and garlic. Blend until well mixed.

3. Spread the mixture on 2 baking sheets, and place in oven for 15 to 20 minutes, just to toast the bread mixture. Shake the pans on occasion to toss.

4. In a small skillet, add the remaining 2 tablespoons of olive oil, and sauté onions and celery until tender.

5. Return the bread to the large mixing bowl, and add the onions, celery, cranberries, and pecans.

6. Drip the chicken broth over the mixture to moisten, and mix well.

7. Transfer to a large casserole dish.

8. Bake, covered, for 45 minutes or until golden brown.

Vegetable Cutlets

A simple and tasty way to get those veggies in on a holiday. Can substitute any of the children's favorites, such as broccoli, squash, etc.

INGREDIENTS | SERVES 12

2 tablespoons olive oil

1 cup red pepper, minced

1 cup yellow pepper, minced

1½ cups carrots, grated

1 (10-ounce) package frozen chopped spinach, defrosted, liquid removed

3 medium potatoes, peeled, boiled, and mashed

1 large onion, chopped finely

3 eggs, lightly beaten

1½ teaspoons salt

Black pepper to taste

1 cup seasoned bread crumbs

Nonstick cooking spray

Looking Like a Pancake

Already this may "go over well" with the young ones. It doesn't look like a vegetable; it looks like a pancake. A light and out-of-the-ordinary holiday veggie, everyone seems to like this unusual dish.

1. In a medium skillet, heat olive oil on low heat. Sauté the peppers until very tender, about 15 minutes.

2. Place all the remaining ingredients in a large mixing bowl. Mix well.

3. Add the peppers to the bowl, and mix well. Batter should be thick.

4. Place in refrigerator for several hours, or even overnight.

5. Preheat oven to 350°F. Bring batter to room temperature before cooking.

6. When ready, form patties using about ¼ cup of vegetable mixture for each patty.

7. Spray nonstick cooking spray on large baking sheets. Place patties on baking sheets and spray top of patties with cooking spray.

8. Bake for 10 to 15 minutes, turn the patties, and bake for another 5 to 7 minutes.

Delightful Tiramisu Trifle

Another tantalizing, light holiday dessert, made a little more healthful. Feel free to change the flavors of the pudding (for instance, banana), change the flavor of the coffee, and the types of berries. Fun to prepare, too.

INGREDIENTS | SERVES 16

1 (8-ounce) package low-fat cream cheese, softened
3 cups low-fat milk, cold
2 (4-ounce) packages fat-free, sugar-free vanilla instant pudding
½ cup instant coffee, brewed
1 teaspoon vanilla extract
8 ounces low-fat whipped topping
50 reduced-fat Nilla Wafers
2 to 3 squares semi-sweet chocolate, grated
1 cup fresh mixed berries

1. With a mixer, beat cream cheese until smooth and creamy.

2. Slowly add milk, pudding mix, brewed coffee, and vanilla extract.

3. Add 2 cups whipped topping and mix.

4. In a trifle bowl, layer bottom and sides with 25 Nilla Wafers.

5. Add half the pudding mixture, and half the grated chocolate.

6. Repeat the layers, starting with the wafers.

7. Top with remaining whipped topping and berries.

8. Refrigerate several hours before serving.

Jolly Jell-O Mold

Lots of variations available here: can substitute Jell-O flavors, juice flavors, and types of canned fruit.

INGREDIENTS | SERVES 10

2 (4-ounce) packages fat-free, sugar-free strawberry-flavored Jell-O

2½ cups boiling water

1 cup orange juice

1 (8-ounce) can crushed pineapple in own juice, drained

1 (11-ounce) can mandarin orange segments in own juice, drained

Nonstick cooking spray

1. Pour Jell-O mix into large mixing bowl. Stir boiling water into Jell-O. Mix for about 3 to 4 minutes, until well blended.

2. Stir in orange juice. Refrigerate 2 hours until Jell-O is thickened.

3. Add in pineapple and mandarin oranges, and mix.

4. Spray nonstick cooking spray into Jell-O mold pan. Add Jell-O mixture and refrigerate about 4 hours, or until firm. Remove from the mold and place on a serving dish.

Delectable Rice Pudding Casserole

Be adventurous (and healthful) and try using half white rice and half brown rice.

INGREDIENTS | SERVES 6

½ cup white rice

3 eggs, well beaten

4 cups low-fat milk

1 teaspoon vanilla extract

3 tablespoons trans-fat-free margarine

⅓ cup sugar

¼ teaspoon salt

Nonstick cooking spray

Pinch of nutmeg

1. Preheat oven to 350°F.

2. Cook rice according to package directions.

3. In a medium mixing bowl, combine cooked rice and eggs, milk, vanilla, margarine, sugar, and salt.

4. In a casserole dish, spray nonstick cooking spray. Pour rice pudding into casserole dish. Sprinkle lightly with nutmeg.

5. Bake for 1 to 1½ hours.

Awesome Apple Pie

A healthful dessert—especially if you only take a few bites of the crust! Try preparing with different fruits, as well, such as fresh peaches or pears. This is so easy!

INGREDIENTS | SERVES 8–10

4 apples, peeled, cored, and sliced thinly

½ cup sugar

1 teaspoon vanilla extract

1 teaspoon cinnamon

2 tablespoons trans-fat-free margarine

Pinch of ground nutmeg

1 (12-inch round) prepared pie crust

1. Preheat oven to 375°F.

2. In a medium saucepan, combine apples, sugar, vanilla, cinnamon, margarine, and nutmeg. Heat on low heat until the apples are soft and the filling is thick, about 20 to 30 minutes.

3. Fill the crust with apple filling.

4. Bake for 40 to 45 minutes, until apples are bubbling.

Pie Crusts Are Usually Deadly

Many pie crusts, commercial ones or the ones you prepare at home, generally taste wonderful due to the fact that they are made with highly saturated fats, lard, and trans fats. Either substitute ingredients for your own pie crusts, or when eating that beautiful pie, just take a bite or two of the crust, and eat the filling—it's bound to be healthier that way!

Famous Filet Mignon

What a family favorite this is—and has been for many years. One of the leanest cuts of beef, filet mignon is always a big hit for the holidays.

INGREDIENTS | SERVES 14–18

7 pounds beef tenderloin

2 to 3 teaspoons salt

2 to 3 teaspoons pepper

1 medium onion, diced

2 to 3 cloves garlic, crushed

2 to 3 teaspoons paprika

Tenderloin—One of the Leanest Cuts of Beef

A special occasion treat (it is kind of expensive), tenderloin is so very delicious, and quite lean. In a 6-ounce serving, there are 350 calories, 15 grams of total fat, and interestingly, as much saturated fat (unhealthier version) as there is monounsaturated fat (healthier version)—6 grams.

1. Preheat oven to 325°F.

2. Place the tenderloin on a baking sheet, with large piece of aluminum foil underneath (large enough for beef to be covered completely after seasoning).

3. Season the meat with dry rub of salt, pepper, onion, and garlic on all sides. Sprinkle with paprika. Seal the foil around the meat.

4. Bake for approximately 2 to 2½ hours, until desired doneness.

Orange Marshmallow Ambrosia

A kid-friendly dessert, a little lighter and healthier! Substitute other favorite canned fruits, if desired.

INGREDIENTS | SERVES 6

4 cups bite-size marshmallows

1 pint low-fat sour cream

1 (15-ounce) can mixed fruit cocktail, in own juice

1 small can mandarin oranges, in own juice

7 ounces shredded coconut

1. In a large mixing bowl, combine marshmallows, sour cream, canned fruits, and coconut.

2. Transfer to a serving dish. Cover and refrigerate for 1 hour, and serve.

What Is the Glycemic Index?

The glycemic index is a number given to a food rating the speed at which a food increases the blood sugar level. It is important to keep blood sugar levels normal. When they are not normal, you can be dealing with diabetes or hypoglycemia. Known for their high glycemic index are white flour, white potatoes, and sugary desserts. You should keep white flour foods to a minimal amount (they generally don't have great nutritional benefits anyway).

Sweet Strawberry Soup

A very refreshing cold soup—substitute low-fat yogurt for sour cream for a higher protein dish; if the white wine doesn't appeal to you, consider light cranberry juice.

INGREDIENTS | SERVES 6

1 pint strawberries, fresh or frozen

1 cup low-fat sour cream

1 cup low-fat milk

¼ cup sugar

1 teaspoon vanilla extract

2 tablespoons white wine

1. Process berries in blender or food processor until puréed.

2. Add sour cream, milk, sugar, vanilla, and white wine, and pulse until well blended.

3. Chill before serving.

Chilled Soups—an Unusual Appetizer or Dessert

Delicious and different, offer cold soups to your children, and to guests. Not only a beautiful presentation, but usually stocked with great nutrients, depending on the fruit or vegetable you make the soup with. Berries and mangos are full of antioxidants and vitamin C. Cold squash or pumpkin soup is a wonderful addition to any meal.

Apple and Cranberry Crumble Tart

Serve warm, giving the family sweet fruits in a delicious treat—alternate the berries!
Even serve with low-fat frozen yogurt for that à la mode feeling!

INGREDIENTS | SERVES 8

½ cup flour

¼ cup plus 2 tablespoons sugar

¼ cup dark brown sugar

¼ cup trans-fat-free margarine, cut in pieces

6 cups Granny Smith or Red Delicious apples, peeled, cored, and sliced

1 cup fresh or frozen cranberries

½ cup orange juice

1 teaspoon vanilla extract

1 tablespoon cornstarch

Nonstick cooking spray

1. Preheat oven to 375°F.

2. Combine flour, ¼ cup of the sugar, brown sugar, and margarine in a small bowl. Mix with a fork, until crumbly.

3. In a large mixing bowl, combine apples and cranberries, remaining sugar, orange juice, vanilla, and cornstarch. Mix well.

4. In a square baking dish, spray nonstick cooking spray. Pour the fruit mixture into the baking dish, and top with flour mixture.

5. Bake for 40 to 45 minutes.

Thanksgiving Sweet Potato Side Dish

Close your eyes and think of sweet potatoes. What comes to mind is Turkey Day, no? Prepare this often,
even when not a holiday—it is a nice healthy dish—taking in those wonderful sweet potatoes.

INGREDIENTS | SERVES 15–20

10 large sweet potatoes, peeled

2 cups trans-fat-free margarine melted

Salt to taste

3 large eggs

2 cans large crushed pineapple with the liquid

1½ cups brown sugar

1 bag large marshmallows

1. In large pot boil potatoes until soft.

2. Drain liquid and add margarine, salt, eggs, pineapple, and brown sugar. Mash all the ingredients together. Place in large glass or aluminum pan.

3. Bake in 350°F oven for 30 minutes

4. Place marshmallows on top in rows about 2 inches apart and bake for 10 more minutes until melted.

5. Serve warm.

Cherry Christmas Cake

A festive holiday favorite—it can become a blueberry, cranberry, or strawberry Christmas cake, too.

INGREDIENTS | SERVES 15–20

1 cup sugar

2 eggs

½ cup canola oil

1 teaspoon vanilla extract

2½ cups all-purpose flour

2½ teaspoons baking powder

⅓ cup orange juice

Nonstick cooking spray

1 large (15-ounce) can cherry pie filling

Streusel topping:

⅓ cup sugar

2 teaspoons cinnamon

½ cup chopped walnuts (optional)

1. Preheat oven to 350°F.

2. In a large mixing bowl, beat sugar and eggs until pale in color, about 1 to 2 minutes.

3. Add oil and vanilla and mix well.

4. In a separate bowl, combine flour and baking powder.

5. Add the flour mixture to the eggs and sugar.

6. Slowly add orange juice. Continue to beat until batter is smooth and thick.

7. Prepare streusel topping by blending sugar, cinnamon, and walnuts.

8. In a 13" × 9" glass dish, spray nonstick cooking spray. Pour half the batter into the baking dish.

9. Top with cherry pie filling; sprinkle with some streusel.

10. Spread remainder of batter on top. Sprinkle remaining streusel topping on top.

11. Bake 40 minutes or until toothpick comes out clean.

CHAPTER 14

Planning a Healthy Party

Sparkling Strawberry Punch

Alcohol-free, of course, but the start to a great party! Go easy, this one is still loaded with lots of calories.

INGREDIENTS | SERVES 10–12

1 pound fresh strawberries, hulled and halved

1 (16-ounce) can frozen lemonade concentrate, thawed

1 (15-ounce) can crushed pineapple, in its own juice

2 to 3 quarts ginger ale

Crushed ice

Mint sprigs, optional

1. In a blender, puree the strawberries. Add lemonade concentrate and pineapple to blender.

2. Pour into a medium-sized punch bowl, adding ginger ale and crushed ice.

3. Garnish with mint sprigs, if desired.

A Great Party!

From start to finish, this will be a spectacular party—for the teenagers, especially. They can pick and choose the items they want to serve—this chapter has awesome party foods. Best of all, they can prepare most of them, too.

Amazing Avocado Salsa

This is a terrific salsa; the avocado add-in really gives it that healthy kick! Serve it with fresh crudités, whole wheat pita triangles, baked tortilla chips, or an assortment of whole grain crackers.

INGREDIENTS | SERVES 4

1 small chili pepper, chopped

1 tablespoon fresh lime juice

2 ripe avocados, peeled, pitted, and chopped

1 (15-ounce) can diced tomatoes, drained completely

1 garlic clove, minced

¼ cup fresh cilantro

Salt and pepper to taste

Tortilla chips, baked

1. In a medium mixing bowl, place chopped chili pepper. Add lime juice and avocado. Mash these ingredients with a potato masher until texture is chunky.

2. Mix tomatoes, garlic, and cilantro into the avocado mixture.

3. Season with salt and pepper.

4. Serve with baked tortilla chips or assorted crackers.

Cheesy Artichoke Squares

Another finger food that's a great little appetizer. Alternate your favorite cheeses.

INGREDIENTS | SERVES 12–16

Nonstick cooking spray

2 tablespoons olive oil

1 medium onion, finely chopped

2 teaspoons minced garlic

1 (15-ounce) can artichoke hearts, drained

1 (8-ounce) package low-fat sharp Cheddar cheese, shredded

4 large eggs

½ cup Italian-style bread crumbs

Salt and pepper to taste

1. Preheat oven to 350°F.

2. Spray an 8-inch square baking dish with nonstick cooking spray.

3. In a medium skillet over low heat, heat the olive oil. Add the chopped onion and garlic, and cook until tender.

4. In a blender or food processor, chop artichoke hearts.

5. Transfer artichoke hearts to a medium mixing bowl, add sautéed onions and garlic, and remaining ingredients. Mix well.

6. Pour into the baking dish, and bake 45 minutes, or until golden brown around the edges.

7. Remove from oven and leave in the pan to cool, about 1 hour.

8. Cut into squares (about 1-inch) and serve immediately.

Feta Cheese and Pita Dip

A delicious dip—or even a great salad topper.

INGREDIENTS | SERVES 8

Nonstick cooking spray
12 scallions, chopped
¼ cup olive oil
2 tablespoons fresh lemon juice
2 teaspoons finely grated lemon zest
1 pound low-fat feta cheese, crumbled
2 cloves garlic, minced
Salt and pepper to taste
8 whole wheat pitas

1. In a small skillet, spray nonstick cooking spray. Sauté scallions until translucent.

2. Place scallions, oil, lemon juice, and zest in a food processor and process until blended.

3. Add the feta, garlic, and salt and pepper to the food processor and blend until combined and smooth.

4. Pour the mixture into a decorative bowl and garnish with additional sliced scallions.

5. Heat pitas and cut them in quarters. Serve with feta dip.

Celebrate the Crab!

A non-fishy fish, this is a great way to get the kids to eat with a little more sophistication.

INGREDIENTS | SERVES 8–10

Nonstick cooking spray
½ medium red pepper
½ medium yellow pepper
4 chopped scallions
1 pound crabmeat, chopped finely
1 (14-ounce) can artichoke hearts, drained and chopped
½ cup grated Parmesan cheese
½ to 1 cup low-fat mayonnaise

1. Preheat oven to 350°F.

2. In medium skillet, spray nonstick cooking spray. Sauté peppers and scallions until tender.

3. In a medium mixing bowl, combine all ingredients, including peppers and scallions, until well blended.

4. Place in pie pan or a small casserole dish and bake for 20 to 30 minutes, or until bubbly.

5. Serve with raw vegetables, hearty whole-grain crackers, or pita quarters.

Paint the Town Six Layers

The six layers could be just about anything. Kidney beans or black beans, alternate cheeses, favorite vegetables, cucumbers, peppers, etc. Whatever appeals to those partying teens!

INGREDIENTS | SERVES 8–10

1 tablespoon olive oil

2 cloves garlic, chopped

2 (15-ounce) cans white beans, drained and rinsed

2 teaspoons chili paste

2 tablespoons water

1 cup shredded low-fat Cheddar cheese

1 cup shredded low-fat mozzarella cheese

1 ripe avocado

½ teaspoon salt

2 teaspoons fresh lemon juice

1½ cups plain low-fat yogurt

5 scallions, chopped finely

½ cup fresh cilantro

2 cups shredded romaine lettuce

2 medium tomatoes, diced

Layers of Great Taste and Great Nutrition!

From the beans to the low-fat cheese, from the avocado to the yogurt, this just can't be beat as a "nutritious dip." Who would have thought something that tasted so good could be that good for you?

1. In a medium skillet, heat olive oil on low heat. Add the garlic, beans, and chili paste and heat 3 to 4 minutes, until beans are soft. Mash the beans with a fork. Remove from heat.

2. Add 2 tablespoons water and continue to mash mixture until smooth.

3. Place bean mixture in the bottom of a 2-quart glass casserole dish. Sprinkle the cheese over the bean mixture.

4. Remove the pit from the avocado, and mash well in a small bowl. Add salt and lemon juice, and mix well.

5. Spread the avocado over the cheese.

6. In a blender or food processor, mix yogurt, 4 chopped scallions and ¼ cup of the cilantro. Set aside the remaining scallions and cilantro for garnish.

7. Spread yogurt mixture over the avocado layer.

8. Layer with lettuce, chopped tomatoes, remaining scallions and cilantro.

9. Serve with baked tortilla or corn chips.

Chunky Chicken Appetizer

An easy "Shake 'n Bake" type appetizer—to spice it up, use a full teaspoon of red pepper flakes. To spice it down, eliminate them altogether. Depends on your crowd.

INGREDIENTS | SERVES 6–8

Chicken and seasonings:

1 pound boneless breast of chicken

½ teaspoon ground cumin

½ teaspoon onion powder

¼ teaspoon red pepper flakes

½ teaspoon garlic powder

½ cup low-fat mayonnaise

¾ cup whole grain crackers, crushed

Nonstick cooking spray

Sauce ingredients:

3 tablespoons low-fat milk

½ cup low-fat mayonnaise

1 cup salsa, spice level as desired

1 teaspoon Dijon mustard

1. Preheat oven to 425°F.

2. Cut chicken into bite-size pieces.

3. Prepare dip mixture by combining cumin, onion powder, red pepper flakes, garlic powder, and mayonnaise.

4. In a small shallow bowl, dip chicken pieces into mayonnaise mixture. Then, coat in crushed crackers.

5. Spray cookie sheet with nonstick cooking spray, place chicken pieces onto pan and bake for 20 minutes.

6. Prepare sauce by combining milk, mayonnaise, salsa, and Dijon mustard and mixing well.

7. Serve immediately with the sauce on the side.

Party Cheese Dip

If you compare any "whipped" cream cheese with a regular low-fat cream cheese, they are quite similar. Air is whipped into the softer cream cheese, and therefore, usually less fat per serving.

INGREDIENTS | SERVES 10–12

1 (8-ounce) container whipped cream cheese

1½ cups low-fat Swiss cheese, shredded

⅓ cup low-fat mayonnaise

2 tablespoons scallions, chopped

⅛ teaspoon nutmeg

Pepper to taste

Nonstick cooking spray

⅓ cup sliced toasted almonds

1. Preheat oven to 350°F.

2. In a medium mixing bowl, mix cream cheese, Swiss cheese, mayonnaise, scallions, nutmeg, and pepper. Blend well.

3. Spray nonstick cooking spray into a round pie plate. Spread the mixture evenly into the dish and sprinkle with almonds.

4. Bake for 15 to 20 minutes until melted and golden brown.

5. Serve with raw vegetables.

Appetizer with Wings

An Asian appetizer that will be the hit of the party—this could really be prepared with any vegetables and any type of nut.

INGREDIENTS | SERVES 4

⅔ cup finely chopped cooked chicken

⅔ cup packaged shredded cabbage with carrots (coleslaw mix)

1 tablespoon chopped peanuts

2 tablespoons bottled hoisin sauce

9 to 12 Bibb or Boston lettuce leaves, cleaned

1. In a medium mixing bowl, combine chicken, cabbage slaw, peanuts, and hoisin sauce.

2. Spoon into lettuce leaves and fold. Serve immediately.

Romaine, Bibb, or Boston Lettuce

Serve your family different varieties of lettuce, such as Romaine, Red Leaf, Bibb, Boston, or Field Greens. The "greener" the lettuce, the more abundant the nutrients. Steer clear of the one type of lettuce with very little nutritional value—iceberg.

Beautiful Broccoli Salad

A twist on that head of broccoli. It is a beautifully presented salad—cauliflower or broccoflower would work nicely, too.

INGREDIENTS | SERVES 6–8

1 cup raisins
3 to 4 cups fresh broccoli florets
1 small onion, finely diced
½ cup low-fat mayonnaise
½ cup sugar
2 teaspoons vinegar
1 cup Spanish peanuts

1. Place raisins in a small bowl of water and wait for them to plump.

2. In a large bowl, combine broccoli, onion, raisins, mayonnaise, sugar, and vinegar. Toss well.

3. Just before serving, add peanuts.

The Dried Fruit Deal

The Beautiful Broccoli Salad contains raisins. Dried fruits have always been a fabulous source of fiber—whether it be dried apricots, prunes, figs, or dates. Today, they are also known for their high sugar content. Since you should be paying attention to "simple" sugars, watch the serving size on dried fruits.

Broiled Tomatoes with Goat Cheese

A tasteful alternative to a "traditional salad." Let's see how savvy your party-goers are! You can also substitute feta cheese.

INGREDIENTS | SERVES 4

Nonstick cooking spray
4 firm ripe tomatoes, sliced each in half lengthwise
3 tablespoons olive oil
Salt and pepper to taste
2 tablespoons fresh oregano, finely chopped
1 cup crumbled goat cheese

1. Preheat broiler.

2. Spray a cookie sheet with nonstick cooking spray and place tomato halves on it.

3. Drizzle tomato halves with olive oil and season with salt and pepper.

4. Sprinkle with oregano and goat cheese.

5. Place tomatoes under broiler and cook until tomatoes are somewhat soft and the cheese is lightly browned, about 3 to 5 minutes. Serve immediately.

Unique Zucchini Casserole

A wonderful soufflé-like dish. It is quite delicious—and low-fat.

INGREDIENTS | SERVES

3 cups zucchini, cut into bite-size pieces

¼ cup trans-fat-free margarine

1 small onion, grated

2 cups carrots, grated

1 (10¾-ounce) can low-fat cream of mushroom soup

½ cup low-fat sour cream

1 (8-ounce) package seasoned bread crumb stuffing

Nonstick cooking spray

¼ cup trans-fat-free margarine, melted

½ cup grated Parmesan cheese

1. Preheat oven to 350°F.

2. In a large mixing bowl, combine zucchini, margarine, onions, carrots, cream of mushroom soup, and sour cream. Mix well.

3. Add ½ of the bread crumb stuffing and mix well.

4. Spray nonstick cooking spray into casserole dish. Pour zucchini mixture into casserole dish.

5. Mix remainder of bread crumb stuffing with melted margarine.

6. Sprinkle top of casserole with bread crumb mixture and Parmesan cheese.

7. Bake for 30 minutes or until golden brown.

Traditional Irish Soda Bread

For a little sweeter bread, add ½ to 1 cup raisins and 2 tablespoons of additional sugar.

INGREDIENTS | SERVES 10–12

4 cups flour

2 tablespoons sugar

½ teaspoon salt

1 teaspoon baking soda

4 tablespoons trans-fat-free margarine, softened

1 egg, lightly beaten

1 cup low-fat buttermilk

Nonstick cooking spray

A Delicious Tradition in Ireland

Irish soda bread is quite the tradition in Ireland. Popular selections include breads with caraway seeds, some with raisins, some with both, some with neither. One of the essential ingredients is buttermilk. The acid in the buttermilk reacts with the baking soda to provide the leavening (rising) of this quick bread. Soda bread tends to dry out quickly, so bake it and eat it in the same day.

1. Preheat oven to 375°F.

2. In a large mixing bowl, combine flour, sugar, salt, and baking soda mix well to blend.

3. Add softened margarine and stir to incorporate the margarine into the flour mixture.

4. Form a well in the flour mixture; add egg and buttermilk. Stir well to form dough.

5. Spray baking sheet with nonstick cooking spray, and place dough in a mound on the baking sheet, forming into a rounded loaf shape.

6. Cut a large "X" in the top of the loaf with a sharp knife.

7. Bake 45 minutes, or until golden brown.

Pasta Shells with Marsala Sauce

This recipe has quite a few steps—however, it is delicious, and worth the work!
It is prepared with ground veal, lower in fat than ground beef.

INGREDIENTS | SERVES 4–6

¼ cup olive oil
1½ cups onion, finely chopped
1½ cups celery, finely diced
1 large carrot, grated
½ pound chopped mushrooms
1 pound ground veal
2 cups chopped tomatoes
2 tablespoons flour
¾ cup dry red wine
1 cup beef broth
Salt and pepper to taste
8 large pasta shells
8 ounces Parmesan cheese, shredded

1. In a heavy skillet, heat olive oil on low heat until sizzling. Add onions, cook for 3 minutes.

2. Add carrots, celery, and mushrooms; cook, stirring constantly for 5 minutes.

3. Stir in veal. Cook until veal is lightly browned.

4. Add chopped tomatoes.

5. Sprinkle flour over mixture. Stir to mix well.

6. Gradually add wine and beef broth. Season with salt and pepper.

7. Simmer for about 2 hours, until thick, stirring constantly.

8. Cook pasta shells as directed on package.

9. Spoon veal mixture into shells, roll up shells, add sauce, and sprinkle with Parmesan cheese.

Roasted Balsamic Asparagus

If you can "dress" up the asparagus with different flavors, the children may eat it.
Be creative—even cook it on the grill—it's really delicious.

INGREDIENTS | SERVES 8

Nonstick cooking spray
2 pounds asparagus spears, trimmed
Salt and pepper to taste
2 tablespoons trans-fat-free margarine
2 teaspoons low-sodium soy sauce
1 teaspoon balsamic vinegar

Asparagus

One of the leaders in the folic acid department, asparagus is an incredibly healthful vegetable, only a difficult one to get the kids to eat. Very low in calories, no fat, little sodium (salt), a great source of potassium, fiber, and vitamin B6—it is hard to beat this veggie!

1. Preheat oven to 400°F.

2. Spray nonstick cooking spray on a large baking sheet. Arrange asparagus in a single layer on the baking sheet. Season with salt and pepper. Bake for about 12 to 15 minutes or until tender.

3. Over low heat, melt margarine in a small skillet until lightly browned.

4. Remove from heat and stir in the soy sauce and vinegar.

5. Drizzle over asparagus, and serve.

Smoked Mozzarella and Corn Potatoes

*What a unique mix of flavors! Feel free to alternate cheeses, even take
out the corn and still have a fabulous mashed potato dish!*

INGREDIENTS | SERVES 8–10

1 tablespoon olive oil

3 cups frozen (or fresh) corn kernels

3 pounds potatoes, quartered, leave skin on

¾ cup low-fat milk

½ cup smoked mozzarella or gouda cheese, shredded

3 tablespoons trans-fat-free margarine

1 tablespoon fresh lime juice

1 teaspoon salt

1 tablespoon garlic powder

Watch Those Carbs

Twenty or so years ago, scientists and the popular press had everyone focusing on fat intake. Today, the focus is on sugar and carbohydrate intake. The solution—moderation. It is not recommended to abandon any food group, just choose the best of the best. Limit the amount of sugary cereals, desserts, white breads, and the like. Though serving several carbohydrates in one meal is not suggested either, this can be the exception—in moderation!

1. Pour olive oil into a large skillet. Heat on low heat. Add corn and sauté 5 minutes or until lightly browned.

2. Place potatoes in a separate saucepan; cover potatoes with water. Bring potatoes to a boil. Reduce heat; simmer 15 to 20 minutes. Pour potatoes into a colander and drain.

3. Return potatoes to the saucepan. Add milk, cheese, and margarine. Mash potato mixture.

4. Turn heat back on and continue cooking until potatoes are hot, stirring constantly.

5. Stir in corn, lime juice, salt, and garlic powder and blend well.

Minted Pineapple Ham

A light and flavorful glaze that can be used on a veal or pork roast, too.

INGREDIENTS | SERVES 10

5 pound ham, uncooked

Nonstick cooking spray

1 cup low-sugar pineapple preserves

1 cup canned crushed pineapple in its own juice (reserve juice)

3 tablespoons pineapple juice

3 tablespoons fresh lime juice

2 teaspoons fresh mint, minced

Pepper to taste

1. Preheat oven to 325°F.

2. Place the ham in a large roasting pan, sprayed with nonstick cooking spray. Cover with foil and cook ham for 1½ hours.

3. Prepare glaze: In a medium bowl, stir together preserves, pineapple, pineapple juice, lime juice, mint, and pepper until well blended.

4. After 1½ hours, pour glaze over ham, and re-cover with foil. Cook an additional hour or so, until cooked through.

Scintillating Savory Vegetables

This is a very colorful dish—and you can choose any vegetables you like.

INGREDIENTS | SERVES 4

1 cup fresh green beans, washed and cut

1 cup fresh baby carrots, washed

1 cup whole baby corn, fresh or frozen

1 cup garbanzo beans, drained and rinsed

2 teaspoons fresh mint, chopped

2 teaspoons Italian parsley, chopped

1. In a microwave safe bowl, cook green beans, carrots, and corn until desired tenderness.

2. In a large mixing bowl, combine cooked green beans and carrots, corn, garbanzo beans, mint, and parsley in medium size bowl. Toss well and serve.

Biscotti for the Big Bash!

This is one of the desserts that works so well using a trans-fat-free margarine, rather than butter. Be quite daring, and use half trans-fat-free margarine, and half olive oil—no one will recognize the difference, and at least the fat used in the recipe is healthier.

INGREDIENTS | SERVES 15–20

1 cup trans-fat-free margarine
1½ cups sugar
4 eggs
2 cups flour
½ teaspoon baking powder
2 teaspoons vanilla
1½ cups chopped walnuts
¾ cup mini chocolate chips
¾ cup chopped Heath bar
Nonstick cooking spray

1. Preheat oven to 350°F.

2. In a large mixing bowl, cream margarine and sugar.

3. Add eggs. Beat until smooth.

4. In a separate bowl, combine the flour and baking powder. Add to egg/sugar mixture.

5. Add vanilla extract. Mix in nuts, chips, and Health bar.

6. Spray three loaf pans with nonstick cooking spray. Divide batter among the three loaf pans. Bake 40 minutes or until firm in the center.

7. Cool biscotti and freeze in aluminum foil.

8. When ready to serve, cut into 1-inch thin slices. In the oven on parchment paper, brown at 325°F for 10 minutes on one side only.

Divine Classic Coconut Cake

*A gorgeous dessert, a family favorite. Generally a very high-fat,
high-calorie dessert—tweaked, yet still delicious.*

INGREDIENTS | SERVES 16–18

1 (2-layer size) package white cake mix

1 (7-ounce) bag coconut flakes

Nonstick cooking spray

1 cup cold low-fat milk

1 (4-ounce) package white chocolate or vanilla instant sugar-free, fat-free pudding

¼ cup powdered sugar

1 (8-ounce) container low-fat whipped topping

1. Prepare cake batter as directed on package. In the mixing bowl, add in 1 cup of the coconut flakes.

2. Spray two 9-inch round cake pans with nonstick cooking spray. Pour batter evenly into the two cake pans. Bake the cakes as directed on the package.

3. Cool for 15 minutes. Remove cake layers from pans and cool completely.

4. In a medium mixing bowl, pour milk, pudding mix, and powdered sugar. Beat with wire whisk 2 minutes or until well blended.

5. Fold in the whipped topping and place in the refrigerator for 30 minutes.

6. Place one of the cake layers on a large plate or serving dish. Spread with ½ of the thickened pudding mixture. Sprinkle with ¾ cup of the remaining coconut. Top with second layer of cake. Spread top and sides with remaining pudding mixture. Sprinkle and depress remaining coconut into "icing" or pudding mixture.

7. Refrigerate for at least 1 hour.

Sinful Ice Cream Dessert

Go easy here. Practice the moderation learned. Serve your favorite ice cream flavors.

INGREDIENTS | SERVES 12–14

1¼ cups chocolate wafer cookie crumbs

3 tablespoons trans-fat-free margarine, melted

1 cup caramel sauce

1 quart chocolate low-fat ice cream, softened

6 (1.4-ounce) English toffee-flavored candy bars, crushed (optional)

1 quart vanilla low-fat ice cream, softened

1 cup chocolate syrup

1 quart cookie dough low-fat ice cream, softened

"It's Low Fat—It Must Be Good for You"!

"Low fat" does not mean "all-you-can-eat." Today's products may say "low in fat," "sugar free," "no sugar added," "trans fat free." Be sure to read the nutrition label always, and look at calorie levels. Don't be fooled by the claims.

1. Preheat oven to 350°F.

2. In a small mixing bowl, combine cookie crumbs and margarine, and mix well. Spread crumb mixture over the bottom of a 10-inch springform pan forming a crust.

3. Bake crust 6 minutes, and cool on a wire rack.

4. Spread ½ cup caramel sauce over crust. Place in freezer until hardened.

5. Spread chocolate ice cream over caramel sauce. Place back in freezer until firm.

6. Mix crushed candy bar with vanilla ice cream. Spread the mixture over the chocolate ice cream. Again, freeze until firm.

7. Spread ½ cup chocolate syrup over the vanilla ice cream. Freeze until hardened.

8. Spread the cookie dough ice cream over the chocolate syrup. Add some caramel sauce to the top for decoration. Cover, and freeze for at least 6 hours.

9. About 10 to 15 minutes prior to serving, remove dessert from freezer. Remove the sides of the springform pan.

10. Serve with the remaining chocolate syrup and caramel sauce.

Magnificent Mint Cookies

For really magnificent cookies, feel free to add chopped walnuts or dark chocolate chips—a little healthy antioxidant thrown in.

INGREDIENTS | **SERVES 12–15**

⅔ cup trans-fat-free margarine, softened

¾ cup sugar

⅓ cup firmly packed dark brown sugar

1 egg

1 teaspoon vanilla extract

1 (1-ounce) square unsweetened chocolate, melted

1½ cups all-purpose flour

1 (10-ounce) package mint chocolate morsels

Nonstick cooking spray

1. Preheat oven to 325°F.

2. In a mixing bowl, beat margarine at medium speed with an electric mixer.

3. Gradually add white and brown sugars. Mix well.

4. Add egg, vanilla extract, and melted chocolate, and continue to beat.

5. Gradually add flour, until batter is smooth.

6. By hand, stir in mint morsels.

7. Spray nonstick cooking spray on a baking sheet. Using a teaspoon, drop large teaspoons-full of dough onto the baking sheet.

8. Bake 10 to 15 minutes. Cool on a wire rack.

For the Cookie Monster

A little health thrown into this chocolate chip, peanut butter, oatmeal cookie—again, feel free to leave in some of these goodies, or take them out.

INGREDIENTS | SERVES 10–20

2 eggs

¼ cup honey

1 cup trans-fat-free peanut butter

1 cup oatmeal flakes, lightly toasted

1½ teaspoons vanilla extract

¼ cup canola oil

3 tablespoons sugar-free pancake syrup

¼ cup low-fat milk

1½ cups flour

½ cup mini chocolate chips

Nonstick cooking spray

1. In a medium mixing bowl, beat eggs until creamy.

2. Add honey and peanut butter. Mix well.

3. Add oatmeal flakes, vanilla, oil, pancake syrup, and milk.

4. Add flour gradually, and then stir in chocolate chips. Blend until batter is smooth.

5. Spray nonstick cooking spray onto a baking sheet. Drop batter by teaspoon onto baking sheet.

6. Bake 8 to 10 minutes, just until golden brown.

Garlic Baked Fries

For garlic lovers only—and remember, don't peel off the skin; that's one of the healthiest parts.

INGREDIENTS | SERVES 6–8

3 pounds baking potatoes, cut into ¼-inch-thick strips

2 tablespoons canola oil

1 teaspoon salt

3 tablespoons minced garlic

Nonstick cooking spray

2 tablespoons finely chopped fresh parsley

4 tablespoons Parmesan cheese, grated

2 tablespoons paprika

1. Preheat oven to 400°F.

2. Combine potatoes, oil, salt, and garlic in a large plastic bag, tossing to coat.

3. Spray baking sheets with nonstick cooking spray. Organize potatoes in a single layer on the baking sheets. Sprinkle with parsley, Parmesan cheese, and paprika.

4. Bake for 30 minutes or until potatoes are tender and golden brown, turning after 20 minutes.

Phenomenally Festive Chocolate Soufflé

Worth the work! Add 30 marshmallows, now it is a chocolate marshmallow soufflé.

INGREDIENTS | SERVES 2

Nonstick cooking spray
2 tablespoons trans-fat-free margarine
1 (1-ounce) square unsweetened chocolate
2 tablespoons all-purpose flour
½ cup low-fat milk
Dash of salt
2 large eggs, separated
¼ cup sugar
1 teaspoon vanilla extract

1. Preheat oven to 325°F.

2. In a 2-cup soufflé dish, spray nonstick cooking spray, and set aside.

3. In a medium saucepan, heat 2 tablespoons margarine and chocolate square in a saucepan over medium heat, until melted.

4. Add flour slowly, stirring until smooth. Lower heat, and cook 1 to 2 minutes, stirring constantly.

5. Add milk gradually. Continue to cook, stirring constantly, until mixture thickens.

6. Stir in salt; remove from heat.

7. With an electric mixer, beat egg yolks and sugar at medium speed until mixture is pale and thick. Stir in vanilla extract.

8. Gradually stir about one-fourth of hot chocolate mixture into yolk mixture. Beat at medium speed until well blended.

9. Gradually add remaining hot chocolate mixture, mixing constantly.

10. In a separate small bowl, beat egg whites until soft peaks form. Fold about one-half of egg whites into chocolate mixture.

11. Fold remaining egg whites into chocolate mixture and blend well.

12. Spoon into soufflé dish. Bake for 35 minutes.

Lively Lemon Torte

Similar to a lemon meringue pie, it is lighter due to the lack of cream and use of a low-fat whipped topping. It is an outstanding and magnificent-looking dessert.

INGREDIENTS | SERVES 10–12

Nonstick cooking spray

2 packages Lady Fingers

5 egg yolks

6 egg whites, separated

¾ cup lemon juice

Zest from 1 lemon

1¼ cups sugar

1 (16-ounce) container low-fat whipped topping

3 tablespoons sugar

1. Spray a 9-inch springform pan with nonstick cooking spray. Line the pan with the Lady Fingers.

2. In a medium mixing bowl, whisk yolks and 2 egg whites together.

3. Add lemon juice plus zest of 1 lemon. Add sugar and mix well. Cook over double boiler until thick, about 3 to 5 minutes. Cool.

4. Fold whipped topping into mixture. Pour into springform pan. Place in freezer minimum of 5 hours.

5. In a separate small bowl, beat remaining 4 egg whites with 3 tablespoons sugar until it forms stiff peaks. Spread over frozen cake.

6. Place under broiler for a few minutes to brown the top.

7. Put in freezer. One hour prior to serving, take out of freezer and refrigerate.

Fluffy Berry Cheesecake

The easiest cheesecake around—vary with your favorite berries.
Different-colored berries give this a beautiful presentation.

INGREDIENTS | SERVES 8

8 ounces whipped cream cheese

⅓ cup sugar

1 cup low-fat sour cream

2 teaspoons vanilla extract

1 (8-ounce) container low-fat whipped topping

1 prepared graham cracker crust

½ pound fresh strawberries, cleaned, hulled, and halved

½ pound blackberries, cleaned

1. In a medium bowl, with an electric mixer, whip the cream cheese until smooth.

2. Slowly beat in the sugar.

3. Add sour cream and vanilla, and mix.

4. Fold in the whipped topping.

5. Pour mixture into the pie crust. Chill in the refrigerator for 4 hours.

6. Just prior to serving, decorate with berries.

APPENDIX A

Nutrition Parenting Resources

Books

Editors of *Cooking Light* Magazine. *Cooking Light Complete Cookbook: A Fresh New Way to Cook*. Birmingham, AL: Oxmoor House, 2008.

Editors of Cooking Light Magazine. *Cooking Light Fresh Food Fast*. Birmingham, AL: Oxmoor House, 2009.

Niehaus, Aisha. *My Food Pyramid*. New York: DK Publishing, 2007.

Litz Julien, Ronni, MS, RD/LDN. *What Should I Feed My Kids? How to Get Your Kids to Eat, but Not Too Much*. Franklin Lakes, NJ: Career Press, 2006.

Litz Julien, Ronni, MS, RD/LDN. *The Trans-Fat-Free Kitchen*. Deerfield Beach, FL: Health Communications, Inc., 2006.

McGraw, Jay. *The Ultimate Weight Solution for Teens*. New York: Free Press, 2003.

Rockwell, Lizzy. *Good Enough to Eat: A Kid's Guide to Food and Nutrition*. New York: Collins Publishing, 2009.

Rogers, Judy. *Fun with Kids in the Kitchen Cookbook*. Hagerstown, MD: Review & Herald Publishing, 1996.

Sharmat, Mitchell. *Gregory, the Terrible Eater*. New York: Scholastic Paperbacks, 1989.

Newsletters

Mayo Clinic Health Letter
P.O. Box 9302
Big Sandy, TX 75755-9302
www.healthletter.mayoclinic.com

Tufts University Health and Nutrition Newsletter
P.O. Box 420235
Palm Coast, FL 32142
www.tuftshealthletter.com

Johns Hopkins Health Alerts
University Health Publishing
500 Fifth Avenue
Suite 1900
New York, NY 10110
www.johnshopkinshealthalerts.com

Nutrition Action Health Letter
Center for Science in the Public Interest
1875 Connecticut Ave. N.W.
Suite 300
Washington, DC 20009
www.cspinet.org

Center for Human Nutrition (University of Texas Southwestern Medical Center) Newsletter
University of Texas Southwestern Medical Center
5323 Harry Hines Boulevard
Dallas, TX 75390

University of California Berkeley Wellness Letter
P.O. Box 420148
Palm Coast, FL 32142
www.wellnessletter.com

TeensHealth Food and Fitness Newsletter
www.kidshealth.org/teen

USDA Team Nutrition E-Newsletter
www.healthymeals.nal.usda.gov

Website Resources

Baylor College of Medicine
www.bcm.edu

Food Guide Pyramid
www.nal.usda.gov

Development of My Pyramid
www.mypyramid.gov

Parents' Place
www.parenting.ivillage.com

National Dairy Council
www.nationaldairycouncil.org

National Dairy Council
www.nutritionexplorations.org

National Dairy Council
www.schoolwellnesskit.org

Nutrition Data/Know What You Eat
www.nutritiondata.com

American Heart Association
www.americanheart.org

Food Safety
www.foodsafety.gov

American Cancer Society/Preventing Cancer
www.cancer.org

Childhood Nutrition
www.keepkidshealthy.com

MedlinePlus Child Nutrition
www.nlm.nih.gov

American Academy of Pediatrics
www.aap.org

The Alliance for a Healthy Generation/Clinton Foundation
www.clintonfoundation.org

American Dietetic Association
www.eatright.org

Childhood Obesity
www.pediatrics.about.com

Fitness and Kids
www.mayoclinic.org

Parents Magazine
www.parents.com

Parenting Magazine
www.parenting.com

APPENDIX B

Growth Charts

Growth charts, based on sex and age, should be found in every child's medical chart in their pediatrician's office. Calculated since the day they were born, and each subsequent visit to the doctor, this chart gives a comprehensive guideline for growth rates through the teenage years. It is important—critical—that children stay on "their own personal growth curve." If there is a consistent drop, the pediatrician should be concerned about medical issues such as failure to thrive, growth hormone deficiencies, thyroid disease, or an eating disorder, to name a few. If there is a consistent rise, again, this brings up issues such as overweight/obesity or thyroid disease, among others.

These charts are not intended to be the only tool for evaluating growth; they are a piece of a puzzle in a clinical and professional setting for determining adequate growth and development.

Learn how to read the growth chart/grid, and follow your child's growth in weight and height changes. When looking at one of the growth charts keep in mind:

- The "lowest" point on the grid is the 5th percentile, whereas the "highest" point on the grid is the 95th percentile. For example, if there were 100 children placed in "height" order, from the shortest to the tallest, once your child is placed on his growth grid, and he is at the 25th percentile, he will be the 25th in line, therefore, on the shorter end of the spectrum. The same concept applies to the weight charts.
- The healthy goal is first and foremost, to follow "their own curve"; however, ideally they will be somewhere in the "average" range—just above or below the 50th percentile.
- A few things to consider: genetic influence of parents' stature and weight, periodic growth spurts, and activity versus caloric intake—which may need to be adjusted once your son makes the soccer team!

Birth to 36 months: Boys
Length-for-age and Weight-for-age percentiles

NAME _____

RECORD # _____

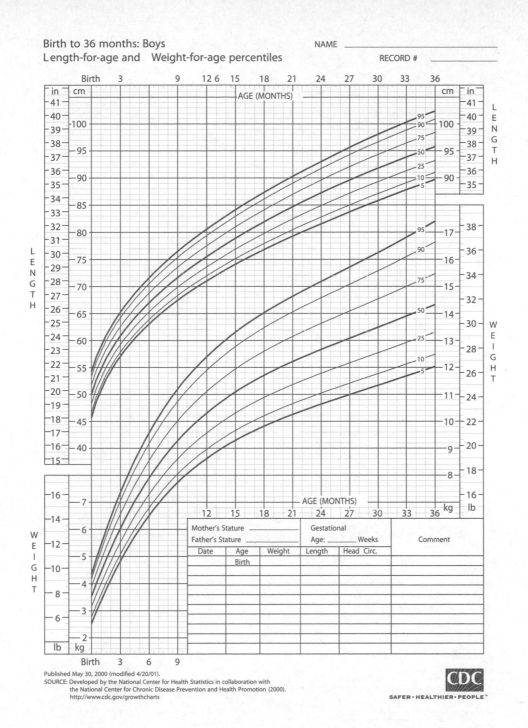

Published May 30, 2000 (modified 4/20/01).
SOURCE: Developed by the National Center for Health Statistics in collaboration with
the National Center for Chronic Disease Prevention and Health Promotion (2000).
http://www.cdc.gov/growthcharts

CDC
SAFER · HEALTHIER · PEOPLE™

Source: Centers for Disease Control—National Center for Health Statistics—growth charts compiled using U.S. children from the National Health and Nutrition Examination Survey (NHANES), latest revision in 2000.

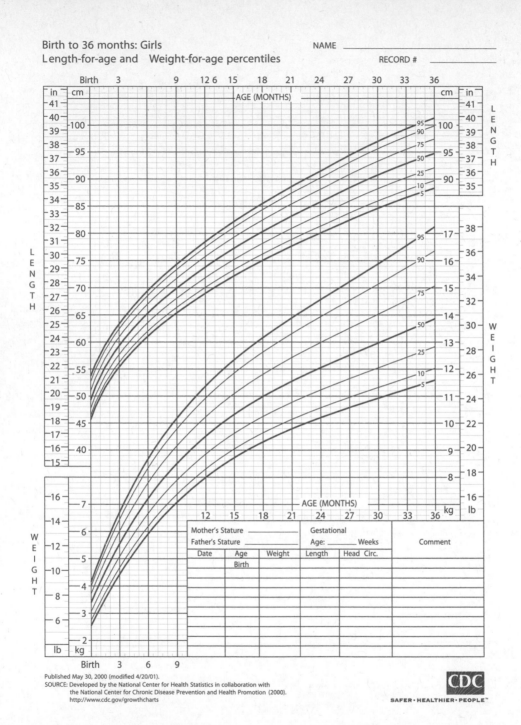

Birth to 36 months: Girls
Length-for-age and   Weight-for-age percentiles

NAME _____

RECORD # _____

Published May 30, 2000 (modified 4/20/01).
SOURCE: Developed by the National Center for Health Statistics in collaboration with
the National Center for Chronic Disease Prevention and Health Promotion (2000).
http://www.cdc.gov/growthcharts

CDC
SAFER · HEALTHIER · PEOPLE™

Source: Centers for Disease Control—National Center for Health Statistics—
growth charts compiled using U.S. children from the National Health and
Nutrition Examination Survey (NHANES), latest revision in 2000.

2 to 20 years: Boys
Stature -for-age and Weight-for-age percentiles

NAME _____

RECORD # _____

Published May 30, 2000 (modified 11/21/00).
SOURCE: Developed by the National Center for Health Statistics in collaboration with
the National Center for Chronic Disease Prevention and Health Promotion (2000).
http://www.cdc.gov/growthcharts

CDC
SAFER · HEALTHIER · PEOPLE™

Source: Centers for Disease Control—National Center for Health Statistics—
growth charts compiled using U.S. children from the National Health and
Nutrition Examination Survey (NHANES), latest revision in 2000.

2 to 20 years: Girls
Stature -for-age and Weight-for-age percentiles

NAME _____

RECORD # _____

Published May 30, 2000 (modified 11/21/00).
SOURCE: Developed by the National Center for Health Statistics in collaboration with
the National Center for Chronic Disease Prevention and Health Promotion (2000).
http://www.cdc.gov/growthcharts

To Calculate BMI: Weight (kg) ÷ Stature (cm) ÷ Stature (cm) x 10,000
or Weight (lb) ÷ Stature (in) ÷ Stature (in) x 703

Source: Centers for Disease Control—National Center for Health Statistics—growth charts compiled using U.S. children from the National Health and Nutrition Examination Survey (NHANES), latest revision in 2000.

BMI charts

New to the medical chart, a BMI growth chart has been created as the most commonly used approach to determining if children are overweight. This chart can be used after the age of two years old.

To calculate BMI manually use the following equation:
(weight in pounds x 703) / height in inches

To calculate BMI electronically go to:
www.nhlbisupport.com/bmi
www.nccd.cdc.gov/dnpabi/Calculator.aspx

BMI categories:
18.5 or less = underweight
18.5 – 24.9 = normal weight
25 – 29.9 = overweight
30 or greater = obese

2 to 20 years: Boys
Body mass index-for-age percentiles

NAME _____

RECORD # _____

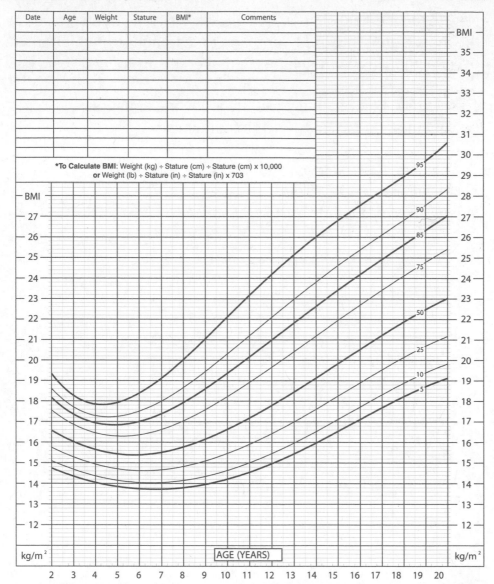

Date	Age	Weight	Stature	BMI*	Comments

*To Calculate BMI: Weight (kg) ÷ Stature (cm) ÷ Stature (cm) x 10,000
or Weight (lb) ÷ Stature (in) ÷ Stature (in) x 703

AGE (YEARS)

Published May 30, 2000 (modified 10/16/00).
SOURCE: Developed by the National Center for Health Statistics in collaboration with
    the National Center for Chronic Disease Prevention and Health Promotion (2000).
    http://www.cdc.gov/growthcharts

SAFER • HEALTHIER • PEOPLE™

Source: Centers for Disease Control—National Center for Health Statistics—
growth charts compiled using U.S. children from the National Health and
Nutrition Examination Survey (NHANES), latest revision in 2000.

2 to 20 years: Girls
Body mass index-for-age percentiles

NAME _____

RECORD # _____

Date	Age	Weight	Stature	BMI*	Comments

*To Calculate BMI: Weight (kg) ÷ Stature (cm) ÷ Stature (cm) x 10,000
or Weight (lb) ÷ Stature (in) ÷ Stature (in) x 703

BMI

35
34
33
32
31
30
29
28
27
26
25
24
23
22
21
20
19
18
17
16
15
14
13
12

kg/m²

AGE (YEARS)

2 3 4 5 6 7 8 9 10 11 12 13 14 15 16 17 18 19 20

95
90
85
75
50
25
10
5

Published May 30, 2000 (modified 10/16/00).
SOURCE: Developed by the National Center for Health Statistics in collaboration with
the National Center for Chronic Disease Prevention and Health Promotion (2000).
http://www.cdc.gov/growthcharts

SAFER · HEALTHIER · PEOPLE™

Source: Centers for Disease Control—National Center for Health Statistics—
growth charts compiled using U.S. children from the National Health and
Nutrition Examination Survey (NHANES), latest revision in 2000.

Index

THE EVERYTHING SERIES!

BUSINESS & PERSONAL FINANCE

Everything® Accounting Book
Everything® Budgeting Book, 2nd Ed.
Everything® Business Planning Book
Everything® Coaching and Mentoring Book, 2nd Ed.
Everything® Fundraising Book
Everything® Get Out of Debt Book
Everything® Grant Writing Book, 2nd Ed.
Everything® Guide to Buying Foreclosures
Everything® Guide to Fundraising, $15.95
Everything® Guide to Mortgages
Everything® Guide to Personal Finance for Single Mothers
Everything® Home-Based Business Book, 2nd Ed.
Everything® Homebuying Book, 3rd Ed., $15.95
Everything® Homeselling Book, 2nd Ed.
Everything® Human Resource Management Book
Everything® Improve Your Credit Book
Everything® Investing Book, 2nd Ed.
Everything® Landlording Book
Everything® Leadership Book, 2nd Ed.
Everything® Managing People Book, 2nd Ed.
Everything® Negotiating Book
Everything® Online Auctions Book
Everything® Online Business Book
Everything® Personal Finance Book
Everything® Personal Finance in Your 20s & 30s Book, 2nd Ed.
Everything® Personal Finance in Your 40s & 50s Book, $15.95
Everything® Project Management Book, 2nd Ed.
Everything® Real Estate Investing Book
Everything® Retirement Planning Book
Everything® Robert's Rules Book, $7.95
Everything® Selling Book
Everything® Start Your Own Business Book, 2nd Ed.
Everything® Wills & Estate Planning Book

COOKING

Everything® Barbecue Cookbook
Everything® Bartender's Book, 2nd Ed., $9.95
Everything® Calorie Counting Cookbook
Everything® Cheese Book
Everything® Chinese Cookbook
Everything® Classic Recipes Book
Everything® Cocktail Parties & Drinks Book
Everything® College Cookbook
Everything® Cooking for Baby and Toddler Book
Everything® Diabetes Cookbook
Everything® Easy Gourmet Cookbook
Everything® Fondue Cookbook
Everything® Food Allergy Cookbook, $15.95
Everything® Fondue Party Book
Everything® Gluten-Free Cookbook
Everything® Glycemic Index Cookbook
Everything® Grilling Cookbook
Everything® Healthy Cooking for Parties Book, $15.95
Everything® Holiday Cookbook
Everything® Indian Cookbook
Everything® Lactose-Free Cookbook
Everything® Low-Cholesterol Cookbook

Everything® Low-Fat High-Flavor Cookbook, 2nd Ed., $15.95
Everything® Low-Salt Cookbook
Everything® Meals for a Month Cookbook
Everything® Meals on a Budget Cookbook
Everything® Mediterranean Cookbook
Everything® Mexican Cookbook
Everything® No Trans Fat Cookbook
Everything® One-Pot Cookbook, 2nd Ed., $15.95
Everything® Organic Cooking for Baby & Toddler Book, $15.95
Everything® Pizza Cookbook
Everything® Quick Meals Cookbook, 2nd Ed., $15.95
Everything® Slow Cooker Cookbook
Everything® Slow Cooking for a Crowd Cookbook
Everything® Soup Cookbook
Everything® Stir-Fry Cookbook
Everything® Sugar-Free Cookbook
Everything® Tapas and Small Plates Cookbook
Everything® Tex-Mex Cookbook
Everything® Thai Cookbook
Everything® Vegetarian Cookbook
Everything® Whole-Grain, High-Fiber Cookbook
Everything® Wild Game Cookbook
Everything® Wine Book, 2nd Ed.

GAMES

Everything® 15-Minute Sudoku Book, $9.95
Everything® 30-Minute Sudoku Book, $9.95
Everything® Bible Crosswords Book, $9.95
Everything® Blackjack Strategy Book
Everything® Brain Strain Book, $9.95
Everything® Bridge Book
Everything® Card Games Book
Everything® Card Tricks Book, $9.95
Everything® Casino Gambling Book, 2nd Ed.
Everything® Chess Basics Book
Everything® Christmas Crosswords Book, $9.95
Everything® Craps Strategy Book
Everything® Crossword and Puzzle Book
Everything® Crosswords and Puzzles for Quote Lovers Book, $9.95
Everything® Crossword Challenge Book
Everything® Crosswords for the Beach Book, $9.95
Everything® Cryptic Crosswords Book, $9.95
Everything® Cryptograms Book, $9.95
Everything® Easy Crosswords Book
Everything® Easy Kakuro Book, $9.95
Everything® Easy Large-Print Crosswords Book
Everything® Games Book, 2nd Ed.
Everything® Giant Book of Crosswords
Everything® Giant Sudoku Book, $9.95
Everything® Giant Word Search Book
Everything® Kakuro Challenge Book, $9.95
Everything® Large-Print Crossword Challenge Book
Everything® Large-Print Crosswords Book
Everything® Large-Print Travel Crosswords Book
Everything® Lateral Thinking Puzzles Book, $9.95
Everything® Literary Crosswords Book, $9.95
Everything® Mazes Book
Everything® Memory Booster Puzzles Book, $9.95

Everything® Movie Crosswords Book, $9.95
Everything® Music Crosswords Book, $9.95
Everything® Online Poker Book
Everything® Pencil Puzzles Book, $9.95
Everything® Poker Strategy Book
Everything® Pool & Billiards Book
Everything® Puzzles for Commuters Book, $9.95
Everything® Puzzles for Dog Lovers Book, $9.95
Everything® Sports Crosswords Book, $9.95
Everything® Test Your IQ Book, $9.95
Everything® Texas Hold 'Em Book, $9.95
Everything® Travel Crosswords Book, $9.95
Everything® Travel Mazes Book, $9.95
Everything® Travel Word Search Book, $9.95
Everything® TV Crosswords Book, $9.95
Everything® Word Games Challenge Book
Everything® Word Scramble Book
Everything® Word Search Book

HEALTH

Everything® Alzheimer's Book
Everything® Diabetes Book
Everything® First Aid Book, $9.95
Everything® Green Living Book
Everything® Health Guide to Addiction and Reco
Everything® Health Guide to Adult Bipolar Disorder
Everything® Health Guide to Arthritis
Everything® Health Guide to Controlling Anxiety
Everything® Health Guide to Depression
Everything® Health Guide to Diabetes, 2nd Ed.
Everything® Health Guide to Fibromyalgia
Everything® Health Guide to Menopause, 2nd Ed.
Everything® Health Guide to Migraines
Everything® Health Guide to Multiple Sclerosis
Everything® Health Guide to OCD
Everything® Health Guide to PMS
Everything® Health Guide to Postpartum Care
Everything® Health Guide to Thyroid Disease
Everything® Hypnosis Book
Everything® Low Cholesterol Book
Everything® Menopause Book
Everything® Nutrition Book
Everything® Reflexology Book
Everything® Stress Management Book
Everything® Superfoods Book, $15.95

HISTORY

Everything® American Government Book
Everything® American History Book, 2nd Ed.
Everything® American Revolution Book, $15.95
Everything® Civil War Book
Everything® Freemasons Book
Everything® Irish History & Heritage Book
Everything® World War II Book, 2nd Ed.

HOBBIES

Everything® Candlemaking Book
Everything® Cartooning Book
Everything® Coin Collecting Book
Everything® Digital Photography Book, 2nd Ed.

Everything® Drawing Book
Everything® Family Tree Book, 2nd Ed.
Everything® Guide to Online Genealogy, $15.95
Everything® Knitting Book
Everything® Knots Book
Everything® Photography Book
Everything® Quilting Book
Everything® Sewing Book
Everything® Soapmaking Book, 2nd Ed.
Everything® Woodworking Book

HOME IMPROVEMENT

Everything® Feng Shui Book
Everything® Feng Shui Decluttering Book, $9.95
Everything® Fix-It Book
Everything® Green Living Book
Everything® Home Decorating Book
Everything® Home Storage Solutions Book
Everything® Homebuilding Book
Everything® Organize Your Home Book, 2nd Ed.

KIDS' BOOKS

All titles are $7.95

Everything® Fairy Tales Book, $14.95
Everything® Kids' Animal Puzzle & Activity Book
Everything® Kids' Astronomy Book
Everything® Kids' Baseball Book, 5th Ed.
Everything® Kids' Bible Trivia Book
Everything® Kids' Bugs Book
Everything® Kids' Cars and Trucks Puzzle and Activity Book
Everything® Kids' Christmas Puzzle & Activity Book
Everything® Kids' Connect the Dots
          Puzzle and Activity Book
Everything® Kids' Cookbook, 2nd Ed.
Everything® Kids' Crazy Puzzles Book
Everything® Kids' Dinosaurs Book
Everything® Kids' Dragons Puzzle and Activity Book
Everything® Kids' Environment Book $7.95
Everything® Kids' Fairies Puzzle and Activity Book
Everything® Kids' First Spanish Puzzle and Activity Book
Everything® Kids' Football Book
Everything® Kids' Geography Book
Everything® Kids' Gross Cookbook
Everything® Kids' Gross Hidden Pictures Book
Everything® Kids' Gross Jokes Book
Everything® Kids' Gross Mazes Book
Everything® Kids' Gross Puzzle & Activity Book
Everything® Kids' Halloween Puzzle & Activity Book
Everything® Kids' Hanukkah Puzzle and Activity Book
Everything® Kids' Hidden Pictures Book
Everything® Kids' Horses Book
Everything® Kids' Joke Book
Everything® Kids' Knock Knock Book
Everything® Kids' Learning French Book
Everything® Kids' Learning Spanish Book
Everything® Kids' Magical Science Experiments Book
Everything® Kids' Math Puzzles Book
Everything® Kids' Mazes Book
Everything® Kids' Money Book, 2nd Ed.
Everything® Kids' Mummies, Pharaoh's, and Pyramids Puzzle and Activity Book
Everything® Kids' Nature Book
Everything® Kids' Pirates Puzzle and Activity Book
Everything® Kids' Presidents Book
Everything® Kids' Princess Puzzle and Activity Book
Everything® Kids' Puzzle Book

Everything® Kids' Racecars Puzzle and Activity Book
Everything® Kids' Riddles & Brain Teasers Book
Everything® Kids' Science Experiments Book
Everything® Kids' Sharks Book
Everything® Kids' Soccer Book
Everything® Kids' Spelling Book
Everything® Kids' Spies Puzzle and Activity Book
Everything® Kids' States Book
Everything® Kids' Travel Activity Book
Everything® Kids' Word Search Puzzle and Activity Book

LANGUAGE

Everything® Conversational Japanese Book with CD, $19.95
Everything® French Grammar Book
Everything® French Phrase Book, $9.95
Everything® French Verb Book, $9.95
Everything® German Phrase Book, $9.95
Everything® German Practice Book with CD, $19.95
Everything® Inglés Book
Everything® Intermediate Spanish Book with CD, $19.95
Everything® Italian Phrase Book, $9.95
Everything® Italian Practice Book with CD, $19.95
Everything® Learning Brazilian Portuguese Book with CD, $19.95
Everything® Learning French Book with CD, 2nd Ed., $19.95
Everything® Learning German Book
Everything® Learning Italian Book
Everything® Learning Latin Book
Everything® Learning Russian Book with CD, $19.95
Everything® Learning Spanish Book
Everything® Learning Spanish Book with CD, 2nd Ed., $19.95
Everything® Russian Practice Book with CD, $19.95
Everything® Sign Language Book, $15.95
Everything® Spanish Grammar Book
Everything® Spanish Phrase Book, $9.95
Everything® Spanish Practice Book with CD, $19.95
Everything® Spanish Verb Book, $9.95
Everything® Speaking Mandarin Chinese Book with CD, $19.95

MUSIC

Everything® Bass Guitar Book with CD, $19.95
Everything® Drums Book with CD, $19.95
Everything® Guitar Book with CD, 2nd Ed., $19.95
Everything® Guitar Chords Book with CD, $19.95
Everything® Guitar Scales Book with CD, $19.95
Everything® Harmonica Book with CD, $15.95
Everything® Home Recording Book
Everything® Music Theory Book with CD, $19.95
Everything® Reading Music Book with CD, $19.95
Everything® Rock & Blues Guitar Book with CD, $19.95
Everything® Rock & Blues Piano Book with CD, $19.95
Everything® Rock Drums Book with CD, $19.95
Everything® Singing Book with CD, $19.95
Everything® Songwriting Book

NEW AGE

Everything® Astrology Book, 2nd Ed.
Everything® Birthday Personology Book
Everything® Celtic Wisdom Book, $15.95
Everything® Dreams Book, 2nd Ed.
Everything® Law of Attraction Book, $15.95
Everything® Love Signs Book, $9.95
Everything® Love Spells Book, $9.95
Everything® Palmistry Book
Everything® Psychic Book
Everything® Reiki Book

Everything® Sex Signs Book, $9.95
Everything® Spells & Charms Book, 2nd Ed.
Everything® Tarot Book, 2nd Ed.
Everything® Toltec Wisdom Book
Everything® Wicca & Witchcraft Book, 2nd Ed.

PARENTING

Everything® Baby Names Book, 2nd Ed.
Everything® Baby Shower Book, 2nd Ed.
Everything® Baby Sign Language Book with DVD
Everything® Baby's First Year Book
Everything® Birthing Book
Everything® Breastfeeding Book
Everything® Father-to-Be Book
Everything® Father's First Year Book
Everything® Get Ready for Baby Book, 2nd Ed.
Everything® Get Your Baby to Sleep Book, $9.95
Everything® Getting Pregnant Book
Everything® Guide to Pregnancy Over 35
Everything® Guide to Raising a One-Year-Old
Everything® Guide to Raising a Two-Year-Old
Everything® Guide to Raising Adolescent Boys
Everything® Guide to Raising Adolescent Girls
Everything® Mother's First Year Book
Everything® Parent's Guide to Childhood Illnesses
Everything® Parent's Guide to Children and Divorce
Everything® Parent's Guide to Children with ADD/ADHD
Everything® Parent's Guide to Children with Asperger's Syndrome
Everything® Parent's Guide to Children with Anxiety
Everything® Parent's Guide to Children with Asthma
Everything® Parent's Guide to Children with Autism
Everything® Parent's Guide to Children with Bipolar Disorder
Everything® Parent's Guide to Children with Depression
Everything® Parent's Guide to Children with Dyslexia
Everything® Parent's Guide to Children with Juvenile Diabetes
Everything® Parent's Guide to Children with OCD
Everything® Parent's Guide to Positive Discipline
Everything® Parent's Guide to Raising Boys
Everything® Parent's Guide to Raising Girls
Everything® Parent's Guide to Raising Siblings
Everything® Parent's Guide to Raising Your Adopted Child
Everything® Parent's Guide to Sensory Integration Disorder
Everything® Parent's Guide to Tantrums
Everything® Parent's Guide to the Strong-Willed Child
Everything® Parenting a Teenager Book
Everything® Potty Training Book, $9.95
Everything® Pregnancy Book, 3rd Ed.
Everything® Pregnancy Fitness Book
Everything® Pregnancy Nutrition Book
Everything® Pregnancy Organizer, 2nd Ed., $16.95
Everything® Toddler Activities Book
Everything® Toddler Book
Everything® Tween Book
Everything® Twins, Triplets, and More Book

PETS

Everything® Aquarium Book
Everything® Boxer Book
Everything® Cat Book, 2nd Ed.
Everything® Chihuahua Book
Everything® Cooking for Dogs Book
Everything® Dachshund Book
Everything® Dog Book, 2nd Ed.
Everything® Dog Grooming Book

Everything® Dog Obedience Book
Everything® Dog Owner's Organizer, $16.95
Everything® Dog Training and Tricks Book
Everything® German Shepherd Book
Everything® Golden Retriever Book
Everything® Horse Book, 2nd Ed., $15.95
Everything® Horse Care Book
Everything® Horseback Riding Book
Everything® Labrador Retriever Book
Everything® Poodle Book
Everything® Pug Book
Everything® Puppy Book
Everything® Small Dogs Book
Everything® Tropical Fish Book
Everything® Yorkshire Terrier Book

REFERENCE

Everything® American Presidents Book
Everything® Blogging Book
Everything® Build Your Vocabulary Book, $9.95
Everything® Car Care Book
Everything® Classical Mythology Book
Everything® Da Vinci Book
Everything® Einstein Book
Everything® Enneagram Book
Everything® Etiquette Book, 2nd Ed.
Everything® Family Christmas Book, $15.95
Everything® Guide to C. S. Lewis & Narnia
Everything® Guide to Divorce, 2nd Ed., $15.95
Everything® Guide to Edgar Allan Poe
Everything® Guide to Understanding Philosophy
Everything® Inventions and Patents Book
Everything® Jacqueline Kennedy Onassis Book
Everything® John F. Kennedy Book
Everything® Mafia Book
Everything® Martin Luther King Jr. Book
Everything® Pirates Book
Everything® Private Investigation Book
Everything® Psychology Book
Everything® Public Speaking Book, $9.95
Everything® Shakespeare Book, 2nd Ed.

RELIGION

Everything® Angels Book
Everything® Bible Book
Everything® Bible Study Book with CD, $19.95
Everything® Buddhism Book
Everything® Catholicism Book
Everything® Christianity Book
Everything® Gnostic Gospels Book
Everything® Hinduism Book, $15.95
Everything® History of the Bible Book
Everything® Jesus Book
Everything® Jewish History & Heritage Book
Everything® Judaism Book
Everything® Kabbalah Book
Everything® Koran Book
Everything® Mary Book
Everything® Mary Magdalene Book
Everything® Prayer Book

Everything® Saints Book, 2nd Ed.
Everything® Torah Book
Everything® Understanding Islam Book
Everything® Women of the Bible Book
Everything® World's Religions Book

SCHOOL & CAREERS

Everything® Career Tests Book
Everything® College Major Test Book
Everything® College Survival Book, 2nd Ed.
Everything® Cover Letter Book, 2nd Ed.
Everything® Filmmaking Book
Everything® Get-a-Job Book, 2nd Ed.
Everything® Guide to Being a Paralegal
Everything® Guide to Being a Personal Trainer
Everything® Guide to Being a Real Estate Agent
Everything® Guide to Being a Sales Rep
Everything® Guide to Being an Event Planner
Everything® Guide to Careers in Health Care
Everything® Guide to Careers in Law Enforcement
Everything® Guide to Government Jobs
Everything® Guide to Starting and Running a Catering
    Business
Everything® Guide to Starting and Running a Restaurant
**Everything® Guide to Starting and Running
    a Retail Store**
Everything® Job Interview Book, 2nd Ed.
Everything® New Nurse Book
Everything® New Teacher Book
Everything® Paying for College Book
Everything® Practice Interview Book
Everything® Resume Book, 3rd Ed.
Everything® Study Book

SELF-HELP

Everything® Body Language Book
Everything® Dating Book, 2nd Ed.
Everything® Great Sex Book
**Everything® Guide to Caring for Aging Parents,
    $15.95**
Everything® Self-Esteem Book
Everything® Self-Hypnosis Book, $9.95
Everything® Tantric Sex Book

SPORTS & FITNESS

Everything® Easy Fitness Book
Everything® Fishing Book
Everything® Guide to Weight Training, $15.95
Everything® Krav Maga for Fitness Book
Everything® Running Book, 2nd Ed.
Everything® Triathlon Training Book, $15.95

TRAVEL

Everything® Family Guide to Coastal Florida
Everything® Family Guide to Cruise Vacations
Everything® Family Guide to Hawaii
Everything® Family Guide to Las Vegas, 2nd Ed.
Everything® Family Guide to Mexico
Everything® Family Guide to New England, 2nd Ed.

Everything® Family Guide to New York City, 3rd Ed.
**Everything® Family Guide to Northern California
    and Lake Tahoe**
Everything® Family Guide to RV Travel & Campgrounds
Everything® Family Guide to the Caribbean
Everything® Family Guide to the Disneyland® Resort, California
    Adventure®, Universal Studios®, and the Anaheim
    Area, 2nd Ed.
Everything® Family Guide to the Walt Disney World Resort®,
    Universal Studios®, and Greater Orlando, 5th Ed.
Everything® Family Guide to Timeshares
Everything® Family Guide to Washington D.C., 2nd Ed.

WEDDINGS

Everything® Bachelorette Party Book, $9.95
Everything® Bridesmaid Book, $9.95
Everything® Destination Wedding Book
Everything® Father of the Bride Book, $9.95
Everything® Green Wedding Book, $15.95
Everything® Groom Book, $9.95
Everything® Jewish Wedding Book, 2nd Ed., $15.95
Everything® Mother of the Bride Book, $9.95
Everything® Outdoor Wedding Book
Everything® Wedding Book, 3rd Ed.
Everything® Wedding Checklist, $9.95
Everything® Wedding Etiquette Book, $9.95
Everything® Wedding Organizer, 2nd Ed., $16.95
Everything® Wedding Shower Book, $9.95
Everything® Wedding Vows Book, 3rd Ed., $9.95
Everything® Wedding Workout Book
Everything® Weddings on a Budget Book, 2nd Ed., $9.95

WRITING

Everything® Creative Writing Book
Everything® Get Published Book, 2nd Ed.
Everything® Grammar and Style Book, 2nd Ed.
Everything® Guide to Magazine Writing
Everything® Guide to Writing a Book Proposal
Everything® Guide to Writing a Novel
Everything® Guide to Writing Children's Books
Everything® Guide to Writing Copy
Everything® Guide to Writing Graphic Novels
Everything® Guide to Writing Research Papers
Everything® Guide to Writing a Romance Novel, $15.9
Everything® Improve Your Writing Book, 2nd Ed.
Everything® Writing Poetry Book